CUTTING EDGE

PRE-INTERMEDIATE

STUDENTS' BOOK

sarah cunningham   peter

with jane

Module	Grammar	Vocabulary	Reading and Listening
Module 1 Leisure and lifestyle page 6 *Do you remember?* page 14	1) Question forms 2) Present Simple *Pronunciation:* weak forms in questions	**Vocabulary:** leisure activities **WB Vocabulary booster:** sports	**Reading:** *My idea of fun!*
Module 2 Important firsts page 15 *Do you remember?* page 22	1) Past Simple 2) Time phrases often used in the past (*in, on, at, ago*) *Pronunciation:* pronunciation of Past Simple forms	**Vocabulary:** words to describe feelings *Pronunciation:* stress in adjectives **Wordspot:** *feel*	**Listening:** *The first time I ever saw your face* (song) **WB Listen and read:** *The magic of movies*
Module 3 The best way to learn page 23 *Do you remember?* page 30	1) *Can, can't, have to, don't have to* 2) *Should/Shouldn't* *Pronunciation:* weak forms of *can/can't*	**Vocabulary:** studying new vocabulary **WB Vocabulary booster:** things in a school	**Reading:** *What's the secret of successful language learning?*
Module 4 Special occasions page 31 *Do you remember?* page 38	1) Present Continuous (and Present Simple) 2) Present Continuous for future arrangements	**Vocabulary:** dates and special occasions *Pronunciation:* th /θ/ or /ð/ **Wordspot:** *day* **WB Vocabulary booster:** special occasions	**Listening:** New Year in two different cultures **WB Listen and read:** *Religious festivals around the world*
Module 5 Appearances page 39 *Do you remember?* page 46	1) Comparatives and superlatives 2) Describing what people look like *Pronunciation:* schwa /ə/	**Wordspot:** *look* *Pronunciation:* counting the number of syllables **WB Vocabulary booster:** parts of the face and body	**Reading:** *You're gorgeous!*
Module 6 Time off page 47	1) Intentions and wishes (*going to, planning to, would like to, would prefer to*) 2) Predictions (*will* and *won't*) *Pronunciation:* contractions of *I am* and *I would* *Pronunciation:* contractions of *will*	**Vocabulary:** holidays **WB Vocabulary booster:** things you take on holiday	**Listening:** the holiday from hell **WB Listen and read:** holiday advertisements

Consolidation Modules 1 – 6 (pages 54 – 55)

Module	Grammar	Vocabulary	Reading and Listening
Module 7 Fame and fortune page 56 *Do you remember?* page 64	1) Present Perfect and Past Simple with *for* 2) Present Perfect and Past Simple with other time words *Pronunciation:* contractions and weak forms	**Vocabulary:** ambitions and dreams **Wordspot:** *know*	**Reading:** *Before they were famous*
Module 8 cultures ge 65	1) Using articles 2) Phrases with and without *the*	**Vocabulary:** geographical features *Pronunciation:* geographical terms **WB Vocabulary booster:** things you find in cities	**WB Listen and read:** *Volcanoes*

found in the Workbook (not including grammar and vocabulary)

Task and Speaking	Writing	Functions and Situations
Preparation for task: read a fact file from a website **Task:** compile a fact file about your partner (extended speaking)	**Optional writing:** write your fact file **WB Improve your writing:** punctuation (1)	*Real life:* questions you can't live without *Pronunciation:* stress and intonation in -wh questions
Preparation for task: people describe the first time they did something (listening) **Task:** tell a first time story (extended speaking)	**Writing:** linking ideas in narrative **WB Spelling:** -ed endings	
Preparation for task: teacher talking about her class contract (listening) **Task:** make a list of guidelines for a language class (extended speaking)	**Optional writing:** write the classroom guidelines **WB Improve your writing:** writing a paragraph **WB Spelling:** finding mistakes	*Real life:* making requests and asking for permission *Pronunciation:* polite intonation
Preparation for task: important dates (listening) **Task:** prepare and talk about a personal calendar (extended speaking)	**Writing:** a letter of invitation **WB Improve your writing:** a letter of invitation **WB Spelling:** -ing forms	*Real life:* phrases for special occasions *Pronunciation:* friendly, positive intonation
Preparation for task: description of a crime **Task:** describe a suspect to the police (extended speaking)	**Optional writing:** write a description of a suspect **WB Improve your writing:** writing a description **WB Spelling:** double letters	*Real life:* social chit-chat *Pronunciation:* intonation for sounding interested
Preparation for task: holiday words and phrases **Task:** plan your dream holiday (extended speaking)	**Writing:** write a postcard **WB Improve your writing:** more postcards **WB Spelling:** words with –ed and -ing	
Preparation for task: discuss questions to ask famous people **Task:** prepare an interview (extended speaking)	**Optional writing:** write your interview **WB Improve your writing:** a mini-biography	*Real life:* checking that you understand *Pronunciation:* stress in questions
Preparation for task: Quiz *How much do you know about New Zealand?* (extended listening) **Task:** complete a map of New Zealand (extended speaking)	**Writing:** formal and informal letters **WB Improve your writing:** formal letters and informal notes **WB Spelling:** plural nouns	

Module	Grammar	Vocabulary	Reading and Listening
Module 9 Old and new page 72 *Do you remember?* page 80	1) *May, might, will definitely*, etc. 2) Present tense after *if, when, before* and other time words *Pronunciation:* won't	**Vocabulary:** modern and traditional **Wordspot:** *change* **Vocabulary booster:** technology	**Reading:** *The changing face of shopping*
Module 10 Take care! page 81 *Do you remember?* page 88	1) *Used to* 2) Past Continuous *Pronunciation:* weak and strong forms of *be*	**Vocabulary:** accidents *Pronunciation:* stress on medical vocabulary	**Reading and listening:** *Health problems: how much do you know?* **Listen and read:** *The secrets of sleep*
Module 11 The best things in life … page 89	1) Gerunds (-*ing* forms), verbs of liking and disliking 2) *Like doing* and *would like to do* (gerunds and infinitives) *Pronunciation:* weak and strong forms of *to*	**Wordspot:** *like* **Vocabulary booster:** -*ed* and -*ing* adjectives	**Reading:** *When an interest becomes an obsession …*

Consolidation Modules 7 – 11 (pages 97 – 98)

Module	Grammar	Vocabulary	Reading and Listening
Module 12 Must have it! page 99 *Do you remember?* page 106	1) Passive forms (past, present, future) 2) Sentences joined with *that, which* and *who* *Pronunciation:* stress and weak forms with the passive	**Vocabulary:** objects	**Listening:** designer goods **Listen and read:** *Diamonds are forever*
Module 13 The right kind of person page 107 *Do you remember?* page 115	1) Present Perfect Simple and Continuous with the 'unfinished past' 2) *How long …?, for, since* and *all* *Pronunciation:* contractions and weak forms	**Vocabulary:** jobs and personal characteristics **Wordspot:** *how* **Vocabulary booster:** jobs	**Reading:** *Jobsearch.com*
Module 14 Building your dreams page 116 *Do you remember?* page 123	1) *Some, any* and quantifiers 2) Describing where things are *Pronunciation:* linking	**Vocabulary:** describing houses and apartments **Vocabulary booster:** things in a house	**Reading:** *Building your dream …*
Module 15 Money, money, money page 124 *Do you remember?* page 130	1) Past Perfect 2) Reported speech *Pronunciation:* contractions of *had* and *will*	**Vocabulary:** verb phrases to do with money **Wordspot:** *make*	**Listen and read:** *The history of money*
Module 16 Imagine … page 131	1) Conditional sentences with *would* 2) *Will* and *would* *Pronunciation:* contractions of *will* and *would*	**Vocabulary booster:** people in politics, religion and public life	**Reading:** John Lennon and Martin Luther King **Listening:** *Imagine* (song) *Pronunciation:* stress in nouns and adjectives

Consolidation Modules 12 – 16 (page 138)

Communication activities (pages 142 – 148)

Task and Speaking	Writing	Functions and Situations
Preparation for task: discuss entering a competition **Task:** decide on five improvements to your school or office (extended speaking and listening)	**Optional writing:** competition entry form	**Real life:** shopping in a department store
Preparation for task: description of a rescue **Task:** describe a rescue and decide who is Hero of the Year (extended speaking)	**Writing:** using adverbs in narrative WB **Improve your writing:** adverbs	
Preparation for task: discuss the most important things in life **Task:** make a list of the most important things in life (extended speaking)	WB **Spelling:** words ending with *-ion*	**Real life:** finding things in common *Pronunciation:* Stress
Preparation for task: people discussing what to take on a trip (listening) **Task:** decide what you need for a trip (extended speaking)	WB **Improve your writing:** joining sentences with *which, who, and, because* and *but* WB **Spelling:** silent *–g* and *-gh*	**Real life:** making suggestions *Pronunciation:* intonation in suggestions
Preparation for task: description of two candidates for mayor of Queenstown (listening) **Task:** select a new mayor for Queenstown (extended speaking)	**Writing:** an application for a job WB **Improve your writing:** error correction	**Real life:** an application for a job
Preparation for task: people talking about their favourite room (listening) **Task:** describe a favourite room (extended speaking)	**Writing:** giving directions WB **Improve your writing:** notes giving directions WB **Spelling:** same pronunciation, different spelling (homophones)	**Real life:** giving directions
Preparation for task: *Is this man Britain's unluckiest criminal?* (reading) **Task:** find the differences between two stories (extended listening and speaking)	WB **Improve your writing:** punctuation in direct speech	**Real life:** dealing with money *Pronunciation:* intonation in questions and requests
Preparation for task: discussing the new planet Hero **Task:** choose people to start a space colony (extended speaking)	**Creative writing:** write a letter to a friend on Earth WB **Improve your writing:** error correction WB **Spelling:** silent 'w'	

Irregular verbs (page 148)   Language summary (pages 149 – 157)   Tapescripts (pages 158 – 169)

module 1
Leisure and lifestyle

▶ Vocabulary: leisure activities
▶ Question forms
▶ Present Simple
Task: compile a fact file about your partner

Vocabulary and speaking

Leisure activities

1 a) Look at the pictures. Which of the activities from the box can you see?

sunbathing   going to the gym
playing computer games   going dancing
playing the guitar   playing football
entertaining friends   surfing the Internet
going for a run   going shopping

b) Discuss the questions in pairs or small groups.
- Which of these things do you do in your free time?
- What else do you do in your free time?

I go to the gym a lot in my free time.

Really? I never go to the gym!

2 A survey asked people in the United Kingdom how they spend their free time. Look at the results. Which statements do you think are true?

- British people spend most of their free time at home.
- British people are very fit and healthy.
- The people who answered were probably old.
- Most British people don't have a very interesting life!

Top 10 Leisure Activities
for adults in the United Kingdom

1 Watching television
2 Visiting/Entertaining friends
3 Listening to the radio
4 Listening to cassettes/CDs
5 Reading books
6 Going to a restaurant
7 Going for a drink
8 Gardening
9 Going for a drive
10 Going for a walk

6

3 a) Make a similar list of the top ten leisure activities for people in your country. The list can be for people of all ages, or just for young people.

b) Compare your list with other students. What are the differences?

4 a) Look back at the phrases in Exercises 1 and 2 and complete the diagrams below. Pay attention to phrases which have *the*, *a*, *to* and *for*.

- going to
  - going to the gym
- going for a
  - going for a run
- going + -ing
- playing
- watching
- listening to

b) Add one more example to the groups above.

c) It is very important to try and remember words that go together (word combinations).

For example: go shopping

What do you think is the best way to remember these phrases?

7

module 1 Leisure and lifestyle

Reading

1 What are the people doing in each picture below? Which countries do you think they are in?

My idea of fun!

People around the world relax in very different ways. We look at favourite leisure activities in three continents …

1 Surfing capital of the world
Any sunny day on the coast of Australia, you can see hundreds of young people going to the beach. They all share Australia's national passion – surfing. 'My friends and I usually go down to the beach before breakfast in the summer,' says 19-year-old Jim Wolfe, 'and come home again for dinner!' At weekends it is quite normal to drive hundreds of kilometres to find that 'perfect wave'. But in Sydney, the biggest city in Australia, you don't have that problem – there are thirty-four beaches close to the city centre!

2 The music of the people
The most popular dance of Brazil, samba, is often called 'the music of the people'. In the 1960s and 1970s people turned to US-style pop music, but these days samba is back again. There are different versions of samba: some that people dance in their villages, others that they practise especially to dance at Carnival. In Rio thousands of people go to samba schools, typically on a Saturday night – to dance, to learn … or just to watch. Thirty-year-old Ana Rita goes every week with her husband '… just because it's fun! Everybody loves to dance, and it's a great way to meet people!'

3 A day in the 'banya'
If you're happy to take a bath in public, then a Russian banya or bath house, is the place for you. Russians of all types meet there … at any time of day. They go there to relax, to talk to their friends or even to discuss business. 'It doesn't matter if you're old or young, fat or thin. Nobody cares, nobody looks at you … it's a wonderful place!' says 24-year-old Masha, a student from St Petersburg. There are cold baths, as well as a hot room where the temperature can reach forty-three degrees.

3 Read the texts and complete the table below. Compare answers with a partner.

	When do people do this?	What kind of people do it?	Why do they do it?
surfing			
samba			
the *banya*			

2 Look at the three parts of the article, and match them to the pictures. Check your answers to Exercise 1.

4 Which of these ways of relaxing would you like to try? Why? If you want to relax, what do you usually do?

8

Language focus 1

Question forms

1 Discuss the following questions in pairs or groups.

- Do you like sport or not? Which sports do you play?
- Do you watch much sport on TV?
- Do you play any games, like chess or cards?

2 How much do you know about sports and games? Work in groups. Answer as many of the questions as you can in **five** minutes.

A question of sport!

a How often do the Winter Olympics happen?
b When were the Barcelona Olympics?
c How does a 100 metres race start?
d Where does the sport of judo come from?
e How long does an ice hockey match last?
f What kind of ball do they use in the game of rugby?
g In which country is baseball the national sport?
h How many spots are there on a dice?
i Who starts in a game of chess: the black or the white player?
j In which sports do players use a racket?
k Why does the referee toss a coin at the beginning of a football match?
l What happens if the score is a draw at the end of the World Cup football final?

3 [1.1] Listen and check your answers. Which group got the highest score?

Grammar analysis

Wh- questions

1 Look at the question words underlined in Exercise 2. Which question word(s) do we use to ask about:
a a person? Who
b a place? Wher
c a thing? What
d a time? When
e the reason for something? Why
f the **way** you do something? how

2 We often add another word to *how*, *what* and *which* to make two-word questions (for example, *how often*). Find **five** examples in Exercise 2.

Word order in questions

In questions, the verb (or auxiliary verb) usually comes **before** the subject of the sentence. Put questions d), e) and f) from Exercise 2 into the correct columns.

Question words	verb/ auxiliary	subject (+ main verb)
When	were	the Barcelona Olympics?
How often	do	the Winter Olympics happen?

▶ Language summary A/B, page 149.

module 1 Leisure and lifestyle

Practice

1 [1.2] Find the correct answers to the questions in the boxes below. Then listen and check.

a 1 When do you usually play football?
   2 Who do you play with?
   3 Where do you usually play football?
   4 Why do you play?

| Some people from college. | On Sunday mornings. |
| In the local park. | It's fun, and it's good exercise. |

b 1 How often do you have English lessons?
   2 How long are the lessons?
   3 Which days are the lessons on?
   4 How many teachers do you have?

| Two. | Twice a week. |
| Tuesdays and Thursdays. | Two hours. |

c 1 What time is it?   3 What date is it?
   2 What day is it?   4 How much is it?

| Monday. | About ten pounds. |
| The sixteenth, I think. | Nearly half past three. |

Pronunciation

[1.3] In the questions above *are*, *do*, and *you* are very weak because they are in the middle of the question. Listen and practise.

/ə/   /djə/
How long **are** the lessons?   Who **do you** play with?

2 Are the statements below true about your teacher? Prepare questions to find out. Ask and check.

1 He/She gets up before eight o'clock at weekends.
   What time do you get up at weekends?
2 He/She goes dancing once a week.
3 He/She comes to school by motorbike.
4 His/Her birthday is in August.
5 He/She likes classical music.
6 His/Her favourite colour is orange.
7 There are five people in his/her family.
8 His/Her journey to school takes more than half an hour.
9 He/She wants to visit Japan and Australia.

Language focus 2
Present Simple

Toshi, from Japan, is training to be a sumo wrestler.

1 Look at the photos of three sports people. Can you guess who:

a has a big lunch (with lots of beer) and then goes to sleep for a few hours?
b doesn't eat very much?
c runs 8 km at least four times a week?
d trains for eight hours every day?
e usually trains before breakfast?
f weighs about 40 kg?
g weighs about 175 kg?
h is 1.5 m tall?
i is 1.95 m tall?
j earns about $50,000 a week?
k receives money from his/her parents every month?

2 [1.4] Listen and check your answers. Whose life sounds the most difficult? Why?

Ania, from Poland, is a champion gymnast.

Dan, from Romania, is a professional footballer. He plays for a top Italian club.

Grammar analysis

Present Simple

1 We use the Present Simple to talk about habits.
*He **has** a big lunch and then **goes** to sleep for a few hours.*
And things that are generally/always true.
*He **earns** about $25,000 a week.*

2 What are the question and negative forms of the examples above?

How often?

1 The phrases below tell us how often things happen. Think of other words to replace those underlined.
every <u>month</u>   on <u>Sundays</u>   <u>five times</u> a <u>week</u>
These phrases are usually at the end (or beginning) of the sentence.
He runs <u>five times a week</u>.
<u>Every month</u> he receives money from his parents.

2 Here are some more phrases that tell us how often something happens. Number them from 1 (= most often) to 6 (= least often).
sometimes ☐   often ☐   usually ☐   never ☐
always [1]   occasionally ☐

These adverbs usually come before the main verb.
*He **never** smokes and he doesn't **usually** eat meat.*

▶ *Language summary C / D, page 149.*

Practice

1 Use the prompts below to make more sentences about the three athletes.

For example: eat/Ania/a healthy diet/always
Ania always eats a healthy diet.

a for many hours/all of them/train/every day
b much money/Ania and Toshi/not earn
c Ania/at 7.00/get up/usually
d never/before midnight/go to bed/she
e live in/Toshi/a special training camp called a *heya*
f on the floor/he/sleep/often
g lots of fan letters/receive/every week/he
h not play/Dan/in every match
i two sports cars/own/he
j miss/he/his family in Romania
k phone/about four times a week/he/his mother

2 a) You are going to interview your partner. Work in groups, A and B. Group A looks at page 139. Group B looks at page 145. Complete the gaps with *are you?* or *do you?*

b) Work in pairs with a person from the other group. Ask and answer the questions.

What time do you usually get up?

Normally about half past six. How about you?

11

module 1 Leisure and lifestyle

Compile a fact file about your partner

Personal vocabulary

Preparation for task

1 Zoe Ball is a radio DJ and children's TV presenter in Britain. Look at the photos. What do you think her life is like?

2 The following fact file about Zoe Ball appeared on a website. Read it for two minutes then close your book. What can you remember about Zoe?

THE ZOE BALL ZONE!

FULL NAME Zoe Louise Ball.

BORN Blackpool, November 1970.

HEIGHT 5'10".

FAMILY Three brothers, two sisters. Father, Johnny Ball, was a children's TV presenter in 1980s.

RELATIONSHIP Married to DJ Fatboy Slim.

EDUCATION Holy Cross Convent School and City Polytechnic (four months only). 'I never did any work, even though I loved school. People at school called me Dumbo because of my big ears!'

JOB Radio DJ, presenter of children's TV programme.

TYPICAL DAY No day is typical: 'It depends if I have to record the TV show, or if I have meetings, or interviews to do.'

HOBBIES Eating, movies, music, dancing.

PETS A cat called Tom – eighteen years old and very weak.

FAVOURITE FOODS Chocolate and banana, but not together!

FAVOURITE BANDS Massive Attack, Pulp, Portishead.

FAVOURITE SONG All the Time in the World, Louis Armstrong.

FAVOURITE FILMS Play it again Sam, Breakfast at Tiffany's.

HERO Woody Allen.

MONEY 'I'm a shopaholic – I love spending money on clothes, holidays, and lots and lots of music.'

AMBITIONS (She says!) to have lots of children, and to train as a teacher (!!!). Not to be famous any more. 'In ten years' time I hope people say, "Zoe Ball? What happened to her?"'

Useful language

"Where/when ... born?"

"How tall ...?"

"How many ...?"

"What is/are your ...?"

"Who's your favourite... ?"

"... married?"

"What's/are your favourite ...?"

"Describe your typical day..."

"Tell me about ..."

"What about ...?"

"Anything else?"

3 With a partner, decide what questions the interviewer asked Zoe.
▶ Useful language

For example: What's your full name?

Though — myśl

Task – zadanie

1 You are going to interview another student in your class for a fact file. You can add extra topics if you want to.
a) Spend a few minutes planning and practising your questions.
▶ *Useful language*

b) Think about your own answers to these questions and ask your teacher for any other words or phrases you need.
▶ *Personal vocabulary*

Fact File
Full name: Patryzji Przydzek
Born: 1987 12 Jun
Occupation:
Typical day: school
Family: sister Weronika
Relationships/Best friends: Magda
Pets: dog
Favourite ways of relaxing:
Favourite … : Sten
Hero/heroine:
Ambitions: finished school god to
Other:

2 a) Work in pairs with someone you do not normally talk to in class. Ask and answer your questions to complete the fact files.

b) Tell the class two things you discovered about your partner.

Optional writing
Write your fact file, and put it on the wall for other students to read. Attach a photo if you can.

Real life

Questions you can't live without

1 Look at the pictures. Discuss which questions in the box below you might hear or ask in each situation.

a In the street.
b Filling in a form at the bank.
c In a restaurant.
d In the classroom.
e In a shop.
f When you start talking to someone for the first time.

Where are you from? f   Can I help you? E   What time is it? A
How do you spell…? b   What's your date of birth? B
Where's the nearest (bank)? A   How long are you going to stay? f
Do you speak English?   How much does this cost? e
Anything else? C   Which part of (Poland) are you from? f
Can we have the bill, please? C   Sorry, could you repeat that, please? d
Where are the toilets, please? C

2 a) [1.5] Listen to three conversations. In which of the situations above do they take place?

b) Listen again. Tick the questions from the box that you heard.

13

Pronunciation

The most important words are stressed (strong) in these questions.

Where are you from?

Notice that normally *wh-* questions go **down** at the end.

1 [1.6] Listen and practise the questions. Copy the voices on the recording. Start with the strong words first like this:

Where ... from? >

Where are you from?

2 Look at the tapescript on page 158 and practise the conversations with a partner. Pay attention to the stress and intonation in the *wh-* questions.

3 With a partner, write similar conversations for the situations in three other pictures on page 13. Practise your conversations.

Do you remember?

1 Discuss in pairs. Where do you do the following?
- play computer games
- go for a run
- listen to CDs or cassettes
- go dancing
- read books or magazines
- go shopping for clothes

2 Cross out the question word which is not correct.
a) *What/When/Who* is your date of birth?
b) *How/What/How often* do you come to class?
c) *How Long/Why/Where* are you learning English?
d) *What colour/How old/When* is your car?
e) *What date/When/What* does your holiday start?

3 Put these questions in the correct order. Ask and answer the questions.
a) your/national/of/What/country/sport/is/the/?
b) spell/surname/you/How/your/do/?
c) teachers/school/many/in/How/there/your/are/?
d) starts/football/Who/and/a/match/stops/?
e) English/start/time/does/What/class/your/?
f) of/listen/What/music/to/you/sort/do/?

4 Which one of the following sentences is correct? Correct the other four.
a) Demi Moore receive a lot of fan letters.
b) I don't get up always late at the weekends.
c) My sister never goes to bed before midnight.
d) She every week writes to her grandparents.
e) My boyfriend doesn't earns much money.

5 Write in the missing preposition and answer the questions using the tapescripts on page 158 to help you.
a) Who trains eight hours a day
b) Who is a diet of rice, meat and beer?
c) Who goes a run most mornings?
d) Who receives money his parents?
e) Who lives her mother in Lublin?

module 2

Important firsts

- Past Simple
- Time phrases often used in the past
- Vocabulary: words to describe feelings
- Wordspot: *feel*
- Task: tell a first time story

Language focus 1

Past Simple

1 Discuss the questions below.

What is your favourite film?
Which of these do you enjoy?
- horror films
- musicals
- gangster movies
- romantic comedies
- historical romances
- detective stories

Do you enjoy old films? If so, which ones and why?

2 You are going to read about the first feature film. First guess the correct answers below.

a The first feature film appeared in:
   1906   1916   1926
b It came from:
   France   Australia   the USA
c It was:
   a comedy   a gangster film
   a romantic film

3 Read the first paragraph to check.

THE STORY OF THE KELLY GANG

Charles Tait, an Australian film director, (1) ...made... the first feature film, The Story of the Kelly Gang, in 1906. The film (2) ...told... the true story of Ned Kelly, a famous Australian gangster and his gang, who (3) .... horses and cattle, (4) .... banks, and often (5) .... metal armour for protection. Although they (6) .... criminals, Kelly and his gang (7) .... heroes to the ordinary people of Australia, because many of them (8) .... the government at that time.

The film (9) ...lasted... for eighty minutes and (10) ...cost... just $450 dollars to make! The Canadian actor who (11) .... Kelly obviously (12) .... there was a future in the movie business, because he (13) .... before the end of filming, and so Tait, the director, (14) .... make the last scenes without him. Because there were no close-ups, no one (15) .... see that it was a different actor playing Kelly!

The film (16) ...opened... at the Athenaeum Hall in Melbourne on 24th December 1906. It (17) ...was... a great success, making over $25,000.

4 Complete the text with the verbs below.

became	disappeared	~~made~~	stole	was
~~cost~~	didn't think	had to	opened	told	were
~~could~~	robbed	~~lasted~~	played	hated	wore

5 [2.1] Listen and check your answers.

module 2 Important firsts

Grammar analysis

1 How do we form the Past Simple of **regular** verbs? <u>Underline</u> six examples in the box in Exercise 4 on page 15.

2 The other (positive) verbs are irregular. Write down the infinitive forms.
became   become

3 How do we form the negative and question forms of these verbs? Notice and remember the special Past Simple form of *be*.

▶ *Language summary A, page 150.*

Famous Firsts Quiz!

1 What nationality was the first woman to receive a university degree?
   a British
   b Italian
   c Russian

2 What did the world's first vending machine sell?
   a chocolate
   b cigarettes
   c postcards

3 When did the first McDonald's restaurant open?
   a in the 1950s
   b in the 1960s
   c in the 1980s

4 What was the first animal in space?
   a a dog
   b a monkey
   c a mouse

Practice

1 Discuss the answers to the quiz below. Then check your answers on page 139.

2 a) Work in pairs or teams, A and B. A looks at the questions and answers on page 139. B looks at the questions and answers on page 143.

b) Put the questions and answers into the correct form of the Past Simple.

c) Take turns to ask and answer the questions.

Pronunciation

1 Look at the Past Simple forms below. If necessary, check the infinitives and meaning in your mini-dictionary.
Which of the pairs rhyme?

	A	B
a	cried	died ✓
b	cut	put ✗
c	appeared	heard ✗
d	paid	played ✓
e	said	stayed ✗
f	saw	wore ✓
g	worried	hurried ✓
h	sent	meant ✓
i	kissed	missed ✓
j	thought	taught ✓

2 [2.2] Listen and check your answers. Practise saying the verbs.

3 Work in pairs. Test your partner like this:

  cry   cried

16

3 a) Write three things and things about yourself. Two should be **true** and one **false**.

- Things you did yesterday.
- Places you went to last year.
- Things you bought last month.
- Films you saw last year.
- Things you didn't like when you were a child.

b) Read out your ideas. Your partner decides which is false.

> Yesterday I went swimming, I sent some e-mails, and I watched TV.

> You didn't go swimming!

> That's right!

Language focus 2

Time phrases often used in the past: *in, on, at, ago*

Number the phrases below 1-12 from the least recent to the most recent.

four months ago ☐	
last weekend ☐	
on Monday morning ☐	
in the 1980s ☐	
in November of last year ☐	
100 years ago ☐	
at eight o'clock this morning ☐	
yesterday afternoon ☐	
in 1998 ☐	
on 1st January this year ☐	
ten hours ago ☐	
in the eighteenth century ☐	

Grammar analysis

1 Complete the rules with *in, on, at* or ø.
  a With times (for example *7.30*) we use ...
  b With days, dates (for example *7th July*) and parts of days (for example *Thursday afternoon*) we use ...
  c With longer periods of time: months, seasons, years, decades and centuries (for example *the 1960s*) we use ...
  d With *last* and *yesterday* (for example, *last night, yesterday morning*) we use ...

2 Which of these phrases is wrong with *ago*?
  ten weeks ago   a long time ago   ten thousand years ago
  a few minutes ago   years and years ago   the summer ago

▶ Language summary B, page 150.

Practice

1 [2.3] Listen and answer questions a–j, using the time phrases in the box in your answers.

2 Play the game *When did you last ...?* You will need a watch.

- Your partner chooses a question to ask you. You talk about that topic for **twenty seconds** without stopping. Use at least one time phrase in your answer.
- If you can't answer, your partner chooses another question.

When did you last ...?

- go to a wedding
- rent a video
- go on a long car journey
- go to a disco or nightclub
- stay up all night
- go for a run
- speak English (apart from in class)
- take an exam
- perform in a play or a concert
- lose something important
- go a whole day without eating

> When did you last go to a wedding?

> The last wedding I went to was my sister's wedding about two years ago.

module 2 Important firsts

Vocabulary

Words to describe feelings

1 How do the people feel in each of the pictures below? Choose one of the adjectives from the box.

> nervous excited disappointed worried bored
> guilty frightened angry relaxed in a good mood
> embarrassed fed up surprised

(a) (b) (c) (d)

2 Which of the words in the box describe:

a positive feelings?   b negative feelings?

3 Use the words from Exercise 1 to answer the questions below. Ask your partner the same questions.

How do you normally feel?
- After an evening at home watching TV
- Just before an important exam
- If you can't remember someone's name
- If you have to speak in front of a lot of people
- If you have to wait in a long queue in a shop
- If you don't go out on a Saturday night
- If you go to a big rock concert
- If you miss a train or a bus
- If you see a big spider
- If a large animal like a cow comes towards you

Pronunciation

[2.4] Listen, write the word and mark the stress like this:

● .
nervous

Listening

The first time ever I saw your face

1 Discuss the questions below in small groups.

- What kind of music do you like best? What are your favourite songs and singers?
- What was the last CD/cassette that you bought?

2 a) Look at the title of the love song on page 19, but not the words. Guess which of the words below you will hear.

> the sun the moon burn gifts
> dark endless flirt joy
> the Earth trembling adore
> flowers cry captive command

b) [2.5] Listen and check.

c) Listen again. If the lines on page 19 are the same as the recording, write **S**. If a word or phrase is different, write **D**. Write in the correct words.

3 a) Which of these words describe the song? Why?

> sad loud romantic cheerful
> dramatic funny slow

b) Did you like the song? Why/Why not?

18

THE FIRST TIME EVER I SAW YOUR FACE

The first time ever I saw
your face   S
I thought the sun rose in
your ~~smile~~ eyes   D
And the moon and the stars
Were the gifts you gave
To the dark and the endless
sea, my love
To the dark and the
endless sea
And the first time ever I
kissed your lips
I saw the Earth move
in my hand
Like the trembling heart
Of a captive bird
That was here at my
command, my love
That was here at my command
The first time ever I saw
your face
I thought the sun rose
in your eyes
And I thought our joy
Would fill the Earth
And last till the end of life,
my love
And it would last till the
end of life

Wordspot

feel

1 The diagram below shows some common uses of *feel*. Tick (✓) the phrases that you already know. Write (?) next to the ones you are not sure about.

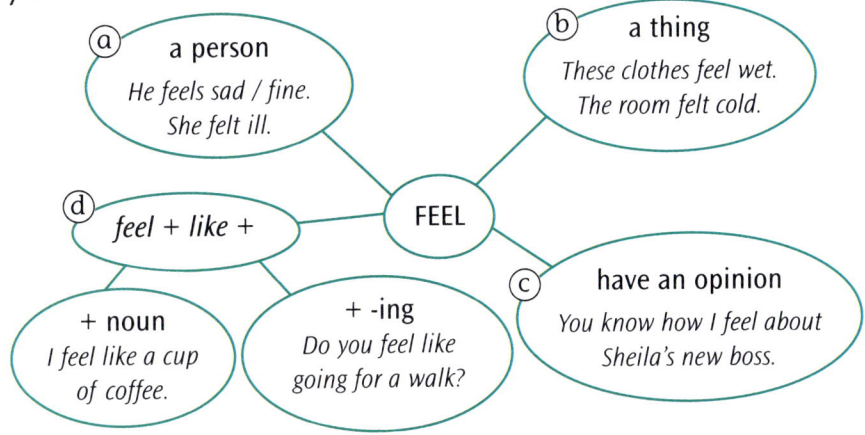

- ⓐ **a person** — He feels sad / fine. She felt ill.
- ⓑ **a thing** — These clothes feel wet. The room felt cold.
- ⓒ **have an opinion** — You know how I feel about Sheila's new boss.
- ⓓ **feel + like +**
  - **+ noun** — I feel like a cup of coffee.
  - **+ -ing** — Do you feel like going for a walk?

FEEL

2 a) Match a sentence from list A with a sentence from list B.

A

1. How's your mum today?
2. What do you feel like doing tonight?
3. What time did you go to bed last night?
4. How do you feel about our new boss?
5. Ooh, your hands feel cold!
6. Do you feel like a rest after your journey?
7. How was work?
8. I feel terrible about what I said to Tina.

B

a. Oh, before nine. I felt really tired.
b. Don't worry – I'm sure she wasn't upset.
c. No, it's OK, I slept a lot on the plane.
d. Oh, she's feeling much better, thanks.
e. Oh, terrible. Sometimes I feel like walking out.
f. I think he's OK. He's got some good ideas.
g. I don't know … what's on at the cinema?
h. I know – I left my gloves at home.

b) [2.6] Listen and check your answers.

3 Work in pairs. Student B closes his/her book and Student A reads out a sentence from list A above. Student B tries to remember the answer from list B above. Then change over.

19

module 2 Important firsts

Tell a first time story

Personal vocabulary

Useful language

a Telling the story

"This is the story of the first time I ..."

"I remember my first (*CD*) very well ..."

"I was (*nine*) at the time ..."

"I was in ..."

"I was with ..."

"I felt very/really ... because ..."

"I remember ... (*go*) -ing"

"At first ..."

"then ..."

b Listening

"Oh no!"

"So what did you do?"

"What happened next?"

"Really?"

Preparation for task

1 Which of these do you remember? Tick (✓) the appropriate boxes.
- your first day at school, college or work ☐
- the first time you travelled alone or went abroad ☐
- your first date ☐
- the first time you met someone important in your life ☐
- the first time you drove a car ☐
- your first English lesson ☐
- your first pet ☐
- the first cassette or CD you bought ☐
- the first time you bought clothes for yourself ☐
- another important first ☐

2 a) You will hear two people (David and Jayne) talking about the first time they did something. Look at the pictures opposite. Which of the things in Exercise 1 are they talking about? Discuss in pairs.

b) Can you guess what happened? Use the words in the boxes opposite to help you.

c) [2.7] Listen and check your answers.

3 Listen to one or both of the stories again and answer these questions. Compare answers with a partner.
a When/Where did it happen?
b Who else was in the story?
c What happened?
d How did he/she feel?

a service station   a coach
a trip   a cream cake

David

Jayne

gorgeous-looking
to cut yourself   blood

Task

1 You are going to tell the story of an important 'first' in your life, either one of the things in *Preparation for task* or an idea of your own. Work individually. Spend a few minutes deciding which story to tell (it should be a true story), and think about the answers to the questions in Exercise 3 above.

2 Ask your teacher for any words or phrases you need.
▶ *Personal vocabulary*

3 Work in pairs. Practise telling your story to your partner.
▶ *Useful language*

4 Work in small groups, with new partners. Listen/Tell your stories to each other.
Who told:
- the funniest story?
- the saddest story?
- the nicest story?

21

module 2 Important firsts

Writing

Linking ideas in narrative

1 a) Read what Marcos wrote about his first trip abroad and complete the text with the phrases 1–9.

1 <u>and</u> I went with three friends
2 because for all four of us it was our first time away from home
3 and I bought a silver ring for my sister
4 because I couldn't find it when I got on the coach that evening!
5 but I got up early and went to
6 so we decided to travel by coach.
7 but we didn't mind
8 so we went to Hyde Park for a game of football
9 then we went shopping in Oxford Street

b) Underline the linking words in Exercise 1.

For example: a <u>and</u>

2 Write the story that you told in the Task on page 21. Use at least three linking words.

The first time I went abroad was when I went to London. It was in the summer holidays about five or six years ago (a) _____ . The plane and train were quite expensive, (b) _____ . We left at five o'clock in the morning and the journey to London took about sixteen hours (c) _____ : we were all very excited (d) _____ .
We stayed in London for three days, in a youth hostel not far from the centre. While we were there we walked a lot. First we went to see all the famous sites – Big Ben, Piccadilly Circus, Buckingham Palace, (e) _____ . On the last morning my friends stayed in bed late, (f) _____ Camden Market. You can buy all kinds of jewellery and clothes there, (g) _____ . It was really hot and sunny in the afternoon, (h) _____ . Unfortunately, I think the ring fell out of my pocket during the game, (i) _____ .
I've been back to London several times since then, but I don't think I'll ever feel as excited as I did that first time.

Do you remember?

1 Think of two reasons for these situations.

a) Ben was late for work.
   Maybe he missed the bus.
   Maybe he didn't ...
b) Sonja didn't go to her cousin's wedding.
c) Lucy didn't eat her lunch.
d) Mike didn't answer the telephone.
e) Martha sold her car.

2 Put in the missing word in each sentence below.

a) When did you _{last} see the doctor?
b) I think the course started about two weeks.
c) He was here at eight o'clock morning.
d) Where did you go for your holidays year?
e) Clothes were very different in 1970s.

3 Rewrite the following sentences with *feel*.

a) I'm very cold and tired.
b) Do you want a drink?
c) This bread is hard: are you sure it's fresh?
d) Do you want a snack?

4 Join the sentences using *then*, *but*, *so* or *because*.

a) We couldn't go. Sue was ill.
b) The bus didn't come. I got a taxi to the station.
c) They loved the film. I didn't.
d) No – you put the sugar in first. You add the cream.

module 3
The best way to learn

▶ *Can, can't, have to, don't have to*
▶ *Vocabulary:* studying new vocabulary
▶ *Should/Shouldn't*
Task: make a list of guidelines for a language class

Language focus 1

Can, can't, have to, don't have to

1 [3.1] Listen to the people in the photos talking about learning foreign languages.

- Which language are they learning?
- Why are they learning?
- Whose reasons are closest to your own?

2 Which verb below did the speakers use? Listen again and check.

Ildiko
a   most foreigners *can/can't* speak Hungarian.

Karina
b   My husband *can/can't* speak Danish.
c   I *have to/don't have to* speak Greek at home.
d   When we go to Greece I *can/can't* talk to my husband's parents.

Ildiko

Karina

Dorothy

Daniel

Dorothy
e   I *have to/don't have* to study Italian for a special reason.

Daniel
f   I *have to/don't have to* learn English for my university exams.
g   If we don't pass we *can/can't* continue into the second year.
h   If we pass, we *can/can't* take another course instead of English.

Grammar analysis

1 Look at the verbs you choose in sentences a-h above. Which verb means:
 • it is possible?   • it is not possible?
 • it is necessary?   • it is not necessary?

2 Notice that *can/can't* show two different types of possibility:
 a ability
 My husband **can** speak Danish.
 I **can't** talk to my husband's parents.
 b permission/prohibition
 If we pass, we **can** take another course.
 If we don't pass, we **can't** continue into the second year.

▶ *Language summary A, page 150.*

module 3 The best way to learn

Practice

1 [3.2] Complete the sentences below with the most appropriate verb: *can, can't, have to* or *don't have to*. Listen and check your answers.

a In Hungary, before they ...*can*... enter university, students ...*have to*... take an exam in a foreign language.

b In Nigeria, 90% of the population ...*can*... speak more than one language.

c Almost 2 million people living in the USA ...*can't*... speak English!

d In Japan, children ...*have to*... know four alphabets by the age of ten.

e People in Sweden understand English so well that English language films ...*don't*... have to subtitles.

f About 75% of the population of Wales ...*can't*... actually speak Welsh.

g In most British secondary schools, children ...*can*... choose between learning French, Spanish or German.

h Children in Switzerland ...*don't have to*... study another language until they are eleven, and then they ...*have to*... study three!

Pronunciation

1 [3.3] Notice the stress and pronunciation of *can/can't* in the middle of a sentence. Listen and copy the pronunciation.
They can /kən/ choose which language they learn.
Most people in Wales can't /kɑːnt/ speak Welsh.

2 Tell other students which of the things below you can/can't do. Practise the sentences so that the other students understand **first** time.
- *can* speak another foreign language
- *can* remember new people's names
- *can't* use a washing machine
- *can* write very quickly
- *can't* sing in tune
- *can't* cook for yourself
- *can* use a computer
- *can* ski
- *can* drive

2 a) [3.4] Listen to Ellen talking about the British education system. What does she say about the things below? Use *can/can't/have to/don't have to* in your answers.

- RE (Religious Education) *have to study once a week*
- PE (Physical Education) *have to study one hour*
- Maths and English
- Geography and History *don't have to*
- Maths GCSE* and university *have to pass*
- the age of fourteen *don't have to study geography history*
- the age of sixteen *don't have stay in school*

* The exams that British pupils take at the age of 16 (General Certificate of Secondary Education).

b) Write five similar sentences about the education system in your country.

24

Reading and vocabulary

1 Which four things below are most important for learning a language?

hard work ☑ A T
enjoying learning ☐ A T
really believing that you will be successful ☐ A
having a good teacher ☐ A T
really wanting to learn (motivation) ☑ A T
studying lots of grammar ☑ T
getting praise from your teacher ☐ T
being realistic about the progress you can make ☐ A
'developing an ear' for the language ☐ A
reading and listening to lots of English ☑ T

2 You are going to read the opinions of two English teachers, Alastair and Teresa. As you read, mark each idea in Exercise 1:

A = Alastair talks about this
T = Teresa talks about this
A/T = Alastair and Teresa talk about this

3 Read the text again. Which words or phrases mean:

a you won't make much progress .... (para. 1)?
b become angry because you can't do what you want to do .... (para. 2)?
c see and pay attention to .... (para. 3)?
d often and carefully, and in an organised way .... (para. 4)?
e alone, without help .... (para. 5)?
f do something that makes you seem stupid .... (para. 6)?

4 Which pieces of advice are most useful? Discuss with other students.

What's the secret of successful language learning?

We asked two experienced teachers of English for their opinion.

Alastair Banton is a teacher at a private language school in the UK. He has also taught English in Japan.

1 I think the most important thing is that you really have to want to learn the language – without that, you won't get very far. You also have to believe that you will do it … imagine yourself using the language confidently, and think, 'Yes, I can do that'.

2 Then there are other things: of course you need to work hard, but at the same time you need to enjoy it and not get frustrated when you feel you're not making much progress. And you have to be realistic – learning a language takes time, and you can't expect to know and understand everything in a few weeks!

3 Also, you should try to 'develop an ear' for the language – not only to recognise the sounds of the language and to understand what people are saying, but also notice the exact words and phrases that people use … and then try to use them yourself. Some people can do this naturally, but others have to learn how to do it – that's where having a good teacher is important!

Teresa Pelc is a teacher of English in Poland. She has taught English in a secondary school for a number of years.

4 For me, motivation is the most important thing. You have to be ready to study grammar, read a lot, listen to English songs, radio and TV, and what's more you have to do these things systematically.

5 It is so easy to forget what you have just learnt … that's why I needed a teacher to force me to study. Even the most motivated students need that extra push sometimes. I believe that only a very few people can learn a language on their own.

6 Learning a language can be quite stressful, especially for adults … suddenly, we speak like children and make fools of ourselves! But if you're motivated, you learn to overcome this. It all sounds like very hard work – and it is. It is also very enjoyable – I praise my students for every thing they do well, however small it is. Many of them are very successful and speak English better than me, and some of them have even become English teachers themselves!

module 3 The best way to learn

Vocabulary and speaking
Studying new vocabulary

1 Here are some things that students do when they read or hear a new word in a foreign language. Which order do **you** normally do them in? Discuss in pairs.

- 3 You **practise saying it**.
- 2 You **look it up** in a dictionary or someone **explains** it **to** you.
- 1 You **write it down** in your notebook.
- You try to **guess** what it means.
- 5 You **think of** a way to remember it.
- 6 You **try hard** to use it in conversation.
- 4 You **check** the pronunciation.

2 Discuss these questions with other students. Be honest!

- Which of the things in Exercise 1 do you **always** do when you read or hear a new word?
- Which do you **sometimes** do?
- Which do you **never** do?
- Should you do any of these things more often?
- What is the best order to do these things in?

3 We can use the words from Exercise 1 in other situations too. Add one more situation for each of the words below. Use your mini-dictionary to help you.

a You can **look up**:
a phone number ☐   the time of a train ☐

b You can **check**:
your e-mails ☐
your answers to an exercise ☐

c You can **find out**:
the date ☐   where something is ☐

d You can **guess**:
the answer to a question ☐
someone's age ☐

e You can **practise**:
a musical instrument ☐   a song ☐

f You can **write down**:
someone's address ☐
the answers to an exercise ☐

Language focus 2
Should/Shouldn't

Read about Stephanie. What advice does she want? Which do you think is the best advice? Do you have any other ideas?

Stephanie has won a competition at her college. The prize is a two-month language course in Edinburgh. She will have English lessons every morning, but she wants to improve her English outside class. Her friends, family and teachers have lots of advice.

Perhaps you should join a sports club or something – then you can make friends and practise your English!

I think you should try to spend two or three hours every afternoon in the school library reading the newspaper and doing grammar exercises.

Why don't you try to get a part-time job in a café, or something? You'll have to speak English and you can earn some money too.

Just try to speak to everyone. You shouldn't worry if you make mistakes, or if you don't understand everything that people say – just try to understand what you can.

26

Grammar analysis

1 Look at the word *should* below. Which is the best explanation of the meaning:

Perhaps you should join a sports club.
• this is necessary?   • this is a good idea/the right thing to do?

2 What are the negative and question forms of *should*?

▶ *Language summary B, pages 150–151.*

Practice

1 **a)** Bruce is studying for some important exams. Look at the room and find the things in the box.

| an ashtray | a cigarette end | the bin | some rubbish |
| his notes | his files | a computer game | a dressing gown |

b) Do you agree with the following sentences? Why/Why not?

His coffee cup shouldn't be on the computer.
He shouldn't smoke so much when he's studying.

c) Find **ten** more things that **you** think he should do differently.

2 Read the following difficult situations. Discuss what each person *should/shouldn't* do.

> Carla's grandmother shouldn't give her money.

1 Carla, a student, is very bad with money. Every month she spends all her money on clothes and going out, and then doesn't have enough for books, etc. Her parents are annoyed with her, and say that she has to learn to be more careful, so they won't give her any extra money. But Carla's grandmother secretly gives her the extra money every time Carla sees her. Carla's parents know what is happening!

2 Nick, who is nineteen, has been going out with his girlfriend, Lucy, since he was sixteen. His parents do not seem to like Lucy. They have never actually said that they dislike her, but they are silent when he talks about her. So now Nick has stopped bringing her to his house, and doesn't talk about her to them.

3 A few years ago, Marina was a bit overweight. She's quite slim now, but she worries about putting on weight again. Instead of eating healthy meals she misses breakfast and lunch. Then in the evening, after a very small meal, she eats chocolate and crisps. Her mother is very worried about her, and tries to force her to eat three meals a day.

module 3 The best way to learn

Make a list of guidelines for a language class

Personal vocabulary

Useful language

a **Useful vocabulary**

"arrive/finish on time"

"interrupt each other/the teacher"

"listen to each other/the teacher"

"use our own language/English"

"make/correct mistakes"

"do/give/mark homework"

"work in pairs and groups"

"give/do tests"

"chat"

b **Talking about what's important**

"We think it's very important to …"

"Everyone should try to …"

"People shouldn't be afraid to …"

"We should always/never …"

"Everyone has to …"

Kristina teaches a class of university students. They meet for three hours a week, and there are about twenty-five students in the class.

Preparation for task

1 a) Kristina and her class worked together to make a set of classroom guidelines: six for the teacher and six for the students. You will hear Kristina talking about the six guidelines **for the teacher**. What do you think they agreed about the following:

1 the teacher speaking their own language/speaking English?
2 giving homework?
3 making the lessons interesting?
4 the teacher answering questions?
5 the coursebook?
6 correcting the students' mistakes?

b) [3.5] Listen to what Kristina and her students agreed about each of the topics above.

2 What do you agree with? What do you disagree with?

28

Real life

Making requests and asking for permission

1 a) Look at the conversations below. Where are the people? What does each person want? What are the missing words?

1 A: ... and one of the things that you can also do is ...
   B: I'm sorry. *Could you speak more* slowly, please?
   A: Sorry. And one of the things that you can also do ... is that OK?
   B: Yes, I can understand much better now *thank* you.

2 A: I'm sorry, *is it ok to leave* the class early today?
   B: Yeah, I suppose so. Is there a problem?
   A: It's my younger sister. I have to take her to the dentist's.
   B: Oh, I see. Sure, *go ahead*. Thanks for *telling me*.

3 A: João, do you have an English-Portuguese dictionary?
   B: Um ... yes ...
   A: *Can I borrow it*, please?
   B: OK, *here you are*.

4 A: *Do you mind if I* change seats?
   B: Yes, all right. *What is the problem*?
   A: I can't see because of the sun.
   B: OK, then. Why don't you sit over there, next to Andrea?

b) [3.6] Listen to the conversations and check your answers. Which speakers are:

- making requests?
- asking for permission?

Pronunciation

1 Notice that intonation is very important if you want to be polite in these situations.

   Is it OK if I ...   Is it OK if I leave early?
   Can I borrow ...   Can I borrow your dictionary, please?
   Could you ...   Could you speak more slowly, please?
   Do you mind if ...   Do you mind if I change seats?

2 [3.7] Listen and repeat the sentences. Copy the voices on the recording.

Task

1 Work in pairs or groups.

Either: make a list of similar guidelines for **your** English class, but be realistic. If the guidelines are too difficult, no one will follow them!

Or: imagine you are teaching a group of foreigners how to speak **your** language. They live in your country and can speak a little of the language. Make a list of ten guidelines to follow.

2 Ask your teacher for any other words and phrases you need.
▶ *Personal vocabulary*
▶ *Useful language*

3 Compare your list to those of other groups. How many of your points were the same and how many were different? Try to agree as a class on the ten most important guidelines.

Optional writing

Write your list of guidelines for teachers and students and put it on the classroom wall. See if you can keep to the guidelines for the rest of this course!

29

module 3 The best way to learn

2 With a partner write four-line conversations for **four** of these situations. Act out some of them for class.

- You're very hot and would like to open the window.
- You can't see the board because the teacher is standing in front of it.
- You need to make an urgent phone call.
- Someone's mobile phone is always ringing during the lesson.
- You don't know how to write a new word that your teacher has just taught you.
- Another student is always talking when you are trying to listen to the teacher.
- The teacher is playing a cassette but it isn't loud enough.
- You would like to borrow another student's rubber.

Do you remember?

1 Complete the gaps with a suitable verb from the box.

> pass   find out   interrupt
> write down   make

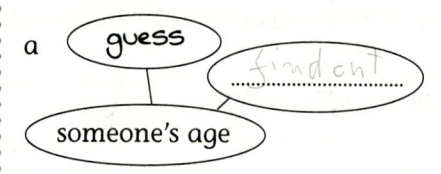

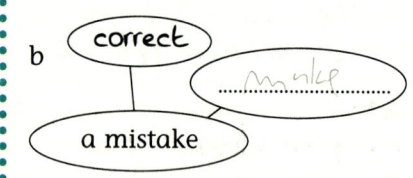

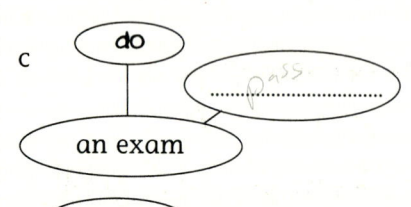

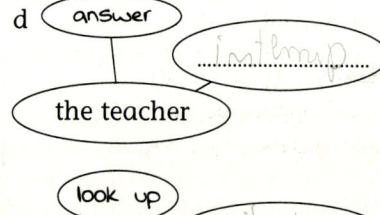

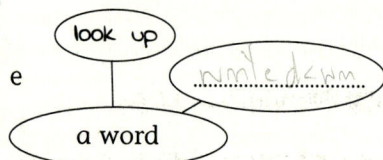

a guess — *find out* — someone's age
b correct — *make* — a mistake
c do — *pass* — an exam
d answer — *interrupt* — the teacher
e look up — *write down* — a word

2 Think of two things:
a) you can do on a beach.
b) you can't do on a plane.
c) you don't have to do when you are three years old.
d) you have to do when you are at school.
e) you should do if you want to lose weight.
f) you shouldn't do if you want to save money.

3 Who usually does these things, the teacher or the students?
a) looks up words in the dictionary
b) does homework
c) checks homework
d) corrects mistakes
e) gives tests
f) writes things down in their notebooks

4 Put the words in the correct order to make questions.
a) you/please/Could/the/open/window/?
b) smoke/I/mind/Do/if/you/?
c) borrow/I/your/Can/please/newspaper/?
d) later/again/Could/phone/you/?
e) your/OK/if/Is/use/printer/it/I/?

5 Match the questions in Exercise 4 with answers from the box below. Ask and answer with a partner.

> Sure, here you are.
> Oh, I'm sorry, it's not working at the moment.
> Yes, it's very hot in here, isn't it?
> No problem, go ahead.
> OK. About eight?

30

module 4
Special occasions

- ▶ Vocabulary: dates and special occasions
- ▶ Present Continuous (and Present Simple)
- ▶ Wordspot: *day*
- ▶ Present Continuous for future arrangements

Task: prepare and talk about a personal calendar

Vocabulary and speaking

Dates and special occasions

1 Which are your favourite months of the year? Why? When's your birthday? Is this a good month to have a birthday?

2 a) Do you celebrate these days in your country? Say **when** they happen. Put them in order.

American Independence Day
New Year's Eve   Halloween
Easter   Chinese New Year
May Day   Christmas Day
St Valentine's Day   Father's Day
Mother's Day

b) [4.1] Listen and make notes about when they happen in Britain/the USA. Which are different in your country?

Pronunciation

1 Notice the difference between the way you write and say dates.

You write: 5.6.2001   or   5th June 2001.
You say: the fifth of June   or   June the fifth.

2 [4.2] Practise saying these dates. Pay attention to the pronunciation of *th* /θ/ or /ð/.

/ð/   /ð/   /ð/ /θ/
April *the* first   *the* first of May   *the* four*th* of July

/ð/   /θ/   /ð/ /θ/
February *the* fourteen*th*   *the* *th*irty-first of October

3 Which other special days do you celebrate in your country? When are they?

4 a) Which of these things do you/your family/your friends do on the special days in Exercises 2 and 3 above?

send cards to people   visit relatives   spend a lot of money
give presents   make a special cake   have a special meal at home
stay out late   have a party   buy flowers   go out for a meal
have the day off work   dress up

b) Think of one other reason why people do these things.

For example: You send a card when someone gets married.

31

module 4 Special occasions

Language focus 1
Present Continuous (and Present Simple)

Imogen
Personal assistant

Carlos
Photographer

Juliet
Editor

1 The people in the picture work for a fashion magazine called *Glitz*. How do you think they spend a normal working day? Who:

a chooses articles for the magazine?
b makes the coffee?
c earns the most money?
d takes a lot of photographs?
e does the photocopying?
f has a lot of business lunches?
g answers the phone?
h has the most interesting job?

What else do they do in their jobs?

2 Today is 1st May, a national holiday, so everybody at *Glitz* has the day off. Read about how Imogen is spending the day.

Imogen is spending her day off with her husband, Alex. Imogen and Alex usually go away at the weekend, either in the countryside or to the beach, or they meet friends. But today they aren't doing anything special – they're just sitting at home, relaxing. Imogen likes her job at Glitz, but she doesn't want to be a PA all her life: that's why she's also doing a course in fashion design at night school. One day, she wants to have her own design company. She's finding the course really useful.

Grammar analysis

1 Find another example of rules a, b and c in Language Focus 1, Exercise 2.

a We use the Present Simple for things that are generally or always true.
They usually go away at the weekend.

b We use the Present Continuous for actions in progress at this moment.
They're sitting at home.

c We use the Present Continuous for actions in progress 'in the present period'.
She's doing a course in fashion design.
(= this year, but not right now)

2 How do we form questions and negatives in the Present Continuous?

3 We don't usually use the Present Continuous for verbs that describe states.
She likes her job.
She doesn't want to be a PA all her life.

Other verbs like this are:
be   have   love   hate
know   think

▶ *Language summary A, page 151.*

Practice

1 Complete the paragraph about Carlos with the Present Simple or Present Continuous.

Carlos (1) _is spending_ (spend) his day off with his family. His family (2) _live_ (live) quite far away, so he (3) _doesn't see_ (not see) them very often. But today is a special day: his parents (4) _are celebrating_ (celebrate) their wedding anniversary. Carlos (5) _spends_ (spend) most of his free time working on his motorbike. He (6) _doesn't like_ (not like) his job at *Glitz* magazine very much, so he (7) _is looking_ (look) for another job. He (8) _wants_ (want) to take photos of motorbikes instead of fashion models!

2 Write some sentences about Juliet using the picture and ideas below to help you. Use your imagination!

- She's spending her day off with _her mother._
- At the weekends she usually _goes out_ _her and her parents home_
- Today she's _painting the rooms_
- Her husband is/isn't _painting because he doesn't like this_
- (S)he doesn't ...
- One day she wants to _have only her and her family house_

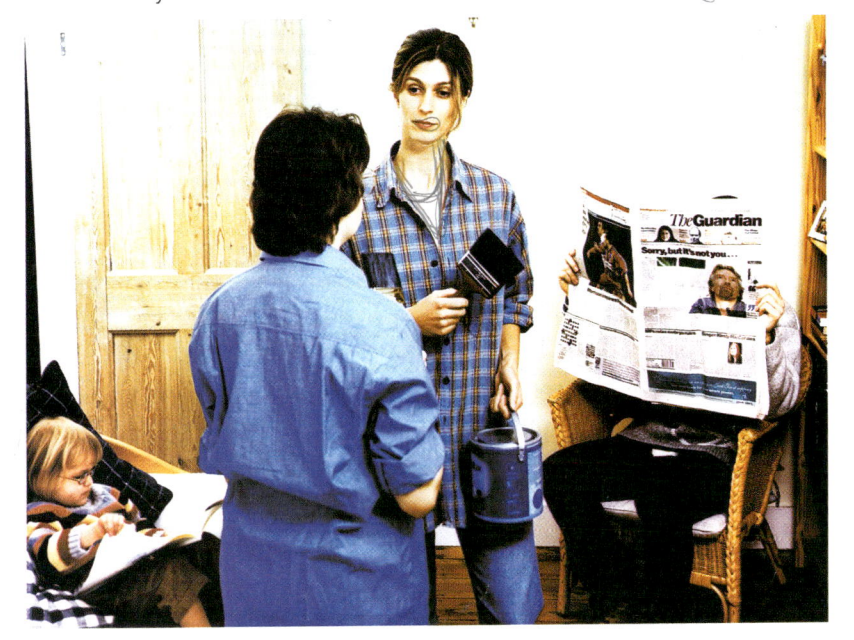

3 a) Choose the correct form in the prompts below to make true sentences about yourself.

1 At the moment, I learn/I'm learning *English/another language/to drive.*
2 I speak/I'm speaking *one language/two languages/more than two languages.*
3 I (don't) like/I'm (not) liking *my job/my school/my English classes.*
4 I never read/I'm never reading *comics/novels/fashion magazines.*
5 At the moment, I read/I'm reading *a book/a good book called … /a boring book called …*
6 Today I (don't) wear/I'm (not) wearing *jeans/a jumper/a suit.*
7 This year, I study/I'm studying *for a school exam/for a university exam/just English.*
8 I usually spend/I'm usually spending Sundays *at home/with my friends/with my family.*
9 At the moment, I try/I'm trying hard to *learn English/stop smoking/find a job.*
10 Right now, I'm (not)/I'm (not) being *very busy/very tired/very well.*

b) Compare answers with a partner. Find at least three things you have in common.

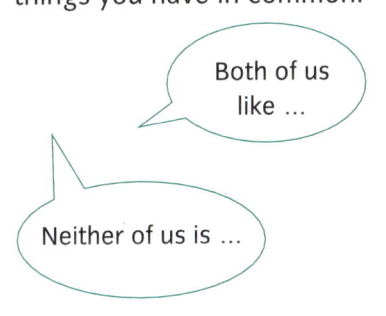

> Both of us like …

> Neither of us is …

33

module 4 Special occasions

Wordspot
day

1 [4.3] Complete the conversations with a word from the box to make a phrase with *day*. Listen and check.

> one   these   the other   every   out   off
> after tomorrow

a A: Do you still go to the gym?
   B: I'm not going much at the moment, I haven't got time. I'm too busy ...these... days.

b A: Do you ever see Joanna Merchant?
   B: Yes, I met her in town ...the other... day.

c A: I'm so tired I need a day ...off... .
   B: You say that ...every... day. Just ask your boss!

d A: When's Joe's birthday? He's so excited about it!
   B: It's the day ...after tomorrow... – we're having a party.

e A: That's 6–4 to me.
   B: Not again! ...One... day I'll beat you!

f A: Did you have a good weekend?
   B: Yes, really nice. We went for a day ...out... in the countryside.

2 Put the phrases from Exercise 1 into the correct section of the diagram below.

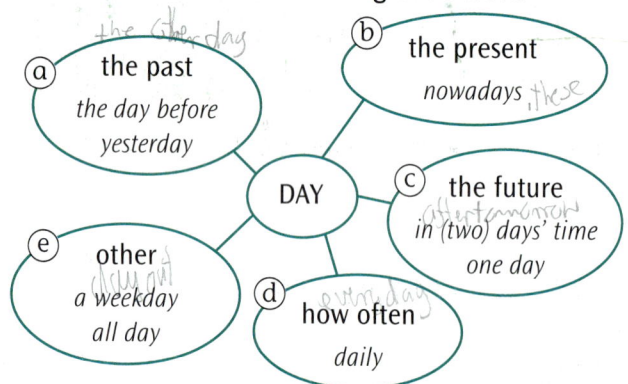

- (a) the past — *the day before yesterday*, the other day
- (b) the present — *nowadays*, these
- (c) the future — *in (two) days' time*, *one day*, after tomorrow
- (d) how often — *daily*, every day
- (e) other — *a weekday*, *all day*, day off

DAY

3 a) [4.4] Listen and write your answers to the questions on a piece of paper. You can write just one word or a short phrase.
For example: I went shopping.

b) Work in pairs. Look at your partner's answers. Try to remember the questions.

Listening
New Year in two different cultures

1 Is New Year an important celebration in your country? What do people usually do?

2 You will hear Karen and Johnny describing Scottish and Chinese New Year. Who do you think mentions these things?

> mushrooms and oysters ☑   fruit cakes ☑
> new clothes ☑   cleaning the house ☑
> little red envelopes of money ☑
> the front and back door ☑

Karen is from Perth, in West Scotland.

Johnny Wong's family live in Hong Kong.

3 a) [4.5] Listen and mark the things **K** if Karen says them, and **J** if Johnny says them.

b) Listen again. Find **one** similarity and **three** differences between the two New Years.

c) Are there any similarities with your country?

34

Language focus 2

Present Continuous for future arrangements

1 It's just before New Year. Read three people's plans. Which verbs below complete each gap?

> cook   rent   go   meet   come   have

Giacomo from Italy

"This New Year my family (a) .... a house in the mountains. Some friends of mine (b) .... to stay. It'll be great!"

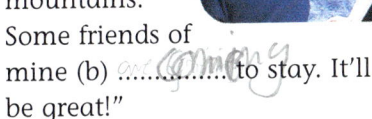

Nick from England

"I (c) .... a party on New Year's Eve. I've invited hundreds of people. I hope they all come!"

Nestor from Brazil

"My mother (d) .... a special dinner for all the family. Then, at twelve o'clock, my friends and I (e) .... to the beach. We (f) .... lots of other people for a big beach party!"

2 🔊 [4.6] Listen and complete the gaps. Whose plans sound most interesting?

Grammar analysis

Tick (✓) the best explanation. The people on the left use the Present Continuous to talk about:

a   things they **want to do** at New Year.
b   things they **think they will probably do** at New Year.
c   things they **have definitely arranged to do** at New Year. ✓

▶ Language summary B, page 151.

Practice

1 Find out about your classmates' plans and arrangements. Decide which questions to ask. Use the words in brackets.

Find someone in your class who ...

a   ... is going out for a meal this evening. (Where?/Who with?)
    Name: ....   Notes: ....
b   ... is doing something unusual this weekend. (What?)
    Name: ....   Notes: ....
c   ... is meeting someone after this lesson. (Who?)
    Name: ....   Notes: ....
d   ... is going shopping today or tomorrow. (Where?/Who with?)
    Name: ....   Notes: ....
e   ... is having a birthday party soon. (When ... party?)
    Name: ....   Notes: ....
f   ... is cooking a meal this evening. (What?/Who for?)
    Name: ....   Notes: ....
g   ... is taking an important exam in the future. (When?)
    Name: ....   Notes: ....
h   ... is going abroad soon. (Where?/Why?)
    Name: ....   Notes: ....

2 Go round the class, asking and answering the questions.

For example:
A: Are you going out for a meal this evening?
B: Yes.
A: Where are you going?
B: I'm going to a new restaurant called Da Corradi.
A: Who are you going with?

You have **ten minutes** to speak to as many people as possible. Write in the names and other information about these people.

3 Compare answers briefly with other students. Is there anything that **nobody** is doing?

... module 4 Special occasions ...

Prepare and talk about a personal calendar

Personal vocabulary

MONTH	1 DATE	2 WHY IT'S IMPORTANT/OTHER INFORMATION
JANUARY	11	Passed test – very nervous before!
FEBRUARY	14	Never send a card but always receive lots!
MARCH		
APRIL		
MAY		Younger sister's birthday. Always phone her and sings heaps (birthday)
JUNE	2	Festa in Rabat – her town – a big party in the street.
JULY		
AUGUST		
SEPTEMBER	21	Independence Day. Country became independent in 1964.
OCTOBER	23	My friend Glen coming from New Zealand.
NOVEMBER		
DECEMBER	1	Parents' 25th wedding anniversary – having a big family party

Useful language

a Explaining your calendar

"(the 2nd of March) is my mother's birthday"

"For (July) I put (the nineteenth) because that's the day when ..."

"In (Spain) the most important date is ... because ..."

"In May we always go to .../ I'm going to .../I went to ... "

b Questions

"What happens/happened/is happening on ...?"

"What do you usually do on ...?"

"Why did you put ...?"

"Why is ... important for you?"

Preparation for task

1 You will hear two people talking about dates that are important for them. What do you think they will talk about?

2 a) [4.7] Listen and complete **only** column 1 in the table.

b) Listen again and complete the notes in column 2 of the table.

Task

1 Work individually. Draw a personal calendar, like the one above. Spend five to ten minutes completing it with important dates in **your** life. Include:

- important dates from the past.
- important things that happen every year, either in your personal life, or in your country.
- arrangements for this year.

36

Real life

Phrases for special occasions

New Year	Birthday	Illness
Christmas	Wedding	Wedding anniversary

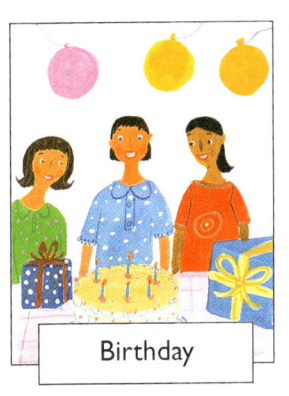

1 Match the phrases below with the occasions in the pictures. (Some of them can be used with more than one picture.)

Happy New Year!　　Happy anniversary!　　Thanks for coming.
It's lovely, thank you very much.　　Happy birthday!
Merry Christmas!　　Congratulations!　　Good health!
I hope you'll be very happy!　　I hope you feel better soon!
Good luck!　　Many happy returns!　　Cheers!
The best of luck for the future/your operation/the New Year ...

Pronunciation

[4.8] It is important to use friendly, positive intonation with these phrases. Listen and repeat.

2 [4.9] Listen to the beginnings of some conversations. When you hear a beep, choose the best phrase from the box above.

3 Work in pairs. Practise the conversations using the tapescript on page 161 to help you. Think of similar conversations of your own. Practise them with your partner.

2 Spend a few minutes planning what you will say.
▶ *Useful language a)*
▶ *Personal vocabulary*

3 Work in pairs or small groups. Tell the other students about your personal calendar. Your partners can ask questions.
▶ *Useful language b)*
What was the most interesting thing you found out?

37

Writing

A letter of invitation

1 Read the letter below quickly. What is the invitation for?

> 43 Amock Terrace
> Edinburgh
>
> April 14th
>
> Dear Sofia
>
> ① How are you? I'm fine. I've got a new job in the marketing department, so I get more money, but it's hard work. It's been a long time since I last saw you. I remember you were very busy helping your friend get ready for her wedding – I hope it all went well and that the weather stayed fine!
>
> ② Actually, I'm writing to tell you about another wedding. My brother Andy and Anushka finally set a date for their wedding – 20th August – we'll send you an invitation in a few weeks. Anyway, my parents want to celebrate the engagement, so we're having a special lunch on Sunday 3rd May. We're inviting relatives and close friends, so there'll be about twenty people at the party, and we'd love to see you.
>
> ③ I know it's quite a long way for you to come, but Rob is driving up, so maybe you could come with him. If not, I can meet you at the station – just let me know when your train gets in.
>
> ④ I'm going away for two weeks tomorrow, but you can phone my parents to tell them if you're coming. Their number is 0131 445892. I really hope you can come!
>
> Love from
> Marina

2 Which paragraph tells Sofia:
- how she can get to the party?
- personal news about Marina since the last time they met?
- the reason for the invitation and details about the event?
- how she can reply to the invitation?

3 Write a letter to a friend, inviting him or her to a special occasion, real or imaginary.

Do you remember?

1 Put the twelve months of the year under the correct stress pattern.

●●●	●●	●●	● ● ●	●
January	April		September	March

2 Think of two reasons why you:
- send a card. *Easter, Valentine's Day, Birthday*
- spend a lot of money. *Christmas, Birthday*
- say congratulations. *Wedding Anniversary*
- give a present. *Birthday, Christmas*

3 Match the words in A with those in B to make phrases from Module 4.

A	B
a) visit	the phone
b) dress	some money
c) earn	your relatives
d) answer	some photographs
e) take	the photocopying
f) do	up

4 What is the *-ing* form of these verbs?
a) sit *ting* b) drive *ing* c) study *ing* d) make *ing*
e) write *ing* f) travel *ling*

5 Circle the correct verb in these sentences.
a) Mum ~~makes~~/*'s making* a cake – it smells great!
b) Anthea *visits*/~~'s visiting~~ her aunt every month.
c) Trude ~~doesn't spend~~/*isn't spending* her holidays with us this year.
d) Carl ~~earns~~/*'s earning* extra money this week.
e) *Do you know*/~~Are you knowing~~ the answer?
f) I ~~celebrate~~/*am celebrating* my birthday on Saturday.

6 Do the phrases mean the same? If not, explain the difference.
a) one day/the other day
b) every day/daily
c) the day after tomorrow/in two days' time
d) have a day off/have a day out
e) nowadays/these days

38

module 5
Appearances

▶ Comparatives and superlatives
▶ Describing what people look like
▶ Wordspot: *look*
Task: describe a suspect to the police

Language focus 1

Comparatives and superlatives

1 Look at the photograph of three sisters. Do they look alike? In what way?

2 [5.1] Listen to Emma talk about her family.

- Which sisters do people think are very similar?
- Do they have similar personalities?

3 Listen again. This is a summary of what Emma says. Complete the gaps.

a Emma is the *oldest*. But her sisters are *taller than* her.
b Emma looks very *similar* to Sophie.
c They both *look like* their father.
d They all have the same colour *eyes* as their father.
e In personality, Emma is very *different from* her sisters.
f They are .... organised *than* Emma.
g Kath is better *than* Emma at remembering *things*.

Emma, 28   Sophie, 26   Kath, 21

Grammar analysis

1 What are the comparatives and superlatives of these adjectives?

1 syllable	tall slim pale
2 syllables ending in -y	pretty friendly
2/3 or more syllables	organised modern
irregular forms	good bad

2 Match the beginning of the sentences in A with the ends of the sentences in B. Notice the prepositions used.

A
a He's **older**
b He's **the tallest**
c It's **the same**
d It's **similar**
e It's **different**
f He **looks**

B
from ours.
like you.
than me.
as mine.
in the class.
to yours.

3 Notice that we can compare nouns using *more*.
She's got **more energy than** me.
He spends **more money** on clothes **than** me.

▶ *Language summary A, page 151.*

39

module 5 Appearances

Practice

1 Make **eight** sentences about the people in your class using comparatives and superlatives. Use some of the ideas below.

> long/short hair   tall/short   young/old   dark/fair hair
> big/small hands   heavy/light bag   number of rings
> warm/cool clothes   bright/dark top   number of books
> number of brothers and sisters

Patrick has got shorter hair than Stefan.

2 Complete the sentences about you and your family. (There are several ways to do this.)

a *Harriet* is the *youngest* person in my family.
b People often say I look like …
c I look very different from …
d My hair is … my mother's/sister's.
e My eyes are … my brother's/my grandmother's.
f I'm … than my brother/sister/cousin.
g My mother's … than my father.
h My father's the … person in my family.
i In my family, … is more organised than …

3 Work in small groups. Tell your partners about the people in your family, without looking at the sentences in Exercise 2.

Pronunciation

1 [5.2] Put the words of the sentences into the correct order. Listen and check.
   a My mother's/my father/than/older
   b I'm/from/very/my sister/different
   c Her hair's/mine/very/similar/to
   d She's/I know/nicest/the/person
   e His nose is/mine/as/same/the

2 [5.3] Notice the short sound /ə/ in these phrases, when you say them in the middle of a sentence. Practise saying them in sentences.

/ə/ /ə/	/ə/ /ə/	/ə/ /ə/
older than	different from	similar to
/ə/	/ə/	/ə/ /ə/
the nicest	the biggest	the same as

You're gorgeous!

Reading and vocabulary

1 a) Who do **you** think is the most attractive man/woman in the world? Why?

b) Which is the best explanation of the saying below? Do you think it is true?

Beauty is in the eye of the beholder.

- It is important to have beautiful eyes.
- Everyone has their own idea about beauty.
- Everyone wants to look at a beautiful person.

2 a) Which pictures above show modern ideas of beauty? Why do you think the people in the pictures were/are considered attractive?

b) Read the text and check your answers.

3 Which of these statements do we **know** are true? Explain your answers.

a Pale skin was more popular than tanned skin until the twentieth century. ✓
b Elizabethan make-up was not very safe.
c In the eighteenth century most fashionable ladies liked mice.
d Ladies in Rubens' times probably never went on diets.
e If Paduang women didn't have a long neck, they couldn't get married.
f People in the eighteenth century thought that it was OK for men to cry.
g Dinka women from Sudan think that thin men are very ugly.

40

1   For many in the 1990s, supermodel Cindy Crawford was the perfect American dream girl: slim, tanned and natural-looking, with long, shiny hair. People have described her as 'The Face of the Decade'.

2   But people have not always had the same ideas about beauty. Until the 1920s, suntans were for poor people, 'ladies' stayed out of the sun to keep their faces as pale as possible. In the times of Queen Elizabeth I of England, fashionable ladies even painted their faces with lead to make them whiter – a very dangerous habit, since lead is poisonous!

3   And people in the eighteenth century would not have thought much of Cindy Crawford's hair! Ladies in those days never went out without their wigs, which were so enormous (and dirty) that it was quite common to find mice living in them. As for the 'perfect beauties' painted by Rubens in the seventeenth century, if they wanted to be supermodels today, they would need to spend months on a diet!

4   Ideas of beauty can be very different according to where you live in the world, too. For the Paduang tribe in South East Asia, traditionally, the most important sign of female beauty was a long neck. So at the age of five or six, girls received their first neck ring, and each year they added new rings. By the time they were old enough to marry, their necks were about twenty-five centimetres long!

5   And what about the ideal man? If you asked people today to name an attractive man, most of them would mention someone like James Bond, Harrison Ford, or Denzel Washington: someone tall and athletic, brave and 'manly'.

6   In the eighteenth century however, 'manliness' was very different from what it is today. As well as wearing wigs, perfume and lots of make-up, a true gentleman showed that he had feelings by crying frequently in public. According to one story, when the British Prime Minister, Lord Spencer Percival, came to give King George IV some bad news, both men sat down and cried!

7   And even now, James Bond might not find it so easy to attract women if he visited the Dinka tribe of Sudan. They have always believed in the saying that 'big is beautiful'. Traditionally, each year, men compete to win the title of 'the fattest man'. The winner is sure to find a wife quickly: for a Dinka woman, if a man is fat, it is also a sign that he is rich and powerful!

4 **a)** Complete the diagram below with words from the text. (You may not find words for every section.)

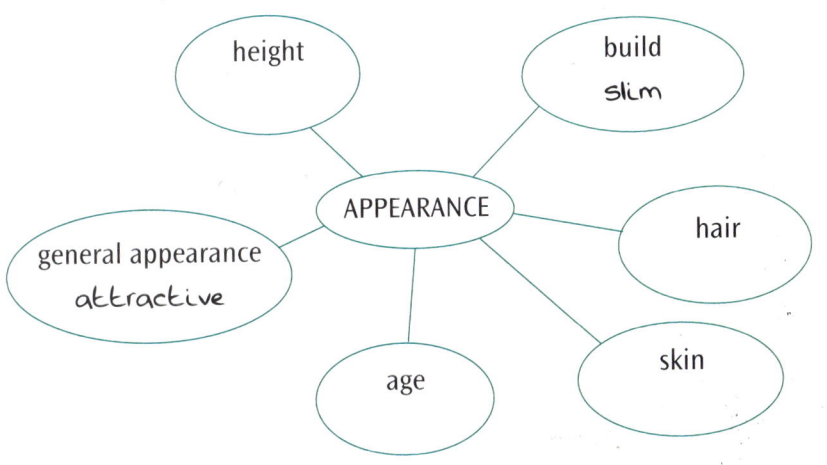

- height
- build — slim
- APPEARANCE
- hair
- general appearance — attractive
- skin
- age

b) Can you add any other words? Look back to Language focus 1 on page 39 to help you.

Pronunciation

1   How many syllables do these adjectives have? Underline the stressed syllables.
For example:

1 2 3
<u>beau</u> – ti – ful

1 2 3
<u>in</u> – teres – ting

gorgeous   well-dressed
tanned   ordinary
fashionable   old-fashioned
ancient   traditional

2   [5.4] Listen and check your answers. Practise saying the words.

module 5 Appearances

Language focus 2
Describing what people look like

1 Match the questions in A with the answers in B.

A
a How old is he?
b How tall is he?
c Is he black or white?
d What does he look like, generally?
e What's his hair like?
f What colour are his eyes?
g Has he got a beard or a moustache?

B
No, he hasn't.
It's dark and wavy and he's going grey.
He's quite slim, and attractive, but he looks a bit untidy sometimes.
I don't know exactly, but I think he's in his forties.
I think they're brown.
White.
He's about average height, I think.

Eddi Murphy

Tom Cruise

2 Which of these film stars is described in the answers? Do you agree with the description?

3 a) [MD] Here are some more possible answers to the questions in A above. Match the answers to the correct questions.

> He's quite good-looking but a bit overweight.   They're grey.
> It's short and dark.   He looks a bit strange.   He's black.
> He's got a moustache, but not a beard.   It's completely white.
> About 1.80 m, I suppose.   He's very tidy and well-dressed.
> He looks very ordinary – average height, average build.
> He's middle-aged, about 55.   He's in his twenties.   He's not very tall.

b) Can you use any of these phrases to describe these film stars? Think of some other phrases to describe them.

Clint Eastwood

Woody Allen

Brad Pitt

Richard Gere

42

Grammar analysis

1 Complete the gaps in the questions and answers. Which use *be* and which use *have got*?

a A: .... colour .... his hair?
  B: .... black.
b A: .... tall .... she?
  B: About 1.72 m.
c A: .... he .... a beard?
  B: No, but he's .... a moustache.
d A: .... old .... she?
  B: She's .... twenties.
e A: What .... her eyes ....?
  B: .... lovely: dark brown and very big.
f A: What .... he ...., generally?
  B: He .... a bit strange, I think.

2 Look at questions e and f. Which asks:
- about a person's appearance?
- for a description/opinion of something?

▶ Language summary B, pages 151–152.

Practice

1 Use these words to make correct sentences/questions.

a What/your new dress?
  (Answer: It's really long and black, it's gorgeous!)
b What/colour/her/eyes?
c He/long hair?
d They/teens.
e What/her husband/look?
f What/her children/look?
g He/glasses and a beard.

2 Work in pairs or teams, A and B. A thinks of a famous person (male or female). B asks up to ten questions to find out who it is. When B guesses, change roles.

Wordspot

look

1 Read the sentences. Add the phrases with *look* to the correct section of the diagram.

a Stop **looking out of** the window and listen.
b That barman **looks like** Brad Pitt, doesn't he!
c **Look** how many people there are on the beach!
d I'm **looking for** a book about cats.
e Are those your photos? Can I **have a look**?
f What a **strange-looking** dog!
g I'm **looking forward** to seeing you.
h **Look**, I don't really know how to tell you this, but I'm going away soon … for two years.
i I know he was bored. He **looked at** his watch every five minutes.
j Could you **look up** Mr White's address, please?

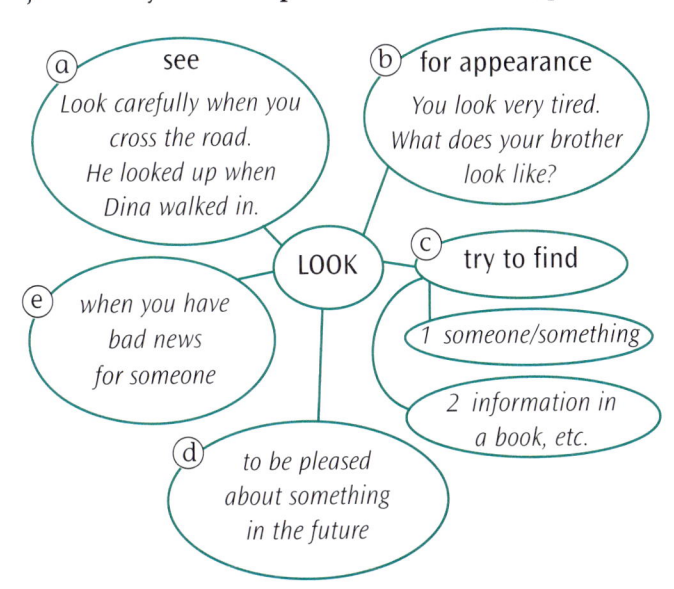

(a) see
Look carefully when you cross the road. He looked up when Dina walked in.

(b) for appearance
You look very tired. What does your brother look like?

(c) try to find
1 someone/something
2 information in a book, etc.

(d) to be pleased about something in the future

(e) when you have bad news for someone

LOOK

2 Finish the sentences below about yourself. Use a phrase with *look* in your answer.

a Why do you:
  • go to the library?   • use a dictionary?
b Finish the sentences below about yourself.
  • I think I look good in ..*blue*...... .
  • I'm really looking forward to ....
  • When I look out of my bedroom window, I can see ....
  • I would like to look like ....
  • I look up about .... new words every English lesson.
  • When I'm on a bus, I look at ....

module 5 Appearances

Describe a suspect to the police

Personal vocabulary

Preparation for task

1 What crime do you think the man in the picture committed? Why is the policeman talking to the woman? What is she telling him?

2 You are going to describe or ask for a description of a crime suspect. Divide into two groups, A and B. Read the cards below and follow the instructions.

A Witnesses

Last weekend you visited your local art gallery. During your visit, art thieves stole a world-famous painting. The police believe that you were in the lift at the same time as one of the thieves, and want you to give a description of this person. Turn to page 146 to see the man you were in the lift with. You were in the lift for two minutes, so you have two minutes to look at the picture. When you have finished, discuss in your group how to describe him. Think about these things.
• age • face • skin • hair • clothes • build • general appearance
Look at the phrases in the *Useful language a)* to help you.

B Police officers

Last weekend thieves stole a world-famous painting from a local art gallery. You know that one of the thieves used the lift just before the painting was stolen. You are going to interview a witness who was in the lift at the same time to get a description of the man. In your group, discuss what questions you will ask the witness. Think about these things.
• age • face • skin • hair • clothes • build • general appearance
Look at the phrases in the *Useful language b)* to help you.

Useful language

a To describe the suspect

"He/She was (*thin/well-dressed/in his thirties*)."

"He/She had (*blond hair/a big nose*)."

"His hair was a bit like …'s (*for example, a student in your class*), but it was shorter."

"He/She was wearing (*a long black coat*)."

b To ask about the suspect

"How old was he/she?"

"What was his/her (*hair/mouth*) like?"

"What colour was/were his/her (*hair/eyes*)?"

"Was his hair longer or shorter than (*mine/Ian's*)?"

"Did he/she have (*glasses/a moustache*)?"

"What was he/she wearing?"

Task

1 Work in pairs, one person from Group A (a witness) and one from Group B (a police officer). The police officer should ask the witness questions and:

Either: make detailed notes about the suspect.

Or: draw a picture of the suspect using the face outline below. Make any extra notes necessary, and ask the witness questions to check that your drawing is accurate.

▶ *Useful language*
▶ *Personal vocabulary*

> Did his hair look like this?

> Yes, but he had more hair than that.

2 a) At the end of the interview, B looks at the ten possible suspects on page 140. Decide which was the man in the lift and ask A to say 'yes' or 'no'.

b) If B chooses the wrong man, A must not point out the correct suspect, but he/she can explain **why** B was wrong.
For example:

> He was younger than that, and his hair was longer.

c) B makes a second and final choice. A says which is the real suspect.

3 How many police officers chose the correct suspect:

- the first time? • the second time?

Did your witness give you a good description? Why/Why not?

Optional writing

Either: choose one of the **other** photos on page 140 and write a description.
Or: write a description of a person your partner knows **without** giving the name. (It can be a famous person, or someone from your class.)
Show your description to your partner. Can he/she guess first time who it is?

Real life

Social chit-chat

chit-chat *n.* informal conversation about everyday things

neighbours

in a taxi

in a shop

work colleagues

1 Which of these topics do people normally talk about in the situations above?

> sport ✓   plans for the day ✓
> health ✓   the weather   family ✓
> personal problems ✓   religion
> what you did at the weekend ✓
> where you're from ✓
> reasons for your visit ✓

2 [5.5] Listen to the four conversations, and tick (✓) the topics you hear discussed.

45

3 [5.6] What were the questions for these answers? Listen again and check.

a A: Nice day isn't it?
B: Yes, it's lovely.

b A: Have you got any plans?
B: No, nothing special. We might go to the park later.

c A: How are you feeling better?
B: Yes, I'm much better.

d A: How is the family?
B: Oh, they're all right. Yes, they're all fine.

e A: Is this your first time in England?
B: Yes, it's our first time here.

f A: Did you have a good weekend?
B: Yeah, it was OK. I didn't do much, really.

g A: Did you see a football game on Sunday?
B: Oh, yeah, fantastic, wasn't it? That goal was brilliant!

Pronunciation

[5.7] Listen to the questions again. Notice how the intonation helps the speaker to sound interested. Practise the questions.

4 a) Have a conversation similar to those on the recording. First, decide:

- what your relationship is (friends/colleagues/strangers).
- where you are (in a shop/in the street/in a café).
- which topics you will talk about (health/family/sport).

b) Act out your conversation. The other students should answer the questions in Exercise 4a above.

46

Do you remember?

1 a) Complete with the comparative or superlative form of the adjective in brackets.

1 Which is ... the nicest (nice) room in your house?
2 Which is ... nearer (near) to your house: a school or a supermarket?
3 Which is ... bigger (big): your bedroom or the kitchen?
4 What is ... the most (unusual) object in your house?
5 Which is ... more (useful) thing to own: a car or a computer?

b) Work in pairs. Ask and answer the questions.

2 What is the opposite of:
a) ugly? beautiful
b) slim? fat
c) pale? tanned
d) fair (hair)? dark
e) long (hair)?

3 Which words are missing from the following sentences?
a) What does she look like?
b) Has he got a moustache?
c) Is her hair similar to mine?
d) My brother looks very different from me.
e) What are her eyes like?

4 Write the missing words.
a) noun: beauty   adjective: beautiful
b) verb: to attract   adjective: attractive
c) noun: fashion   adjective: fashionable
d) verb: describe   noun: description

5 Match the beginnings in A with an ending in B. In pairs, ask and answer the questions.

A
1 Did you have
2 Have you got any plans
3 Did you see
4 So are you here
5 Are you feeling
6 How's
7 Is this your first time

B
in (New York)?
the family?
on business?
a good holiday?
for tomorrow?
any films at the weekend?
OK today?

module 6

Time off

▶ **Intentions and wishes:** *going to, planning to, would like to, would prefer to*
▶ **Vocabulary:** holidays
▶ **Predictions:** *will* and *won't*
Task: plan your dream holiday

Language focus 1

Intentions and wishes: *going to, planning to, would like to, would prefer to*

1 Discuss with other students.

- Are you usually free at the weekend, or do you have to do a lot of work or study?
- How many weeks holiday from work or school do you have every year? Is it enough?
- Do you think people in your country have enough free time, generally? (Think about people in different types of job.)

2 Do you like to keep busy or do you prefer to take life easy? Do the quiz with a partner to find out.

3 What do your partner's answers show about him/her? Do you ever make resolutions about your free time? Give examples.

Live wire or couch potato?

Bath

1 Unexpectedly, you have two or three hours off work/school this afternoon, are you going to:
a tidy your desk, sort out your papers and answer some letters?
b phone a couple of friends or send a few e-mails?
c lie on the sofa and watch an old film on TV?

2 Next weekend, are you planning to:
a meet a few friends, and do a bit of shopping?
b decorate your bedroom, make a new dress or mend your motorbike?
c sleep?

3 You enter a competition. Which of the following would you prefer to win?
a a Jacuzzi for your bathroom
b a really good mountain bike
c a year's membership of a health club

4 What kind of holiday would you least like to go on?
a a sightseeing holiday in a busy city
b a cycling, climbing and camping holiday
c a beach holiday with nothing else to do

module 6 Time off

Grammar analysis

1 Which sentence below shows that the person has thought more about the plan and how to do it?
   a **I'm going to phone** some friends this evening.
   b **I'm planning to repair** my motorbike this weekend.

2 Read sentences c) and d). Which means:
   • I want to do this?
   • I want to do this more than something else?
   c **I'd prefer to win** a mountain bike.
   d **I'd like to go** on a sightseeing holiday.

3 What form do we use after *be going*, *be planning*, *would like* and *would prefer*?

▶ Language summary A, page 152.

Practice

1 a) Use the words below to make **six** good resolutions for the future.

For example:
I'm not going to argue with my mother any more.
I'm going to spend less on clothes.

- argue (with my sister)
- spend (more/less) time (reading)
- save money for (a new computer)
- spend more/less money on (cigarettes)
- eat more/less (chocolate)
- study (English every weekend)
- keep in touch with (old friends)
- learn to (drive)
- stop (smoking)
- join (a gym)
- do (more sport)
- remember (birthdays)

b) Work in groups. Read out your resolutions.

2 When you have some free time, do you go away for the day/weekend? Use the prompts below to make questions, then ask two partners.

		Partner A	Partner B
a	(plan/have) any days or weekends away in the next few weeks? Who (plan/go) with?		
b	Which places near your home (like/visit) for the day?		
c	Which other parts of your country (like/visit) for a weekend or a few days?		
d	For a really nice weekend away, (prefer/go) the country, the seaside, or a city?		
e	Which of these cities (prefer/visit) for a long weekend: New York, London or Dublin?		
f	Are there any other cities (really/like/go to)?		

Pronunciation

1 [6.1] Write the number of words you hear. Contractions (for example, *I'm*) = 2 words.

2 Notice that the vowel sound in *to* is pronounced /ə/. Practise saying the following phrases.

I'm planning > *I'm planning to have*
I'm going > *I'm going to see*
I'd like > *I'd like to go*
I'd prefer > *I'd prefer to travel*

3 Practise saying the complete sentences from Exercise 1.

48

Vocabulary and speaking

Holidays

1 a) Which of these are most important to you on holiday? Discuss.

- the weather
- the food
- accommodation
- shops
- sightseeing/culture
- the scenery
- the nightlife
- who you go with

b) What can you see in the photos above? Do they show positive or negative things about holidays?

2 a) If necessary, check the meaning and pronunciation of the words in **bold** below. Divide the ideas into the following groups.

ideal holiday   awful holiday   not sure/neither

- your plane is **delayed**
- the place you visit is **lively** and full of people
- the water is too **polluted** to swim in
- the hotel staff are **rude** and **unhelpful**
- the food in the hotel is **disgusting**
- there are **views** of the city from your hotel room
- there's no **entertainment** or **nightlife**
- the **atmosphere** is **peaceful** and **relaxing**
- the weather's **wet** and **windy**
- the weather's **really hot**
- the hotel has views of a **building site**
- there are lots of **shops**

b) Compare answers in pairs or small groups. Explain your answers if necessary. Can you add any other ideas to each group?

3 a) Tell your partners about a holiday you have had that was either really good, or awful. Use some of the phrases above.

b) Listen to your partner's story: has anything similar ever happened to you?

module 6 Time off

Listening and speaking
The holiday from hell

1 Last year Mark and Rosa saved up and booked their dream holiday, in the Caribbean. Read what the holiday brochure said.

- luxurious hotel close to beautiful sandy beach
- three swimming pools, tennis, golf and watersports
- three beach bars and first class restaurant
- average temperatures 28 to 30°C; average hours of sunshine per day 8 to 9 hours
- flying time eight and a half hours
- airport fifteen minutes by bus from the hotel

2 Work in pairs (A and B) and act out the following conversation.

A is Mark/Rosa. Tell a friend about the holiday you are planning. (Invent any details that you do not know from the brochure above.)

B is Mark/Rosa's friend. Ask about the holiday.
Where are you going?
What's the hotel like?
How long is the journey?

3 [6.2] Unfortunately, the holiday was awful. In fact, Mark and Rosa appeared on a programme called *Holidays in Hell* to describe it. You will hear the story in two parts.

a) Listen to Part 1 and look back at the list of problems in Exercise 2, page 49. Underline the problems they mention.

b) What do you think happened next? Listen to Part 2 and check.

4 Listen and answer the questions below.

Part 1: complete the sentences.
a The holiday cost .... each.
b They went in the month of .... because the brochure said ....
c Their flight was delayed because ....
d The flight was .... hours late.
e They couldn't fly to San Antonio because ....
f They flew to .... instead.

Part 2: true or false?
a The Hotel Paradiso was a typical five-star hotel.
b There was a sandy beach next to the hotel.
c The swimming pool was empty.
d They had vegetables for breakfast.
e There were lots of ants in the bowl of lettuce.
f The most frightening part of the holiday was the flight to San Antonio.
g They arrived in San Antonio five days late.
h Hurricane George never got to San Antonio.

5 a) Work in pairs, A and B. Mark and Rosa are talking to their friend again after the holiday. Start the conversation like this:

A: So did you have a nice holiday?
B: No, it was awful. It was a nightmare!
A: Why? What happened?

b) What do **you** think was the worst part of the holiday?

Language focus 2

Predictions: *will* and *won't*

Matt, from London, is visiting the capital city of your country in August. What do you say to him?

a It'll be very hot.
b You'll have a wonderful time.
c There'll be lots of tourists.
d You won't see the city at its best.
e It won't be very crowded.
f You'll have to take warm clothes with you.
g There'll be lots of insects.
h You won't be able to find a hotel.

Grammar analysis

1 Tick (✓) the correct answer. Sentences a) – h) above describe:
   a things you **plan to do**. ☐
   b things you **expect to happen**. ☐
   c things you **want to happen**. ☐

2 a Which verb form do we use in a) – c) above?
   b Change sentence a into a question.
   c Change sentence h into the present.

▶ *Language summary B, page 152.*

Practice

1 Work in pairs, A and B. Act out the conversation between you and Matt:

A: I'm planning to visit (name of city) in August next year.
B: You'll have a great time – it won't be very crowded. Most people will be away on holiday.
A: Oh good. What about the weather?

2 Matt may stay in your country for a while. Here are some other things he may do.

> open a bank account   go to the hairdresser
> go to the doctor   go on a coach tour of the city
> travel by train from the capital to the second city

a) Match the beginnings in A with the endings in B to make questions for Matt.

	A	B
1	Will I have to make	will it take?
2	Will I have to leave	will I need?
3	Will I have to	crowded?
4	Will I need to book	an appointment?
5	Will it be	pay?
6	Will it be	to speak English?
7	Will the people be able	a tip?
8	How long	to sleep?
9	What documents	expensive?
10	Will there be anywhere	a seat?

b) Work in pairs. Choose two things for Matt to do. Which of the questions will he need? Act out the conversation between you and Matt.

> I'm going to open a bank account tomorrow – but I don't know very much about it.

> OK. How can I help?

> Well, what documents …?

Pronunciation

1 Complete the sentences with *It'll*, *You'll* or *There'll*.

   a … have a great time!
   b … need to take an umbrella.
   c … be lots of things for children to do.
   d … be quite cold at that time of year.
   e … be very crowded.

2 [6.3] Listen and check your answers. Practise saying the sentences.

module 6 Time off

Plan your dream holiday

Personal vocabulary

Useful language

a Discussing the different possibilities

"Personally, I'd like to … because it will be …"

"I'd prefer to … because …"

"Well, how about … or we could …?"

b Asking about holidays

"Where/When are you going?"

"How long are you going for?"

"Why did you choose that holiday?"

"Which excursions are you going on?"

c Telling people about your holiday

"We're going to … for … days/weeks."

"I chose this holiday because …"

"We're going to stay in a hotel."

African Wildlife Safari: South Africa, Zimbabwe and Botswana
A truly grand tour of Southern Africa: for many, the holiday experience of a lifetime.

European City Tour: London–Paris–Amsterdam
What could be better than to combine three of Europe's greatest cities into one fabulous holiday?

Preparation for task

1 a) Look at the advertisements for three dream holidays above. Which places do you visit on each holiday?

b) Which holiday do the words and phrases below relate to? Check the meaning and pronunciation of any unknown words.

a safari lodge   the dry season   an ostrich   a cruise   a canal
a theme park   a motel   self-catering accommodation
dolphins and killer whales   sailing   an excursion

2 Discuss the questions below with the class.

- How will people spend their time on each of these holidays?
- What will they see?
- What will be the best things about each holiday?

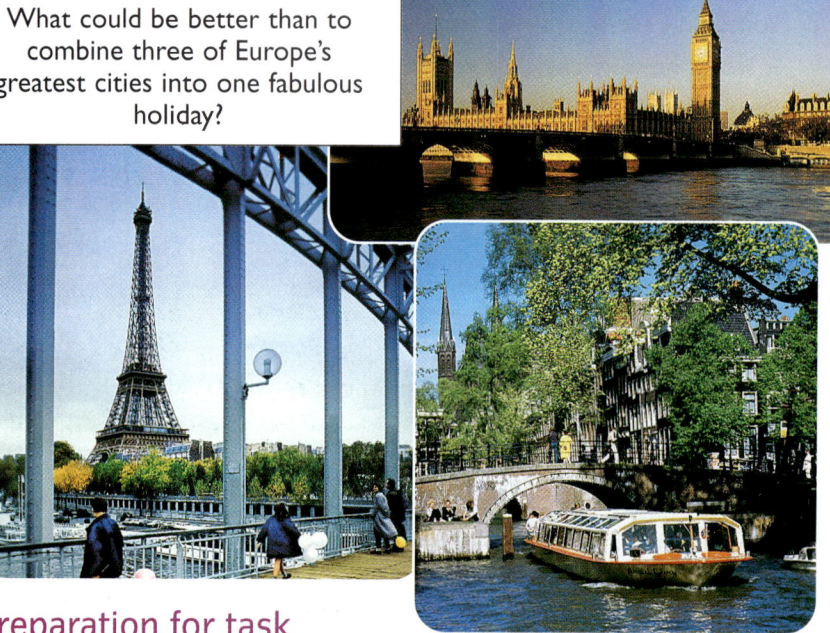

The Florida Experience
Discover fantastic Florida, fun capital of the USA!

Task

1 Work in pairs or small groups. You are going to plan a dream holiday (money is no problem). Decide together which holiday you would like to go on, and why.

2 a) Read the fact file about your holiday (Safari page 140, European cities page 146, Florida page 144) and complete the tables.

b) Discuss the different possibilities.
▶ *Useful language a)*
▶ *Personal vocabulary*

3 Work with a new partner who has planned a different holiday from you. Ask/Tell each other about the holiday you have planned.
▶ *Useful language b) and c)*

Writing

Write a postcard

1 a) Neil and Claudia are on holiday in Spain. In the following pairs of phrases, underline the one that is suitable for a postcard to a friend. Why are the other phrases **not** suitable?

a Hi Tim!/Dear Mr Buchanan
b I am pleased to tell you that we have arrived …/Here we are …
c The weather is warm, with a maximum temperature of 26.5 degrees./It's lovely and sunny.
d The food is really tasty/Meals usually cost between $15 and $20 and are of excellent quality.
e We're staying in …/Our postal address is …
f … on the 25th July./… when we get home
g Bye for now!/Yours sincerely
h There are plenty of clubs and things to do/There are 126 nightclubs and over a thousand restaurants.

b) Complete the postcard with phrases from Exercise 1.

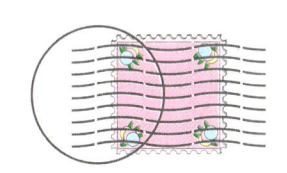

(1) Hi Tim,
(2) Here we are in sunny Spain! We arrived in Barcelona a week ago and after a few days sightseeing there, (3) _____ a place called Llafranc. (4) _____ and there's a marina and a very nice little beach. (5) The food is really tasty (especially the seafood!) We'll both definitely have to go on a diet (6) _____ (7) _____ in the evening. Give our love to everyone at college.
(8) _____.
Neil and Claudia

Tim Buchanan
Flat A
156 Rutherford Rd
Leeds
LS4 9FT

2 You are on holiday. Write a postcard to someone you know, using some of the phrases above. Include:

- the name and address of the person you're writing to.
- a greeting.
- where you are now and information about it.
- other places you've visited.
- information about the weather, food, evening entertainment.
- signing off.

53

Consolidation modules 1–6

A Present tenses, should, can

1 Check the meaning of these words/phrases.

| a murderer | to escape from prison |

2 Complete the gaps in the text below. Use the Present Simple, Present Continuous, or put *should/shouldn't* or *can/can't* in front of the verb.

Police officers in Burton (1)........(look for) 38-year-old Brian Poole, a murderer, who escaped from prison this morning.
'This man is extremely dangerous,' said Superintendent Michael Walsh earlier today. 'Anyone who (2)........ (see) him (3)........ try to talk to him or go near him, but (4)........ phone the police immediately.'
There is also another man that officers (5)........ (want) to interview – a witness saw him sitting in a car near the prison, just before the escape. 'We (6)........ (think) the car was dark blue, but I (7)........ give you any more details about it at the moment,' said the Superintendent. 'We would like to hear from anyone who (8)........ remember seeing a dark blue or black car in that area.' People who (9)........ (live) near the prison (10)........ (ask) how Poole was able to escape from the 'high security' prison. 'It's disgusting,' said mother-of-four Mrs Jane Thompson, 'the government (11)........ do something about it – we (12)........ (not/feel) safe, and we certainly (13)........ go out after dark.' A government representative (14)........ (visit) the prison tomorrow.

B Vocabulary: revision

Work in pairs. Read the definitions and find words from Modules 1–6 (the Module number is in brackets). The first letter of each word is the same as the last letter of the word before.

1 Another word for pretty or handsome. (5) attractive
2 If you don't understand, ask the teacher to ... again. (3) e........
3 How you feel before an important exam. (2)........
4 Something from a place you visited. (6)........
5 Members of your family. (4)........
6 Don't ... too much money! (4)........
7 His hair's not black, but it's ... than yours. (5)........
8 Feeling calm and not worried. (2)........
9 If the flight is late, it is ... (6)........
10 A word to describe horrible food. (6)........
11 Very beautiful or attractive. (5)........
12 You can do this lying on the beach. (1)........
13 Similar in meaning to number 1 above. (5)........
14 If you don't know the answer, you (3)........

C Comparative and superlative adjectives

Complete the gaps in the article below with an adjective from the box, in the comparative or superlative form.

| heavy | large | important | ancient | long |
| accurate | big (x 2) | tall |

> **Found: (1)........ animal that ever walked the planet**
>
> It was (2)........ than a giraffe and (3)........ than five elephants. The baluchitherium lived in Asia between 25 and 40 million years ago, and was (4)........ than any other animal that lived on the Earth. Scientists who found the graves of twenty of the animals say that this is (5)........ discovery of its kind, and that they can now make an (6)........ picture of the (7)........ creature. Adult baluchitheriums were about nine metres long and six metres (8)........ . They were vegetarians and used their (9)........ necks to eat leaves from the tops of the trees!

54

D Vocabulary: pairs

1 How quickly can you find nine pairs of opposites from Modules 1–6 in the box below?

pleased	stay up late	clean	excited
go to work	tanned	fashionable	
correct yourself	polluted	make a mistake	
visit relatives	go to bed early	pale	
old-fashioned	have the day off	bored	
entertain friends	disappointed		

2 Compare your answers with a partner and explain why you put the words/phrases together.

3 Test your partner. Read out one word or phrase from a pair. Can your partner tell you the other one?

E Plans, wishes and predictions

1 Circle the best verb form in the article below.

> **Here is your horoscope for Friday 23rd.**
>
> Not feeling very healthy at the moment? Well, if (1) *you'd like to lose/you're losing* a few kilos, today is a good day to start. Join a gym today and start eating sensibly, and (2) *you're planning to see/you'll see* results in a few weeks. Your horoscope for the weekend looks excellent. Those of you who (3) *will go/are planning to go* away, don't take an umbrella – (4) *you'll need/you won't need* it: the weather (5) *will be/won't be* warm and sunny. If (6) *you'd prefer to stay/you won't stay* at home, now is a good time to plant some flowers – it's good exercise and (7) *you're going to get/you'll get* lots of fresh air! Finally, have you got some extra money this week? Invest now and make your fortune. Like King Midas, everything you touch (8) *will turn/won't turn* to gold!

2 [1] Listen and check your answers.

3 Invent a horoscope for your partner. Include some of these topics:

> home   work   school   money   love
> weather   relationships

4 Take it in turns to tell your partner what you predict.

F Listening and grammar: Present and Past Simple

1 You will hear a song called *You are everything*. What kind of song do you think it is?

2 Match words from A and B to make six phrases from the song. Do not look at the song yet!

A	B
see	the corner
feel	memories
look	your name
turn	face
call out	ashamed
bring back	like you

3 [2] Listen to the song without looking at the words. Number the phrases as you hear them.

4 Here are the words of the song. Listen again and circle the correct verb form.

> Today I (1) *see/saw* somebody who
> (2) *looks/looked* just like you
> She (3) *walks/walked* like you do – I
> (4) *think/thought* it (5) *is/was* you
> As she (6) *turns/turned* the corner, I
> (7) *call out/called out* your name
> I (8) *feel/felt* so ashamed when it
> (9) *isn't/wasn't* you
>
> You are everything and everything is you
>
> How (10) *can/could* I forget when each face
> that I (11) *see/saw*
> (12) *Brings/Brought* back memories of being with you?
> I just (13) *can't/couldn't* go on living life as I do, comparing each girl with you
> When they just won't do – (14) *they're not/they weren't* you
>
> You are everything and everything is you

5 Discuss these questions.

What was the relationship between the singers? What is it now? How do they feel?

55

module 7
Fame and fortune

- Vocabulary: ambitions and dreams
- Present Perfect and Past Simple with *for*
- Present Perfect and Past Simple with other time words
- Wordspot: *know*

Task: prepare an interview

Vocabulary and speaking

Ambitions and dreams

1 a) What were your ambitions when you were younger?

> I wanted to be a farmer and have lots of children!

> I wanted to be really good at singing!

b) Would you still like to do these things now? Were your ambitions realistic or not?

2 Look at the list of ambitions opposite. Divide them into three categories. Compare and explain your answers.

1 realistic ambitions
2 dreams
3 it depends/not sure

---

learn how to drive   become famous   start your own business
go abroad   go to university and get a degree   have a large family
become a millionaire   write a novel or a poem   get married
play in an orchestra   buy your own home
become really good at a sport or a musical instrument
get an interesting job with a good salary   travel around the world
appear on TV or in a film

3 Which of these things would you like to do? Do you have any other ambitions? Compare your answers.

4 It is important to remember the verbs that we use in these phrases (word combinations). Underline some more examples of word combinations in Exercise 2.

For example:

<u>have</u> children   <u>get</u> married   <u>go</u> abroad   <u>become</u> famous

56

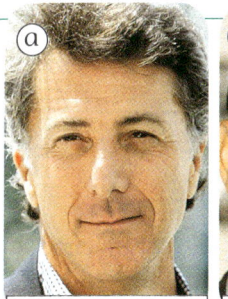

a Dustin Hoffman
b Tom Hanks 
c Harrison Ford 
d Michael Caine 
e Roseanne Barr 
f Antonio Banderas 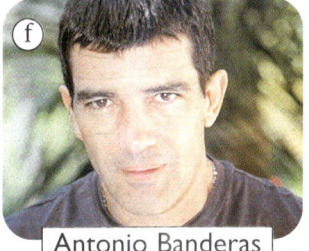
g Ewan McGregor 

Reading

1 How many people in the pictures do you recognise? What do you know about them?

2 Here are some jobs these people did before they were famous. Can you guess who did each job? Read and check your answers.

assistant chef   bellman   street musician
carpenter   soldier   waiter   model

3 Answer the questions in pairs. Which of the people above:

a   wasn't very good at his previous job?
b   needed a job because he had a wife and children?
c   had a bad relationship with his/her boss?
d   found his/her job useful when he/she became an actor?
e   seemed to like his/her previous job?
f   thought he received good money in his job?
g   hated his/her job?

4 Discuss in pairs. Have you ever had a holiday job, or a temporary job? What was it like?

Before they were famous

1 One day in the early 1960s, Hollywood producer Sam Spiegel was having lunch in a New York restaurant when a nervous-looking waiter spilled coffee over him.
'I'm sorry,' said the waiter, 'I'm not really a waiter. Actually, I'm an actor.'
'No,' replied Spiegel angrily, 'from now on, you're a waiter.'
But Spiegel was wrong. The young man was in fact Dustin Hoffman, who went on to win two Oscars and to appear in huge Hollywood films like *The Graduate*, *Kramer vs Kramer* and *Rain Man*.

2 Hoffman isn't the only Hollywood star who made a living from ordinary jobs before becoming famous. Imagine Harrison Ford supporting his young family by working as a carpenter; actor Antonio Banderas working as a model for mail-order catalogues; or comedienne Roseanne Barr as an assistant chef in an expensive French restaurant (she left after arguing with her boss, and went away to become an actress). And if you used the London Underground in the early 90s, perhaps you saw the future star of *Trainspotting* and *Star Wars Part 1*, Ewan McGregor, performing as a street musician. 'I made about £20 a day,' says McGregor.

3 For many actors and actresses, this early experience came in useful in their acting career. Academy Award winning actor, Tom Hanks, worked as a bellman in the Hilton hotel in Los Angeles in the 1970s, an experience which he says helped prepare him for acting. 'You put on your bellman suit and then play the role of bellman,' he told a magazine. 'You make good tips and a nice wage, working three, four days a week.'

4 And British actor Michael Caine – who has appeared in over ninety films in a movie career lasting over forty years – found his experience of military service helped him in a different way. Caine spent two years in the army, serving in Germany and Korea. Although he hated life as a soldier, he says, 'In Korea I noticed that heroes weren't all tall, with perfect teeth … but ordinary guys. So that's the way I always try to play them.'

5 So next time you see a waiter spill someone's drink, or you stop to watch a street musician, take a good look – he or she might be the next Hollywood sensation!

module 7 Fame and fortune

Language focus 1
Present Perfect and Past Simple with *for*

Grammar analysis

1 Match the sentences with the correct timeline.
   a *I was in New York for two weeks.*
   b *I've been in New York for two weeks.*
   c *I'm in New York for two weeks.*

   ① 2 weeks — past | now | future
   ② 2 weeks — past | now | future
   ③ 2 weeks — past | now | future

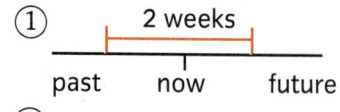

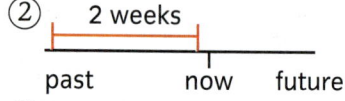

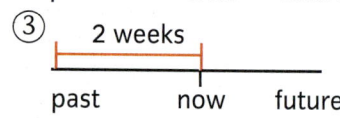

2 What are the Past Simple and Present Perfect forms of these verbs?
   a **regular**   work
   b **irregular**   know
   How do we form the questions and negatives?

3 Notice these questions with *How long*?
   *How long **has** he **been** famous?*
   *How long **was** he a model?*

▶ *Language summary A/B, page 152.*

1 Compare the two sentences below.

Antonio Banderas has been a famous actor for many years now.

Before he became famous, he was a model for a while.

a Which action:
 • is finished?   • continues up to the present?
b Which sentence uses:
 • the Present Perfect?   • the Past Simple?

2 Look at the text on page 57 and make similar sentences about the following.

a Tom Hanks   c Michael Caine
b Roseanne Barr

Practice

1 Use **eight** of these prompts to make true sentences about yourself/people you know.

For example:
I've had my CD player for three months.

a I *have had/had* my .... for ....
b *I've been/was* a .... for ....
c I *have been/was* at .... school for .... years.
d Before that, I *have gone/went* to .... school.
e I *have lived/lived* in .... for ....
f I *have known/knew* .... for .... years.
g My grandparents *have been/were* married for .... years.
h My father *has worked/worked* as a .... for .... years.
i .... (my teacher) *has been/was* a teacher for .... years.

58

Pronunciation

1. ▭ [7.1] Listen and count the number of words you hear (*I've* = 2 words).

2. Listen again. Write down the complete sentences. Notice how the words change when we speak quickly.
   /ə/
   I've known Anna for about eight years.

3. Listen again and practise.

2 Which of these verbs are regular and which are irregular? What are the Past Simple and past participles forms?

a	see	f	make
b	have	g	notice
c	leave	h	reply
d	appear	i	find
e	win	j	put

3 It is important to learn irregular verbs. Which of these ideas would help?

a Gradually learning the verbs from the list on page 148 using the 'look–cover–write–check' method.

b Remembering irregular verbs as you meet them.

c Learning a few irregular verbs each day by making up sentences with them.

d Repeating the irregular verbs to yourself, again and again.

e Asking another student (or your teacher) to test you.

Try one or more of these ideas for a week. Tell the class how well the method is working.

Language focus 2

Present Perfect and Past Simple with other time words

1 Robbie left school in 1990. He is remembering his old school friends. Complete the sentences using the verbs below.

> wanted   didn't go   spent   was   went   studied
> didn't enjoy   liked   had   decided

Ameet was always interested in business – he always (1)............ lots of brilliant ideas for making money and his ambition (2)............ to be a millionaire by the age of twenty-five!
Lucy was a film addict – she sometimes (3)............ to the cinema four or five times a week. She (4)............ to become a famous film actress like her heroine, Michelle Pfeiffer.
Edward was always very quiet, and he (5)............ out very much – he (6)............ most of his time at home in his bedroom, playing games on his computer.
Kate (7)............ for at least three hours every evening – when she was eighteen years old, she (8)............ to become an ecologist and help save the planet.
Hannah (9)............ school at all – for some reason, the only subject she (10)............ was Geography.

2 Robbie contacted his friends by e-mail. What do you think they are doing now? Look at the next page and find out.

module 7 Fame and fortune

During the last ten years, **Ameet** has had ten different jobs: he has worked in the import-export business, he has been an estate agent and now he has just started his own company which sells mobile phones – but he hasn't made a million pounds yet!

Edward has moved to the United States, where he now works, designing computer games. His most popular game, Death Rider, has already sold over ten million copies, and has made him very rich! He isn't married, in fact, he's never had a girlfriend, and he still spends most of his time playing computer games in his bedroom.

Lucy is an actress and a part-time waitress. In the last few years, she's appeared in several plays and a couple of TV commercials – but there has been no call from Hollywood yet!

Since leaving university with a brilliant degree, **Kate** has worked for Greenpeace and other similar organisations, first as a volunteer and now as a manager. She's just had her first baby.

In the last ten years, **Hannah** has been married three times, and has lived in Italy, Egypt, France and Australia. At present, she is running a small restaurant and bar on the Greek island of Kos with her third husband, Nikos.

3 Answer the following questions in pairs.

a Say two things that each person has/hasn't done.

b Whose experiences in the last few years are:
- the most surprising?
- the most interesting?

Grammar analysis

1 Look at Exercises 1 and 2 on pages 58–59.
   a Which information is about:
   - a past time that is finished?
   - a period of time that continues from the past to the present?
   b Which uses: the Past Simple/the Present Perfect?
   Underline all the verbs in these tenses.

Time phrases

2 a Past Simple
   in 1990   five years ago
   when she was eighteen years old
   yesterday   last year
   If we give a definite past time like this, we cannot use the Present Perfect.

   b Present Perfect
   Often, there is no time phrase here.
   We do not know exactly when the action happened.
   She's lived in Italy, Egypt and France.

   We often use these time words with the Present Perfect. They do not give a definite past time. Notice the word order.
   *She's **just** had her first baby.*
   *It's **already** sold over ten million copies.*
   *He hasn't made a million pounds **yet**.*
   *He's **never** had a girlfriend.*

▶ *Language summary C, page 153.*

Practice

1 a) Use the prompts to make sentences in the Present Perfect.

For example:
just/I go/the hairdresser's/to
I've just been to the hairdresser's.

1 not/I/yet/finish/school
2 just/lunch/I/have
3 I/on holiday/already/go/this year
4 an arm or a leg/never/I/break
5 I/go/yet this year/not/to/the dentist's
6 I/do/anything exciting/not/this week

7 I/anyone famous/never/meet
8 I/on a plane/this year/travel/not
9 not/I/do/any sport/this week
10 I/never/anything/steal

b) Which of these sentences is true for you? Compare answers.

> 'I haven't done any sport this week.' False ... I've played football every day. How about you?

2 Work in pairs. Ask and answer these questions. In the last five/ten years:

a which cities/foreign countries have you visited?
b how many times have you changed school/job?
c how many times have you moved house?
d which important skills have you learnt?
e which new sports or other interests have you taken up?
f what other important things have happened to you?

> I've visited five different countries.

> I haven't moved house!

3 Think of a group of people that you knew five/ten years ago (for example, colleagues/neighbours). Write a paragraph about what has happened to them, like Robbie's on page 60.

Wordspot

know

1 Match a phrase/question in A with an ending/response in B.

A
a Yes, I know Ally.
b Are you coming next weekend?
c Have you got that book for me?
d Jon, why weren't you at the meeting?
e Do you know how to programme this video?
f What can we get Mum for her birthday?
g I think you should ask Daniel,
h You don't need a map.
i Do you know Sylvia's new phone number?

B
You know, the one you borrowed last week.
I'm sorry, I didn't know about it.
I was at school with her.
I know. What about some perfume?
You know the way to Marta's house, don't you?
he knows a lot about cars.
Yes ... I wrote it down somewhere ...
I'm not sure. I'll let you know tomorrow.
Yes, first press VCR on the remote control, then ...

2 The diagram below shows some important uses of *know*. Add the phrases with *know* from Exercise 1 to the correct section of the diagram.

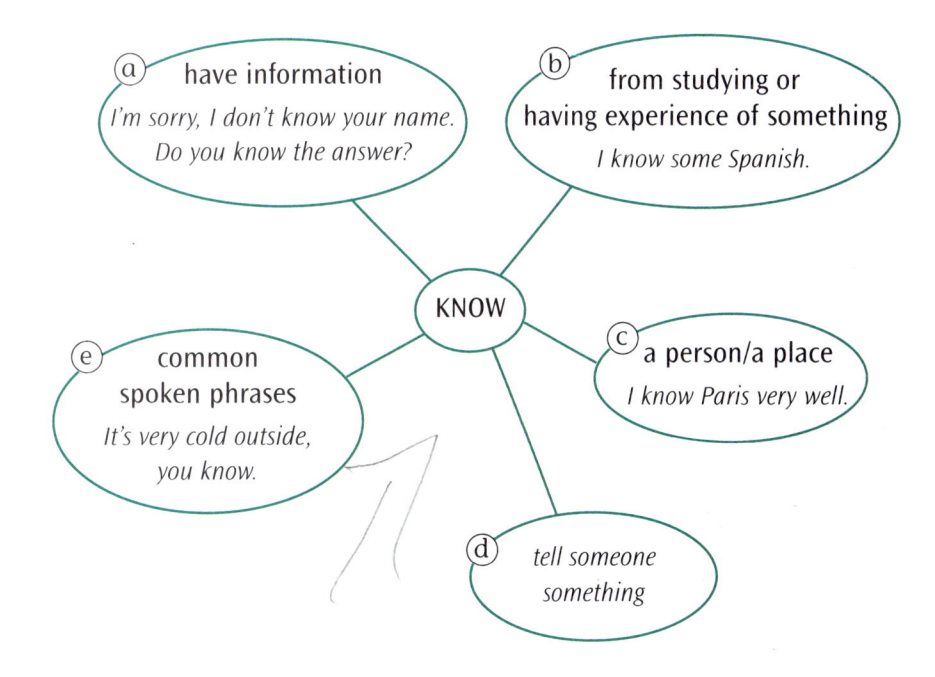

- ⓐ **have information**
  I'm sorry, I don't know your name. Do you know the answer?
- ⓑ **from studying or having experience of something**
  I know some Spanish.
- ⓒ **a person/a place**
  I know Paris very well.
- ⓓ **tell someone something**
- ⓔ **common spoken phrases**
  It's very cold outside, you know.

KNOW

3 Work in pairs, A and B. A looks at the questions on page 140 and B looks at the questions on page 144. Take turns to ask and answer the questions.

61

module 7 Fame and fortune

Prepare an interview

Gwyneth Paltrow

Tony Blair

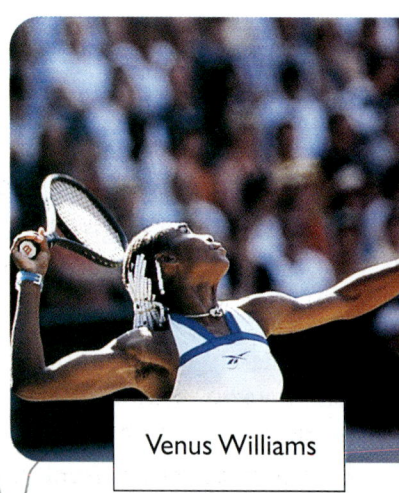

Venus Williams

Edgar Davids

Steven Spielberg

Madonna

Preparation for task

1. Do you know who these people are, and why they are famous?

2. Work in pairs. A journalist is going to interview each of these people. Choose the best questions to ask each one.

- Have you always wanted to be a politician/tennis player, etc.?
- Have you achieved all your ambitions?
- What are you working on at the moment?
- What have been the best/worst moments in your career so far?
- How many films have you starred in?
- How many records have you sold, altogether?
- Describe a typical working day.
- How do you relax?
- What's the best/worst thing about your job?
- Is it difficult to find enough time for your family and friends when you're so busy?
- Is there any special relationship in your life at the moment?
- How would you like people to remember you?

Useful language

"Why are you in (*Spain*)?"

"Is it true that …?"

"Can you tell us something about …?"

"What about …?"

"How long have you …?"

"How many (*films*) have you …?"

"When did you …?"

"Why did you …?"

Task

1 Work in pairs. You are going to prepare a list of questions to interview a famous person. Decide who you want to interview. It could be:

- somebody who is in the news at the moment.
- a famous person from your country.
- a famous person who is visiting from abroad.
- someone you really admire.

2 Prepare a list of ten questions. Use questions from Exercise 2 on page 62, but you must prepare at least four of your own.
▶ *Useful language*

3 With your partner, practise the interview. (If you don't know some of the answers, invent them!)

4 *Either:* act out your interview for the class. Do not say who the famous person is. The other students have to guess.
Or: record your interview onto an audio or video cassette.

Optional writing

Write up your interview as a magazine article like this:

> **YOU:** So what's been the best moment in your career so far?
>
> **VENUS:** Oh, definitely when I won the US Open in 1999.

Real life

Checking that you understand

1 [7.2] Complete the conversations below with the phrases in the box. Listen and check your answers.

> Could you say that again, please?   Sorry, what was that?
> I'm sorry, I don't understand.   What exactly is a warranty agreement?
> What do you mean exactly?   How do you spell it?
> Can you explain what 'beyin tavası' is?   What does 'ordövr' mean?

a

SALESMAN: ... so if you take <u>out a warranty agreement</u> ...
CUSTOMER: ....
SALESMAN: Yes, if you take out a warranty agreement ...
CUSTOMER: ....
SALESMAN: It's ... um ... an agreement, where you pay some money and if the machine breaks down, the repairs are free.
CUSTOMER: I see. Thank you.

b

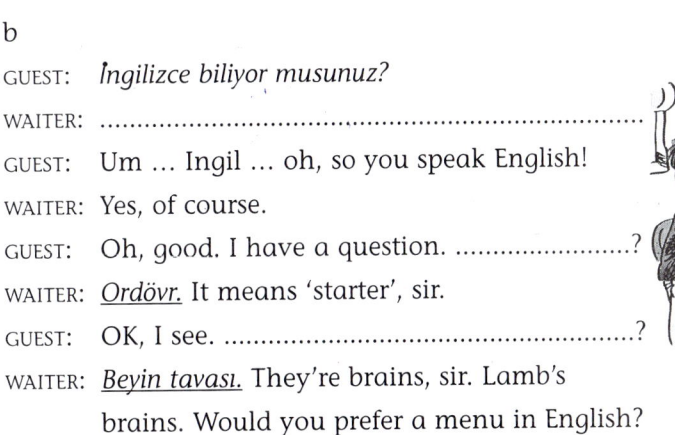

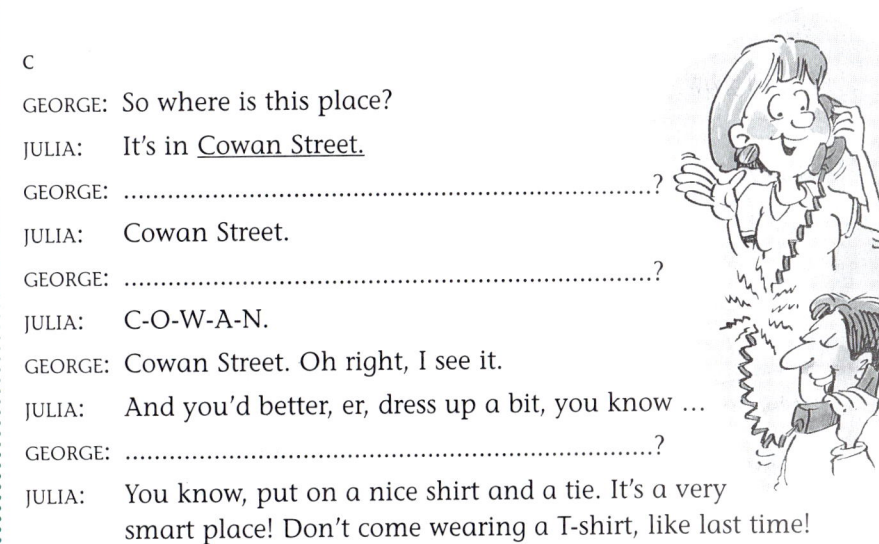

GUEST: *İngilizce biliyor musunuz?*
WAITER: ....
GUEST: Um ... Ingil ... oh, so you speak English!
WAITER: Yes, of course.
GUEST: Oh, good. I have a question. ....?
WAITER: *Ordövr.* It means 'starter', sir.
GUEST: OK, I see. ....?
WAITER: *Beyin tavası.* They're brains, sir. Lamb's brains. Would you prefer a menu in English?

c

GEORGE: So where is this place?
JULIA: It's in <u>Cowan Street</u>.
GEORGE: ....?
JULIA: Cowan Street.
GEORGE: ....?
JULIA: C-O-W-A-N.
GEORGE: Cowan Street. Oh right, I see it.
JULIA: And you'd better, er, dress up a bit, you know ...
GEORGE: ....?
JULIA: You know, put on a nice shirt and a tie. It's a very smart place! Don't come wearing a T-shirt, like last time!

63

module 7 Fame and fortune

Pronunciation

1 Listen to the conversations in Exercise 1 again. Pay attention to the phrases for checking that you understand. Which words are stressed?

What exactly is a warranty agreement?

2 In pairs, practise the conversations. Copy the voices on the recording.

2 Work in pairs. Make similar conversations to those in Exercise 1 on page 63. Substitute some of the words underlined in each conversation with the ideas in the boxes below. Use your mini-dictionary to help you with the explanations for these words.

a) pay in instalments   have six months' interest free credit

b) beverages   bagels   rocket   parsley

c) Beresford Square   Coombe Grove   Highbury Road

Do you remember?

1 Complete the gaps with the correct form of one of the verbs in the box below.

get   become   have

a) When did you ...get... your degree?
b) Why did you decide to ...become... an actress?
c) Do you ...get... a lot of tips in this job?
d) I'm not speaking to Tom. We ...had... a row last night.
e) Antonio Banderas ...became... famous after he appeared in Mambo Kings.
f) I'd like to ...have... children one day, but not yet.
g) I ...became... really good at skiing when I lived in Italy.
h) Did you know that Liz ...got... that job in New York?

2 a) Find seven pairs of rhyming past participles.

spoken   rung   driven   flown
chosen   bought   broken
thought   frozen   caught
given   sung   known   taught

b) Circle the past participle which does not have the same vowel sound.

1 won   got   come
2 made   taken   said
3 rung   run   put
4 gone   become   done
5 stolen   found   known

3 Put the word in brackets into an appropriate place in each of the sentences.

a) Have you been to the cinema? (this week)
b) We've moved to this area. (just)
c) I think we've seen this film. (already)
d) I'm sorry, I haven't phoned the bank. (yet)
e) That book's wonderful: I've read it. (three times)
f) He's been abroad. (never)
g) Have you finished in the bathroom? (yet)

4 Circle the correct verb form in the following sentences.

a) *I lived*/*I've lived* here until I was eighteen.
b) Happy Anniversary! How long *were you*/*have you been* married?
c) *She lived*/*She's lived* in that house all her life and she doesn't want to move.
d) *I had*/*I've had* my bike for ten years before *I sold*/*I've sold* it.
e) *They moved*/*They've moved* house three times last year.

64

module 8
Countries and cultures

- Using articles
- Vocabulary: geographical features
- Phrases with and without *the*

Task: complete a map of New Zealand

Just a myth?

1 English businessmen carry umbrellas and wear bowler hats.
2 Italian families eat pasta every day.
3 Japanese tourists take photos all the time.
4 French women are very well-dressed.
5 It's often foggy in London.
6 People in Brazil love dancing.
7 Scottish men normally wear kilts.
8 New York is a dangerous city.
9 People in Japan eat rice for breakfast.
10 English people drink tea every day at five o'clock.
11 It never rains in Egypt.
12 People in Australia have a lot of barbecues.

Language focus 1

Using articles

1 Discuss with other students. Which of the ideas in the text are true? Which are just myths?

2 [8.1] Listen to some people from these countries giving their opinion. Do they agree or not?

3 What do people say about people from your country? Are these things true or not?

Grammar analysis

1 Complete the rules.
   a We normally use/do not normally use *the* when we talk in general about a group of things or people.
   b We normally use/do not normally use *the* with names of people and places.

   Underline all the examples in the text that show this.

2 Exceptions!
   We use *the* with these place names.
   Seas and oceans: the Pacific   the Mediterranean   the Atlantic
   Rivers: the Nile   the Danube   the Amazon
   Ranges of mountains: the Himalayas   the Andes   the Alps
   Some countries, etc.: the United Kingdom   the United States   the European Union   the Netherlands

▶ Language summary A, page 153.

65

module 8 Countries and cultures

Practice

1 a) Work in pairs. Use the words below to make as many general statements as possible. Use a word from b, c and e. Add phrases from a and d if you want.

For example: Most Spanish people don't drink tea.

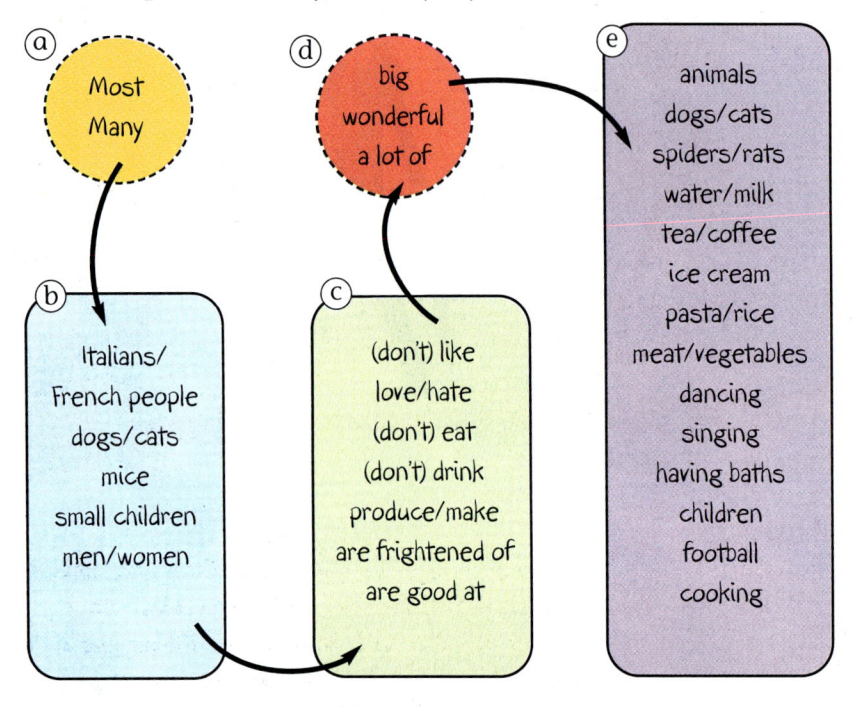

a) Most / Many

b) Italians / French people / dogs/cats / mice / small children / men/women

c) (don't) like / love/hate / (don't) eat / (don't) drink / produce/make / are frightened of / are good at

d) big / wonderful / a lot of

e) animals / dogs/cats / spiders/rats / water/milk / tea/coffee / ice cream / pasta/rice / meat/vegetables / dancing / singing / having baths / children / football / cooking

b) Read out some of your sentences to other students. Do they agree with you or not?

2 a) Complete the gaps in the statements below with *the* or Ø. Decide which of the statements are true and which are false.

1 .... France, ... Italy and .... United Kingdom are all members of .... European Union.
2 .... river Nile is the longest river in .... Asia.
3 .... San José and .... San Diego are cities in .... California.
4 The longest mountain range in the world is .... Andes in .... South America, which stretches over 7,000 km.
5 .... Hawaii, ... Tahiti and .... Madagascar are all islands in .... Pacific Ocean.
6 .... Lake Superior, on the border between .... Canada and .... United States, is the largest lake in the world.
7 .... river Rhine, which flows through .... Switzerland, and .... Germany is the longest river in .... Europe.

b) [8.2] Listen to the correct answers. Change the sentences so they are true.

Vocabulary

Geographical features

1 a) Check the meaning of the words in **bold**.

1 one of the largest **rivers** in the world
2 countries with **lakes** and **forests**
3 a country with no **coast**
4 a country with a lot of **islands**
5 a city famous for its **canals**
6 a country with large areas of **desert**
7 a country which has a **border** with France
8 a capital city which is a **port**
9 a city with a famous **cathedral**
10 a city with a lot of **historical monuments**
11 a country with a hot **climate**
12 a country which has **volcanoes**
13 a country famous for its beautiful **scenery**

b) Work in teams. Find places on the map with these features. Which team can find them first? Check your answers on page 143.

Pronunciation

[8.3] How do you pronounce the sounds underlined? Listen and check. Practise saying the words.

forest   climate   volcano
island   mountain   scenery
beach   coast   canal
desert

66

2 Read the following descriptions. Which place on the map is being described in each one?

a This lake is in Europe, in the Alps. It's not in Switzerland, but it's very near to the Swiss border, just north-east of Milan, in Italy.

b This is an island in the East Mediterranean. It's north of Egypt and south of Athens. It's the largest of the Greek islands.

3 With a partner, write three similar descriptions of places on the map or in your country. Do not say the name. Read out the descriptions. Can they guess where it is?

b) ... was amazed to meet Joe Stafford, who I haven't seen since we were at school! What a coincidence! He said he was on holiday here as well, staying at his villa on the coast, only about 25 kilometres from here. So anyway, we had a good long talk about the old days, and we've arranged to ...

c) There are several important industries in the south of the country, especially coal mining and shipbuilding. The main coal mining area is around Yelin, an industrial city on the border with Zenda. The main shipbuilding area is ...

Language focus 2

Phrases with and without *the*

1 Read passages a) – c) quickly. Which of them comes from:

- a letter to a friend?
- a guidebook for tourists?
- an encyclopedia?

a) ... makes the city a popular destination for tourists. Edinburgh Castle is in the city centre. On the left as you walk down Princes Street, from the station, it stands at the top of a hill called Castle Rock, and dominates the city skyline. Perhaps the best time to see it is at night, when the castle is illuminated by ...

2 a) Look at the phrases underlined in passage a).

with *the*	in the city centre
	on the left
	at the top
without *the*	at night

b) Underline similar phrases in the other passages (b and c) with these words.

Passage b: school   holiday   coast
Passage c: south   border

module 8 Countries and cultures

Grammar analysis

1 It is important to learn and remember whether phrases take *the*. However, there are some patterns. Use the phrases in Exercise 2 on page 67 to add *the* or Ø to the following phrases.

in ... east   on ... right   at ... university
in ... north-west   on ... wall   in ... suburbs
at ... bottom   on ... ceiling

2 Notice this exception.
at night BUT *in the morning/afternoon/evening*

▶ Language summary B, page 153.

Practice

1 Write seven sentences about yourself on a piece of paper, using the ideas below.

a My home is *in the city centre/town centre/near the town centre/in the suburbs*.

b At 2 p.m. I'm usually *at home/at school/at university/at work/other*.

c I prefer to study *in the morning/in the afternoon/in the evening/at night*.

d My favourite place to go on holiday is *on the coast/in the north (south/east/west) of* (my country).

e My school/college/office is *in the centre/in the east (west/north/south) of* (my town).

f I usually sit *on the right/on the left/in the middle of* the class.

g My name is *at the top/at the bottom* of this piece of paper. (write your name)

2 Your teacher will give you another student's piece of paper. Read out the sentences to the class, but do not say who wrote them. The other students guess who wrote them.

Complete a map of New Zealand

Preparation for task

1 Look at the map. Which country does it show? Can you answer the questions?

How much do you know about New Zealand?

1 New Zealand is:
a in the south-west of Australia.
b in the South Pacific.
c in the Indian Ocean.

2 It is about the same size as:
a Great Britain.   b Spain.   c Jamaica.

3 The climate in the north of New Zealand is:
a cold.   b warm.   c hot.

4 The population of New Zealand is:
a 1 million.   b 5 million.   c 3.5 million.

5 The official language is:
a Maori.   b English.
c both Maori and English.

6 Which of these can you find in New Zealand?
a mountains   b farmland   c volcanoes
d fjords   e glaciers   f beaches

7 New Zealand is most famous for:
a its lamb.   b its scenery.   c its wool.

2 [8.4] Jenny, a tour guide from New Zealand, is telling a group of tourists about the country. Listen and check your answers.

68

Task

Choose one of the instruction cards below.

> **1** Work in pairs, A and B. You are going to find out more about New Zealand. A looks at the map of North Island on page 141. B looks at South Island on page 144.
>
> **2** Look at the features marked in red. You are going to explain to your partner exactly where they are. (Look at the phrases in the *Useful language* box.)
>
> **3** Take turns to describe the features. Find out what they are/why they are important.
>
> A marks the following places on South Island on this page.
> - Lake Wanaka
> - Christchurch
> - Mount Cook
> - Queenstown
> - Fox Glacier
>
> B marks the following places on North Island on this page.
> - the two most important airports
> - the active volcanoes
> - the Bay of Islands
> - Lake Taupo
>
> **4** You are the tourists in Jenny's group. Plan a short tour of New Zealand.

> **1** Work individually. Draw two rough maps of your own country. On the first mark only the capital city. On the second, mark ten important geographical features. For example:
> - the second, third, etc. cities
> - important rivers, forests, volcanoes
> - popular places to go on holiday
>
> **2** Work with a partner from a different country. Give your partner the blank map. Explain where the ten important features are so that your partner can complete the map.
>
> **3** Check your answers on each other's maps.
>
> **4** Which of the places that your partner described would you most like to see?

3 a) [8.5] Look at the map and listen to Jenny describing some of the main geographical features. Write the correct numbers next to these features.

Auckland ☐   Stewart Island ☐
The Cook Straits ☐   Wellington ☐
Northland ☐   The Southern Alps ☐

b) Listen again. What else do you learn about these places? Make notes, then compare them with a partner.

Useful language

"It's in the north of ..., near ..."

"It's on the east coast"

"It's the highest mountain/longest river"

"It's an important (*industrial*) area."

module 8 Countries and cultures

Writing

Formal and informal letters

1 a) Look at these two letters. Who is writing to who, in each case? Why?

b) Which letter is formal, and which is informal? How do you know?

---

a)

BAY PLAZA HOTEL

Bay Plaza Hotel
40–44 Oriental Parade
Wellington
New Zealand

22 March 2001

Mr J. Williams
31 Harbour Heights
Sydney
Australia

Dear Mr Williams

I am pleased to confirm your reservation for 15th August for two nights, in a single room with private bathroom, at the rate of $95 per night.

I will reserve a parking space for you as requested. The hotel is approximately 20 minutes drive from the airport and I enclose a map of the area to help you to find us.

Please do not hesitate to contact me if you have any further queries. I look forward to welcoming you to the Bay Plaza Hotel and hope that you will have a pleasant stay with us.

Yours sincerely

B. Chapman

Reservations Dept.

---

b)

Auckland
10th July

Dear Sam,

It was great to hear from you and I'm so pleased that you're finally coming to see New Zealand. It's fine for you to stay here for the first week of September – but please stay as long as you like! Yes, I think it's a very good idea to hire a car at the airport, then you can see much more of the country. It's about 20 minutes drive to the house and I'll make sure there's somewhere for you to park – don't worry.

I'm sending you some photos of Lake Taupo, and some of the beaches on the coast of Northland, to give you an idea of how fantastic the scenery is here... what do you think? The weather should still be quite warm in September, so you'll be able to do lots of swimming and sunbathing. I'm sure you'll have a great time here!

Anyway, do get in touch if you've got any questions, but if not I'll see you on the 2nd. I can't wait to see you again.

Love
Andi

70

2 a) Look at the addresses and dates on the two letters. How are they different?

b) Which letter has contractions (*I'm*)?

c) Match the beginnings in A with the endings in B.

A

| 1 Dear Sir |
| 2 Dear Mrs Kemble |
| 3 Dear Kate |
| 4 My darling Joanna |

B

| Love |
| Yours faithfully |
| With all my love |
| Yours sincerely |

3 Look at the phrases <u>underlined</u> in the informal letter. Find phrases in the formal letter which have a similar meaning.

4 Write a letter to a friend to say he/she can stay with you. First, think about these questions.

- When is he/she coming?
- How long is he/she staying?
- How is he/she getting to your house (or do you need to go and meet him/her)?
- What is he/she planning to do in your city/country?
- Are you sending anything (photos/map) in the letter?

Do you remember?

1 Make general statements using the endings below.
a) <u>Children are/Rome is</u> noisy.
b) … dangerous.
c) … expensive.
d) … horrible.
e) … good for you.
f) … bad for you.

2 Find the odd ones out in the groups below. Can you explain why?
a) the Alps, the Andes, the Atlantic, the Himalayas
b) the Pacific, the Mediterranean, the Nile, the North Sea
c) the Danube, the Rhine, the Suez, the Amazon
d) the Sun, the Moon, the sky, the Earth

3 Find the answers to the following questions in the box below.
a) When is the best time to see the Moon?
b) In Great Britain, which side of the road do people drive on?
c) Where do you study for a degree?
d) Where is the number 71 on this page?
e) Where in the USA is New Orleans?
f) Where in a room do you find the light switch?
g) Where in Spain is Barcelona?
h) Where is the dot in this circle?

on the left   at the bottom   on the north-east coast
in the middle   at university   in the south   at night   on the wall

4 Explain the difference between these pairs of words.
a) a lake/a sea
b) a forest/a tree
c) a river/a canal
d) a beach/a desert
e) the weather/the climate
f) a volcano/a mountain

module 9
Old and new

- Vocabulary: modern and traditional
- *May, might, will, definitely,* etc.
- Wordspot: *change*
- Present tense after *if, when, before* and other time words
- Task: decide on five improvements to your school or office

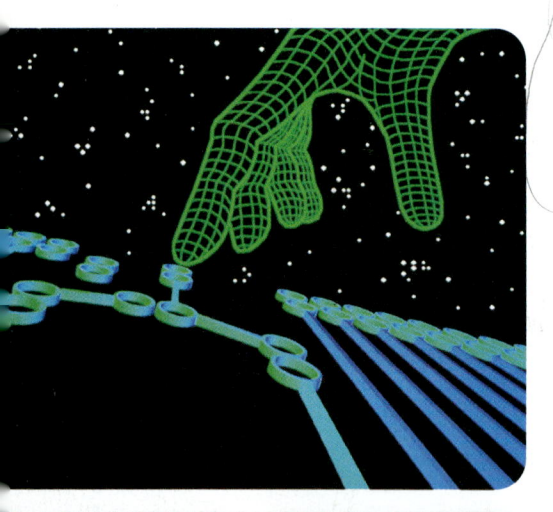

Vocabulary and speaking

Modern and traditional

1 Match the modern items in A below with the more traditional items in B.

A) a fast food restaurant   e-mail   a personal computer   a rock concert   a shopping mall   a CD player   an electronic organiser   a CD-ROM   a computer game   a microwave   a hypermarket   a theme park

B) a market   letters and telegrams   a diary and an address book   a cooker   a board game   a corner shop   a cassette player   a traditional restaurant   a fair   a typewriter   an encyclopedia   a circus

2 Which box do these belong to, A or B?

a mobile phone   the Internet   a library   air conditioning   a photocopier   a fax machine   a motorway   a bicycle   a skyscraper

3 Discuss these questions.

a Choose three pairs of items above and decide what the advantages and disadvantages of the old and new items are.

> Fast food restaurants are cheaper, but they can be very noisy.

> Traditional restaurants are comfortable and you usually have a lot of choice, but sometimes you have to wait!

b Do you ever have any problems with any of these things (new or old)? Explain why.

72

Reading and vocabulary

1 Discuss in groups. Where do you/your family usually buy the things in the box below?

- a hypermarket
- an open air market
- a shopping mall
- small local shops

paper and pens	furniture
food	clothes	CDs
electrical goods	books

2 a) Read about three people who sell these goods. Match the pictures with the paragraphs.

b) Answer these questions.

- What are the differences between their 'shops'?
- What are the advantages of each type of shopping?

THE CHANGING FACE OF SHOPPING

1 For the past eighteen years, Dilip Sardesai and his wife Andrija have run a small stationer's shop in the university city of Newcastle, in the north-east of England. As well as selling paper, pens, computer and office equipment, they also offer a photocopying and fax service. They work long hours to keep the shop going, and both of their children help them after school. Dilip sees the personal contact he has with his customers as the most important part of his job. 'Many of our customers are from the university,' says Dilip. 'We've seen generations of students come and go – we like to offer them the kind of personal service they can't get in a larger shop. We're never too busy to stop and chat about exams … or whatever they want to talk about …'

2 Nicole Parnot is the manageress of a Forum hypermarket, situated 20 kilometres from Arras, a town in the north-east of France. Forum has 600 stores in five different countries and plans to expand into Eastern Europe. The huge hypermarket employs over 300 people, and has parking spaces for over 3,000 cars. 'People nowadays have busy lives,' says Nicole, 'so we try to attract families by offering them a complete shopping experience, including a full restaurant service and free entertainment for the children. We try to make it possible for shoppers to do all their weekly shopping in one place. People come here not only for food and household goods, but also clothes, electrical goods, books, CDs … in fact, we sell everything from peanuts to personal computers!'

3 Five years ago, Dave Stirling had the idea of selling CDs over the Internet. The business he started from his home in Ohio, USA, now sells 500,000 CDs a year and has made him into a millionaire at the age of twenty-four. 'I could see right away that this was the future of shopping,' says Stirling. 'Why should you pay $15 for a CD – and spend the time and money getting to the store and parking your car – when, by clicking on your computer, you can have the same CD brought to your door for half the cost? And of course, there's the choice – we promise to find any CD and deliver it within seventy-two hours!' According to Stirling, this is only the beginning. 'I believe that one day we will do all our shopping over the Net: it's easier, quicker and cheaper. Shops and supermarkets will soon be a thing of the past.'

3 Discuss with other students.

- How do you prefer to shop?
- Which method of shopping don't you like?

module 9 Old and new

Language focus 1

May, might, will, definitely, etc.

1 What changes do you expect to see in the future? Discuss these three questions in groups.

a Will hypermarkets replace small local shops?
b Will people do all their shopping over the Internet?
c Will the Internet replace libraries and newspapers?

2 a) [9.1] You will hear Lucy, Mary and Stefan talking about the questions above. Which question is each person answering?

b) Listen to the three people again and complete the gaps.

Grammar analysis

1 Put the sentences below in order from 1 (= most probable) to 5 (= least probable).
People'll probably use the Internet to do all their shopping. ☐
People probably won't use the Internet to do all their shopping. ☐
People definitely won't use the Internet to do all their shopping. ☐
People may/might use the Internet to do all their shopping. ☐
People will definitely use the Internet to do all their shopping. ☐

2 a What do you notice about the position of *probably* and *definitely*:
• in positive sentences?
• in negative sentences?

b What are the negative forms of *may* and *might*?

▶ Language summary A, page 153.

Lucy
" No, people (1) .... all their shopping over the Net. A lot of things you want to see and touch before you buy them, like fresh food, you know, or clothes. They'll (2) .... more things like electrical goods, and books, because they'll be cheaper – but some people are worried about security, about giving a credit card number on the Net – I mean, I think that (3) .... some people. "

Mary
" I don't know, I think it'll (4) .... more and more difficult for small shops to survive, because of the prices, really. And you can get everything in one place in a hypermarket, of course. But then people will always need local shops, I mean, if you just want some milk or something, you don't want to drive a long way. So they (5) .... completely. "

Stefan
" Well, you can already read newspapers on the Net, but it's a bit difficult if you want to read one on the train! So it (6) .... them completely, and of course it's not very relaxing to sit and read something at your computer, is it? I mean, if you want to read a novel for example, or something like that, that you find in libraries – but not a reference book. I think people (7) .... the Net for that kind of information. You know, children doing a project for school or something. "

Practice

1 a) Use the prompts below to make sentences. Give a reason for your answer.

1 mobile phones/replace/ordinary phones

Mobile phones probably won't replace ordinary phones because most people will have both.

2 faxes and e-mails/replace/letters
3 microwaves/replace/cookers
4 credit cards/replace/cash
5 computer games/replace/board games
6 planes/replace/trains
7 CD-ROMs/replace/encyclopedias
8 computers/replace/teachers

b) Compare answers with a partner.

2 Complete these sentences about yourself. Compare your answers with other students.

a I _might_ live to be a hundred years old.
b I .... have more than two children.
c I .... have grey hair when I'm older.
d I .... live here all my life.
e I .... learn to speak English as well as my teacher.
f I .... visit the United States.
g I .... go to live in another country.
h I .... become a millionaire.

Pronunciation

1 [9.2] Listen to these three phrases. Does *won't* rhyme with *want* or *don't*?
You won't believe me.
You want to believe me.
You don't believe me.

2 [9.3] Listen to some predictions and repeat.
a I probably won't live to be a hundred.
b I definitely won't become a millionaire.
c I probably won't live here all my life.
d I'll definitely have grey hair when I'm older.
e I'll probably have more than two children.

Wordspot

Change

1 The diagram shows the most common uses of *change*. Read the examples. Then put the sentences below into the correct section.

a Have you changed your hair?
b Change places/trains.
c You know Harry – he'll never change.
d Have you got any change for the coffee machine?
e I'll just go upstairs and change.
f I've changed my mind about Dean – he's quite nice really.

a become different
Sue hasn't changed. She looks exactly the same.
Look! The sky's changing colour.

b make something/someone different
We're going to change the garage into an office.

f money
I need to change this £50 note.
Can you change this into dollars?
Keep the change.

CHANGE

c from one thing to another
change your name/address/job/the subject

e clothes
Go and change your shoes, Tim – they're all wet!
Are you going to change into a dress for the party?

d a plan or decision
Oh, please change your mind and come with us!

75

module 9 Old and new

2 **a)** Think of three:

- things that can change colour.
- ways you can change your appearance.
- reasons why you might need some change.

b) What happens when:

- you move house?
- you are in a foreign country and only have money from your own country?
- you buy a £12 train ticket with a £50 note?
- a princess kisses a frog?

(Use *change* in your answers.)

3 Talk to other students and find someone who:

a has changed his/her phone number recently.
b has got a lot of change in his/her pocket.
c would like to change his/her name.
d has changed his/her school/job more than twice.
e changes into more comfortable clothes when he/she gets home in the evening.
f changes his/her mind a lot before making a decision.
g changes trains/buses on his/her way to school/work.
h thinks he/she has changed in the last few years.

Language focus 2

Present tense after *if*, *when*, *before* and other time words

1 Read about the new leisure complex and look at the two possible sites. Briefly, what are the good and bad points of each site?

The town council is going to build a new leisure complex. It will have a multi-screen cinema, fast food restaurants and a video arcade. There are two possible sites, one in the town centre on the site of an old cinema, and one out of town, in a large park near a residential area.

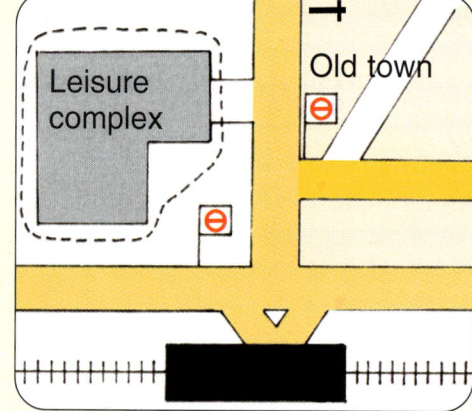

Site A

The site is close to shops and public transport, but there is no space for a car park and there is a lot of traffic already. There are a lot of cafés and restaurants in the old town nearby.

Site B

The site is in a park, an area of natural beauty. There is no public transport, but there is room for a large car park. The roads in the residential area around the park are quite small. There are no cafés, restaurants or other kinds of entertainment in the area.

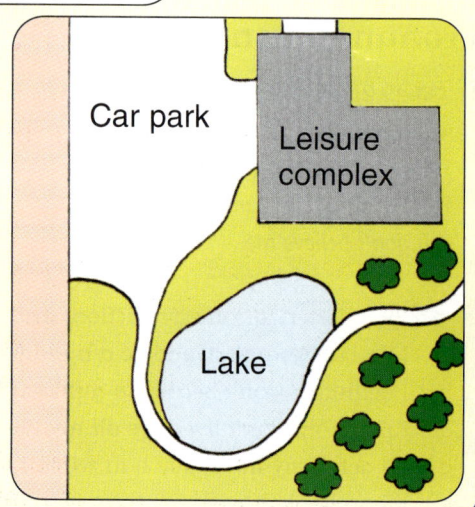

2 Discuss in pairs. Are the statements below:
- true of Site A/Site B?
- equally true of both/true of neither?

a When the complex opens, a lot of people will come from out of town to use it.
b If they build the complex on this site, they'll probably need to cut down a lot of trees.
c If they build the complex on this site, there may be serious traffic problems.
d As soon as the complex opens, local people will start complaining about it.
e If they build the complex on this site, people without cars won't be able to get there.
f More people will use the complex if it is built on this site.
g Before they start building, they should ask local people what they think.

Grammar analysis

1 Are the sentences above about:
   a the present?   b the future?

2 a Which verb form comes after *if, when, before* and *as soon as*?

   b Which verb forms can you find in the other part (the main clause) of the sentences?

▶ *Language summary B, page 154.*

Practice

1 a) Complete the sentences with the correct form of the verbs in brackets.

1 Many cafés and restaurants in the old town ..will lose.. (*lose*) business if the complex ..opens... (*open*) near them.
2 If the complex ..is.......... (*be*) in the park, the local residents ....will...... (*complain*) about the noise and rubbish.
3 When the complex ..opens..... (*open*), it ..will............. (*create*) a lot of jobs for local people.
4 If people ..don't have.. (*not have*) a car, they .... (*need*) a special bus service to get to the park site.
5 There may .... (*be*) serious traffic problems if they ..don't......... (*not build*) bigger roads near the site.
6 The area by the lake ..will........ (*lose*) its character if they ....put........ (*put*) the complex there.
7 The builders should .... (*find out*) more about traffic and transport problems before they .... (*make*) a decision.
8 If they .... (*build*) the complex in the city centre, many people ..won't........ (*not able/park*).
   be able to park

b) Write three more sentences of your own about the leisure complex. Which site do you think is best? Why?

2 Work in pairs. Complete the conversations below with your own ideas. Practise reading your conversations aloud.

a A: Oliver, could you do your homework now?
   B: Oh, Mum, I'll do it when …
b A: Are you going anywhere nice this weekend?
   B: We might go for a picnic in the country if …
c A: We haven't got any milk!
   B: Oh no! I'll go and buy some when/as soon as … the shop opens
d A: Are you enjoying your new job more now?
   B: No, I hate it! I want to leave as soon as I get.. money
e A: So when are we going to see each other again?
   B: I don't know, I'm very busy at work at the moment, and I'm going away soon, but I'll phone you if/when .I. have free time
f A: Are you going to have a holiday this year?
   B: I hope so, if ..I. have money and time

3 [9.4] Listen and compare your answers with those on the recording.

module 9 Old and new

Decide on five improvements to your school or office

Personal vocabulary

[handwritten notes:] I'd like to make my English classroom into better one. I want to make it bigger and more comfortable. Buy new better chairs and computers. Buy new table, and new window.

Useful language

a To make suggestions and discuss possibilities

"How about …?"

"I think we should …"

"I'd like to …"

"If we …, it will (*probably/definitely*) be much better for …"

"I'd prefer to …"

b Useful verbs

"put a … near the/in the …"

"build a new …"

"make the … into a …"

"make … bigger"

"have a … instead of …"

"redecorate the …"

"change the … into a …"

"improve the …"

Preparation for task

1 Discuss the following questions in pairs or small groups.

- What competitions do you find in magazines or newspapers? What prizes can you win?
- Do you know anyone who has won a competition like this?

2 Look at the competition entry form and pictures opposite. What kind of competition is it? Read the form and answer the questions.

a What is the prize? What do you have to spend it on?
b What examples do they give of how you could spend the money?
c Which things do you have to explain?
d Do you have to give the cost of the improvements yourself?

Task

1 You are going to enter the competition. Spend five minutes thinking how **you** will spend the money. Ask your teacher about any words or phrases you need.
▶ *Personal vocabulary*

2 Work in pairs or small groups. Explain and compare ideas with your partner.
▶ *Useful language*

3 a) As a class, write a list of your ideas on the board. Each group explains their ideas.

b) Vote for the five best ideas from the class list. Each student can vote a maximum of three times.

4 [9.5] Listen to four people talking about how they would improve their school or office. Complete the table below.

	School or office?	Improvements?	Why?
a			
b			
c			
d			

Optional writing

Write your entry for the competition, explaining what changes you plan to make to your school/workplace, and why.

EXCITING NEW COMPETITION!
Give your workplace a spring facelift!

Living magazine is offering three prizes of between £10,000 and £50,000 to be spent on improving the school, college or office where you spend so many hours each day! If you win, the money will be yours to spend as you wish, whether you need basic equipment, or one or two little luxuries to make life more pleasant.

Just think! You could spend it on any of the following:
- improving the appearance of the place (redecoration, new furniture, pictures or carpets).
- better study facilities (a computer room, language laboratory or a small library).
- improving the outside area (making a garden or car park for example).
- better sports facilities (a small gym or tennis court).
- making the environment more comfortable for people who work there (sofas, plants, lifts!).

To enter, all you have to do is to write below:
- five ways you intend to spend the money if you win.
- what you want to include (for example, what exactly will you have in your new computer room?).
- where you want to put the new features and why.
- why these changes will make your workplace a better place to be!

(Remember, if you win, *Living* magazine will decide the cost of the improvements, and exactly what your money will buy, so you do not need to include this in your entry.)
I would like to enter .... school/college/company for the *Living* magazine Spring Facelift competition. If I win, I plan to make the following improvements:

....

....

79

Real life

Shopping in a department store

1 You are in a department store. Where can you hear the sentences below?

- cash desk
- clothes department
- anywhere in the store

a Can I help you?
   I'm just looking thanks

b Excuse me, do you sell plants?
   on the ground floor near the entrance

c Can I pay by credit card?
   Sorry madam we don't accept credit card check or cash

d Excuse me, have you got this T-shirt in white?
   We only what's there I'm afraid

e Where are the changing rooms, please?
   Just over there on the right can you see them

f Can I bring it back if it's the wrong colour?
   Certainly if you keep receipt

g Have you got these trousers in a size 40?
   Sorry we haven't got any any left

h Here's your receipt and your change.
   Thank you

i Is there a toilet in here?
   yes just next the restaurant on the 4 floor

2 [9.6] Listen and write in the replies. Practise the conversations, in pairs.

3 [9.7] Listen to some more situations. When there is a pause, decide what to say. Compare your answer with the one on the recording.

Do you remember?

1 Look at these children's predictions. Find and correct two grammatical mistakes.

a) We'll probably be able to talk to the television.
b) We'll have cars with wings, which fly.
c) I'll be a princess and I'll be live in a castle.
d) We might not won't have telephones.
e) There'll definitely be cities on the moon.

2 Put the sentences below in order. Make them true for you.
a) TV/get/I/watch/home/when/might/I
b) some/shopping/I/tomorrow/go/if/I'll/CDs/buy
c) this/I'll/if/time/English/I/study/have/weekend
d) can/when/I'm/work/I/well/speak/English/going to/in the USA
e) my/I/hair/I'll/as soon as/wash/get up

3 Match a word from A with a word/phrase from B to make phrases from Module 9.

A	B
a) pay	some letters
b) expand	about the weather
c) keep	by cheque
d) deliver	your receipt
e) chat	your business

4 Which words are missing from the sentences below?
a) Have you got this jacket ~~~~ brown?
b) Have you got any change ~~~~ the parking meter?
c) Can I bring it ~~back~~ if she doesn't like it?
d) I need to change ~~into~~ some dry clothes.
e) The café? – It's ~~on~~ the fourth floor.
f) Can we have a sofa here instead ~~of~~ these chairs?

module 10
Take care!

- *Used to*
- **Vocabulary:** health problems, accidents
- *Past Continuous*

Task: describe a rescue and decide who is Hero of the Year

Reading, listening and vocabulary

1 a) Make a list of common health problems.

For example: a bad cold

b) Read the quiz quickly. Which problems from your list are mentioned? Which others are mentioned?

2 Do the quiz in pairs. Which answers do you think are correct? (More than one answer is possible.)

3 [10.1] Listen to Dr Sandra Cabot and check your answers. Did any of her answers surprise you?

4 How many more word combinations can you find using these verbs from the quiz?

I've got .... a headache
              a bad cold
to take .... medicine

to put ....   some cream ....
              on it

Health problems
How much do you know?

1 If you burn yourself on a hot pan:
 a you should put butter or oil on the burn.
 b you should put a plaster on it.
 c you should put lots of cold water on it.

2 If you've got a temperature:
 a you should stay in bed and keep warm.
 b you should take aspirin or paracetamol.
 c you should rest and keep cool.

3 If you've got a bad cold:
 a you should go to the doctor's and get some medicine.
 b you should take asprin.
 c you should go to bed and have a hot drink.

4 If you want to lose weight in a healthy way:
 a you should stop eating potatoes, bread and pasta.
 b you should take regular exercise.
 c you should eat less fat and sugar, and more fruit and vegetables.

5 If you are taking a prescription of antibiotics:
 a you should take them at exactly the same time every day.
 b you should finish the prescription.
 c you should never drink alcohol.

6 If you've got bad backache:
 a you should go to bed and rest until it gets better.
 b you should go for short walks and keep moving.
 c you shouldn't lift anything heavy.

module 10 Take care!

Pronunciation

1 Mark the stress on the following words.

medicine   plaster   aspirin
antibiotics   exercise
headache   healthy
prescription   temperature

2 [10.2] Listen and check.

5 a) Prepare short conversations in small groups. A has a health problem, B and C give advice. Some is good, some is bad!

For example:

A: I've got terrible backache!
B: Well, you should go to bed and rest.
A: Really?
C: Mmm... I'm not so sure. I think you should keep moving – go for short walks and things like that.
A: Oh, right.

b) Act out some of your conversations for other students.

Language focus 1

Used to

1 Two or three hundred years ago most people didn't live as long as we do today. Think of three reasons why.

2 Match the pictures a) – d) with the paragraphs 1 – 4 opposite.

Did you know ... ?

1   Two or three centuries ago people had much shorter lives – the average age was forty-five. But this was mainly because a lot of babies used to die. If people survived to be adults, they could often live to be seventy or even eighty, like today.

2   Having children was much more dangerous than it is today. Families often used to have ten or twelve children, but many babies died, and unfortunately many women died in childbirth.

3   In those days they didn't know how to cure all the diseases that we can cure now. Many people didn't use to have enough to eat, or did not have enough money to pay for doctors. Even if you had a doctor, some of their methods were very strange. They used to believe that cutting open their patients and 'bleeding' cured almost any problem – unfortunately, it often killed them instead!

4   And people knew less about hygiene in the past. Even rich people didn't use to wash very often, and most poor people didn't have toilets or clean water. It was difficult to keep food fresh too, so they used to cook with a lot of strong spices to cover the taste of the bad meat.

Grammar analysis

1 Underline all the examples of *used to* above. Cross out (✗) the **wrong** explanation below.

We use *used to* for:
a things that happened more than once in the past.
b feelings, thoughts, ideas, etc. in the past (past states).
c things that happened only once in the past.

2 What are the negative and question forms?

▶ *Language summary A, page 154.*

82

Practice

1 Write sentences with *used to/didn't use to* using ideas from A and B below.

For example:
A long time ago people used to think the Earth was flat.

A long time/200 years ago ...

A

People/not/have
People/think
People/send
Poor children
People/believe

B

messages by pigeons.
the Earth was flat.
electricity in their houses.
not/wear/shoes.
not/go/to school.
in witches.

Pronunciation

[10.3] Listen and practise saying the phrases.

think > used to think > people used to think ...
have > didn't use to have > people didn't use to have cars

2 Complete these sentences about yourself.

When I was a small child ...
a I used to think that ...
b I used to be frightened of ...
c I used to/didn't use to love ...
d My favourite toy used to be ...
e I used to spend hours ...(read)-ing.
f I never used to ...

Vocabulary

Accidents

1 Which of the words in **bold** below can you find in the pictures? Check any unknown words if necessary.

A
a If you **bump into** the corner of a table,
b If you **fall over** in the street,
c If you **slip** on some ice,
d If you **cut yourself** with a sharp knife,
e If you **drop** a glass on the floor,
f If you **touch** a hot pan,

B
you'll probably **get a bruise**.
you might **cut yourself**.
you might **hurt yourself badly**.
you will probably **burn yourself**.
you might **break an arm** or a **leg**.
you will probably **bleed**.
you will only probably **hurt yourself slightly**.

2 Work in pairs. Look at the accidents in A and match them with the consequences in B. (There are many possibilities.)

If you slip on some ice, you'll probably get a bruise ...

3 Why should you be careful in the following situations?

a if you're using the iron
b if your floor is wet
c if you're carrying sharp scissors
d if a small child is in the kitchen while you're cooking
e if there are clothes or toys all over the floor

module 10 Take care!

Language focus 2

Past Continuous

1 Look at the pictures of minor car accidents. Explain in your own words what happened in each accident.

2 If you have a car accident, you may need to make an insurance claim. Read what the four drivers above wrote on their claim forms. Match the extracts to the appropriate pictures.

① I was driving slowly down the high street. At the traffic lights, I knocked over a man who was crossing the road. He admitted it was his fault, because the same thing has happened to him before.

② As I was coming home from work, I accidentally turned into the wrong house and crashed into a tree that I do not have.

③ While I was waiting in a traffic jam, I unfortunately bumped into a cyclist, who passed my car on the other side from where I was looking ...

④ I was driving carefully down a country lane when a cow walked into the side of my car. I learnt afterwards that the cow was half-witted*...

* very stupid

Grammar analysis

Past Simple and Past Continuous

1 Look at the Past Simple and Past Continuous verbs in the sentence below.

I **was driving** slowly down the high street. At the traffic lights, I **knocked over** a man **who was crossing** the road.

Which verb describes the **main event** in this story?
Which describes the **situation** at the time?
Which action(s) started first?

driving along — knocked over a man
past ——————————— now

2 <u>Underline</u> the other examples of the Past Simple and Past Continuous in the insurance claims.

3 What are the negative and question forms?

Time words

We can join the Past Simple and Past Continuous parts of a sentence with a time word.

While I was waiting in a traffic jam, I **bumped into** a cyclist.

Find another time word like this in the insurance claims.

▶ Language summary B, page 154.

84

Practice

1 You witnessed accident c on page 84. On page 142 you will see a picture of the scene just before the accident. Find the motorist (Mr Smith) and the cyclist.

a) You have exactly one minute to study the picture. Memorise as many details as possible.

b) Work in pairs, A and B. Test each other's memories using the questions below.

For example: What car/the motorist/drive?
What car was the motorist driving?

Questions for A

a Why/Mr Smith/look the other way from the cyclist?
b What/the motorist in the red car/try to do?
c Mr Smith and the other motorist/talk/politely?
d Who/sit in the back seat of Mr Smith's car?
e they/sit/still? What/they/do?
f Who/cross the road? What/she/carry?

Questions for B

a What/the cyclist/wear?
b the cyclist/concentrate/on the road/when the accident/happen?
c What/his friend/do?
d How many people/stand/at the bus stop?
e What/they/do?
f How many men/repair/road? What/they do?

c) Whose fault do you think the accident was?

Pronunciation

1 [10.4] Listen to these sentences and notice the pronunciation of *be*. Practise the sentences.
  a An old lady *was* /wəz/ crossing the road.
  b The cyclist *wasn't* /wəzənt/ concentrating.
  c The children *weren't* /wɜ:nt/ sitting still.
  d They *were* /wə/ fighting.

2 [10.5] Listen and write down the six sentences you hear. Practise the sentences.

---

2 Complete the story with the correct verb form, Past Simple or Past Continuous.

One cold December evening, an Austrian electrician called Karl Emminger (1).......... (go) to a party at a friend's house. Soon after midnight, Karl and his wife (2).......... (leave) the party. It (3).......... (snow), so they (4).......... (walk) quickly to the bus stop to catch the last bus home. Ten minutes later, they (5).......... (stand) at the bus stop when a bus, driven by Oskar Schillab, (6).......... (drive) past them without stopping. Furious, Karl (7).......... (stop) a taxi and (8).......... (tell) the driver to 'Follow that bus!' A few moments later, they (9).......... (see) the bus, which (10).......... (wait) at a red traffic light. Karl (11).......... (jump) out of the taxi, onto the bus and (12).......... (hit) Oskar on the nose. Shocked, Oskar (13).......... (take) his foot off the brake. The bus, which (14).......... (stand) on a hill, (15).......... (move) forward and (16).......... (crash) into a shop window, causing thousands of pounds of damage!

3 a) Complete the following sentences about yourself using the Past Continuous. Compare answers with a partner.

1 I once had an accident when I ...
2 When I left the house this morning, the sun ...
3 I met ... when I ...
4 At eight o'clock last night, I think I ...
5 At seven o'clock this morning I ...
6 When I arrived at this lesson, ... (name) was ...
7 When the teacher arrived at this lesson, I ...

b) Close your books. How many of your partner's answers can you remember?

... module 10 Take care!

Describe a rescue and decide who is Hero of the Year

Preparation for task

1 a) A newspaper has decided to give a £10,000 first prize for the 'Hero of the Year'. Look at the pictures of the three finalists below. They all rescued someone. What do you think happened?

b) Which questions in the table can you complete?

Kathy Reynolds, 32

Shirley Yeats, 67

Simon Roland, 10

Heroine with a cigarette lighter!

Kathy Reynolds, 32, was walking home one afternoon when she stopped to light a cigarette. A car stopped behind her and a man jumped out. To Kathy's horror, the man pulled out a knife and demanded money from an old woman, Eileen Murphy, 73, who was waiting at a bus stop. Kathy – who is only 1.55 m tall – took her cigarette lighter and set fire to the back of the mugger's trousers! The man was so shocked he dropped his knife, and with the help of Mrs Murphy, Kathy knocked the man to the ground, sat on him and tied his arms and legs together with a shoelace! She then called the police using her mobile phone – and moments later the police came to arrest the man!

2 a) The pictures opposite show what happened to Kathy Reynolds. Put them in the correct order. Read the newspaper story above to check.

b) Complete the first column of the table below.

		Kathy Reynolds	Shirley Yeats	Simon Roland
1	age of finalist	32	67	10
2	Where did the rescue happen?	in the street	at the ship	on the beach
3	Who did he/she rescue?	Mrs. Murphy	passengers	a young man
4	Why did these people need help?	she was about to be mugged	the ship was sinking	he was drowning
5	Why was the 'hero' there and what was he/she doing?		go back to her cab	he was playing on the beach
6	What did he/she do to help?	set fire	telephoned	he took him out
7	Are there any other reasons why he/she was very brave?	she was only 1.55 m tall	she was old	he was very young

Task

1 a) Work in two groups, A and B. Find out what happened to one of the other finalists.

- Group A looks at page 141 (Shirley Yeats).
- Group B looks at page 145 (Simon Roland).

b) Work with someone from **your own** group. Complete the information about your story in the table above.

2 Now work with a student from the other group. Ask/Answer the questions from the table to complete the final column.

Writing

Using adverbs in narrative

1 To make a story more interesting, we often use adverbs like those in the box below.

> suddenly   immediately   fortunately
> unfortunately   eventually   certainly

MD Look in your mini-dictionary and find an example of how each adverb is used.

2 Look at the rough draft of the story of Shirley Yeats. It is correct, but it would be more interesting with more adverbs. Add a suitable adverb from the box above where you see ∧.

Shirley Yeats is ∧ a very brave woman! At the age of sixty-seven, the retired school teacher decided to take the holiday of a lifetime, and went on a cruise sailing round the coast of Malaysia. She was having a wonderful holiday, relaxing and sunbathing. But one day, she was going into her cabin, when she ∧ noticed that smoke was coming out of another cabin, ∧, she phoned the captain from her cabin and told him about the fire. Then she went up on deck to see what she could do to help. ∧ the fire spread very quickly, and soon it was out of control, so the captain decided to get all the passengers off the ship. Many of them were very frightened, but Shirley stayed calm. She helped the other passengers to get into lifeboats and even gave first aid to other passengers who were hurt. ∧ all 1,100 passengers were in the lifeboats, and ∧ not one passenger died in the fire. Shirley was one of the last to leave. Later she told journalists: 'I was very frightened but I knew what I had to do – I think all my time as a teacher helped – all those years of telling people what to do!'

3 Find at least six other words that link the story together and circle them, as in the example.

3 In small groups discuss who should win the prizes in the competition, and why.

▶ *Useful language*

1st prize (£10,000) ....
2nd prize (£5,000) ....
3rd prize (£2,000) ....

Useful language

"... should get first prize because he/she ..."

"I think ... was the bravest because ..."

"He/She was very calm/quick-thinking."

"She/He saved ...'s life."

"He/She was in danger ..."

87

module 10 Take care!

4 a) Write a rough draft of a story.

Either: write the story of Simon Roland using the pictures on page 145 and the words next to them to help you. Add extra details to make the story more interesting if you want to.

Or: write a story of your own (true or imaginary) of a rescue or accident. Ask your teacher for any words or phrases you need.

b) Either alone or with a partner, read through your story. Add adverbs and linking words where necessary. Write the final draft for homework.

Do you remember?

1 Cross out (X) the word which is not possible with each verb below. Then add a word which is possible.

a) take | aspirin / ~~a headache~~ medicine / exercise

b) I've got | a pain in my chest. / stomachache. / ~~exercise~~. headache

c) put | a plaster / cold water / a prescription | on it — butter cream

d) keep | warm / ~~to bed~~ the change, cold / moving

2 In which of the sentences below can we use *used to* instead of the Past Simple?

a) Sorry, I forgot to post that letter.
b) My ~~dad told~~ used to tell me funny stories every night, when I was a child. used to
c) I ~~loved~~ going to the park in the summer.
d) You didn't tell me about Kim's accident! about it used to
e) She ~~didn't~~ eat meat as a teenager.
f) I met him at Teri's party.

3 Write answers to the questions below. Ask and answer in pairs.

What were you doing:
a) at 3 p.m. yesterday? I was reading the newspaper.
b) between eight and nine last night? I was watching TV
c) before you started this exercise? I was watching TV
d) ten minutes before this lesson started? I was going to class
e) the last time you hurt yourself? I was running to school

4 Put a word from the box into the correct place in the sentences below.

> over   yourself   on (x2)   into (x2)
> herself   myself

a) He went off the road and crashed into a tree.
b) Be careful – you'll cut with that knife!
c) I've dropped a contact lens the floor and I can't find it.
d) Grandma couldn't see in the dark and she bumped the door.
e) She hurt while she was playing in the garden, doctor.
f) I think I slipped some oil on the kitchen floor.
g) He's too old to drive now – I'm worried that he'll knock someone. over myself
h) Can you see where I burnt on the iron?

5 Circle the best adverb in these sentences.

a) It rained and rained for hours. *Eventually/ Immediately*, the rain stopped and we went for a walk.
b) Don't worry, I've only hurt my leg *badly/slightly*.
c) She slipped on the stair and dropped the beautiful vase. *Certainly/Fortunately*, it didn't break.
d) I *accidentally/unfortunately* took your car keys this morning. I'm so sorry.
e) We were all having dinner, when *immediately/suddenly* the lights went out and everyone stopped talking.

module 11
The best things in life ...

- Gerunds (-ing forms) verbs of liking and disliking
- *Like doing* and *would like to do* (gerunds and infinitives)
- Wordspot: *like*

Task: make a list of the most important things in life

When an interest becomes an obsession ...

Whether it's collecting coins, supporting your favourite football team, or just shopping, most people have some kind of hobby. But what happens when that interest becomes the most important thing in your life? When a hobby becomes an obsession?

Take Colin Duffy, for example. When he was six, his father took him to see his local football team, Liverpool. Since then, Colin, now thirty-six, has seen a total of 1,729 matches, and has travelled over 75,000 miles to watch his team. Colin and his wife spent their honeymoon in Leeds (where Liverpool were playing that weekend!) and named their first son Kenny Dalglish Owen Duffy - after his two favourite players.

Colin may be Britain's number one football fan, but 22-year-old Beverley Bloom is Britain's biggest shopper. Every week she writes a newspaper column about her addiction. Fortunately, Beverley's credit card bills go to her father ... a millionaire property tycoon. 'I don't think I'd like to tell you what Beverley spends,' he says, admitting that it is well over £50,000 a year.

But even Beverley cannot beat champion shopper Imelda Marcos, wife of the ex-president of the Philippines. She was so obsessed with buying shoes that when her husband fell from power, more than 3,000 pairs were found in their palace, together with over 1,000 unopened packets of tights.

Most children are interested in collecting stamps or dolls at some time, but few go as far as twenty-eight year old Tony Mattia, who fills his house with thousands of Barbie dolls. He spends hours every day combing their hair and changes all their costumes once a month. And, it seems that, the more unusual the collection, the bigger the obsession. For example, US collector Hugh Hicks has about 60,000 light bulbs and Nick Vermeulen from the Netherlands has over 2,000 aeroplane sick bags.

But such obsessions can have unfortunate results. John Weintraub became obsessed with collecting plastic figures of US presidents given as free gifts in packets of breakfast cereal. After two years he had the whole set except for Thomas Jefferson. Weintraub was so desperate to get the last one that he broke into a factory and opened every box of cereal he could find. He was seen by a guard, arrested and sent to prison. 'It's OK though,' he said, 'because at my first prison breakfast out came the statue of Jefferson.'

Reading and vocabulary

1 Work in groups and discuss these questions.

a What are the most popular hobbies and interests in your country? Do you have any special interests yourself?

b Do you know anyone who is mad about:
- a sport?
- shopping?
- collecting something?

2 a) Which of these things do people collect? What other things do they collect?

> coins   shoes   light bulbs
> stamps   pairs of tights   dolls
> plastic toys from breakfast cereals

b) Read the article. Which of the things above are mentioned? What other hobbies and collections are mentioned?

89

module 11 The best things in life ...

3 How much can you remember about each person? Complete the first column in the table. Check your answers on page 89 and complete the second column.

Name	Obsession	How we know they are obsessed
Colin Duffy	Liverpool football club	he's seen 1,729 matches
Beverley Bloom	shopping	he spends 50,000 $ a year
Imelda Marcos	shoes	he has 3,000 pairs
Tony Mattia	dolls	he has 1000 dolls
Hugh Hicks	light bulbs	60,000 light bulbs
Nick Vermeulen	sick bags	2,000 sick bags
John Weintraub	plastic toys	he broke into a factory to take the Jefersons statued figure

4 Use the clues to complete the puzzle below with words from the text on page 89. What is the hidden word? (See page 139 for the answer.)

a U N F O R T U N A T E
b O B S E S S E D
c U N U S U A L
d S H O P P E R
e D E S P E R A T E
f I N T E R E S T E D
g C O L L E C T I N G
h F A V O U R I T E
i C H A M P I O N

CLUES

a The opposite of *fortunate*.
b If you are crazy about something and can't think of anything else, you are ...
c The opposite of *usual*.
d Someone who goes shopping is a ...
e If you want something very, very much, you are ... to have it.
f The opposite of *bored*.
g A lot of people have a stamp or coin ...
h The one you like best is your ...
i If you are better than anyone else at doing something, you are a ...

Language focus 1

Gerunds (*-ing* forms), verbs of liking and disliking

1 Which of these things do/don't you like?

a chocolates
b ice cream
c spiders
d washing-up
e being with your family for special occasions

Helena, age 21

Oliver, age 8

David, age 32

Melissa, age 24

Julia, age 35

2 [11.1] Listen to what five people are talking about in Exercise 1. Match the topic to the person. Do you think their feelings are unusual or not?

3 Listen again. Which words from the box below does each person use to describe their feelings?

> disgusting   sweet   cold and horrible
> boring   lovely and furry   relaxing

Grammar analysis

1 We use gerunds (-*ing* forms) in the same way as nouns and pronouns.
  a They can be the subject of the sentence.
  Spending holidays with my family | *is not my idea of fun.*
  A family holiday
  b They can be the object of the sentence.
  I find | wash**ing**-up | really relaxing.
        | it
  c We use them after prepositions.
  She's crazy about | *shopping.*
                      | *football.*

2 A number of verbs and phrases to express likes and dislikes are followed by a gerund (or noun). Put these examples in **bold** in the correct place on the line below.

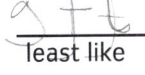

  _____
  least like   most like

  a He's **crazy about** football.
  b I really **enjoy** washing-up.
  c She's very **keen on** shopping.
  d I **don't mind** sweets or biscuits.
  e He's **interested in** collecting coins.
  f She **can't stand** spiders.
  g I **absolutely loathe** chocolate.
  h I **love** spiders.
  i I **hate** looking at dirty plates.
  j He **doesn't really like** swimming.

▶ Language summary A, page 154.

Practice

1 a) Do you have any unusual likes/dislikes? Are any of the possibilities below true for you? Discuss your answers in pairs.

A	B
I love I really like I really enjoy I quite like I don't mind	mice and rats taking exams cleaning the house long train journeys sitting in traffic jams getting up early in winter doing my English homework
I hate I can't stand I don't really like I'm not very keen on	small babies sunbathing chocolate pop music football hot weather going to parties the countryside meeting new people buying presents shopping

> Well, I really like long train journeys.

> Really. Why?

> Because I can read my book and talk to other people

b) Tell your partner your opinion about some of the other things in B above.

> I really hate the winter.

module 11 The best things in life ...

2 Make these sentences true using the *-ing* form.

a I find ..cooking.. very relaxing.
b .... can be stressful.
c I'm (not) very interested in ..shopping..
d .... is boring, I think.
e I think .... is good fun.
f ..Smoking.. is bad for you.
g ..Doing exercise.. is good for you.
h My friend (name) .... is crazy about ..fishing football..
i I think ..learning.. is disgusting.
j ..Smoking.. can be dangerous.

Grammar analysis

1 Look at sentences 1–8 below again. Underline the verbs followed by a gerund (*-ing* form) like this ...., and those followed by an infinitive (*to* + verb) like this ~~~~~ .

2 (Circle) the correct answer for the rules below.
  a *She likes being with children.   She loves travelling.*
    Like | + verb + *-ing*: means *enjoys/wants to*.
    Love |
  b *She'd like to have at least four children.*
    He'd love to own a Ferrari.
    Would like/love + *to* + verb: means *enjoys/wants to*.
  Which form is used to describe a general feeling? Which is used to describe something you want to do in the future?

▶ Language summary B, page 155.

Language focus 2

Like doing and *would like to do* (gerunds and infinitives)

Match the sentences to the pictures.
1 He's crazy about cars.
2 She plans to go to India for her next trip.
3 She really likes being with children.
4 He'd love to own a Ferrari.
5 She'd like to have at least four children of her own.
6 He loves dancing.
7 He hopes to become a professional dancer one day.
8 She really loves travelling.

92

Practice

1 a) Work in pairs, A and B. A looks at the card on page 141 and B looks at the card on 144.

b) Put the verbs in brackets into the correct form with *do* or *would*. Ask and answer the questions with your partner.

2 [11.2] How do these conversations finish? (There is more than one possibility.) Compare your answers with the recording.

a A: Would you like to stay for something to eat?
   B: Thanks, I ....

b A: Have you been to the Egyptian Exhibition at the British Museum yet?
   B: Not yet, but I ....

c A: Are you going to Caroline's party on Saturday night?
   B: I don't know. To be honest, I don't really ....

d A: Are you having a holiday this summer?
   B: Yes, we ....

Pronunciation

1 Notice how *to* is pronounced:
• in the **middle** of a sentence or clause.
Are you going to /tə/ *Caroline's party?*
• at the **end**.
I don't really want to /tuː/.

2 Listen again and practise the conversations with a partner.

Wordspot

like

1 Choose a word from the box to complete the sentences below. (There is more than one possibility.)

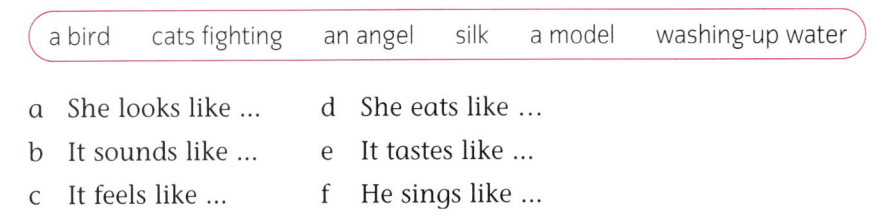

> a bird   cats fighting   an angel   silk   a model   washing-up water

a She looks like …
b It sounds like …
c It feels like …
d She eats like …
e It tastes like …
f He sings like …

2 Put the word *like* into the correct place in these sentences.

a He's so young. He doesn't look ∧ a doctor. *(like)*
b Which do you best – chocolate or ice cream?
c Would you something to eat?
d What does that soup taste?
e Open it at the top, this.
f Your eyes are your brother's.
g I'll come and meet you at the airport if you.
h What was the concert?

3 Add the phrases with *like* to the correct section of the diagram below.

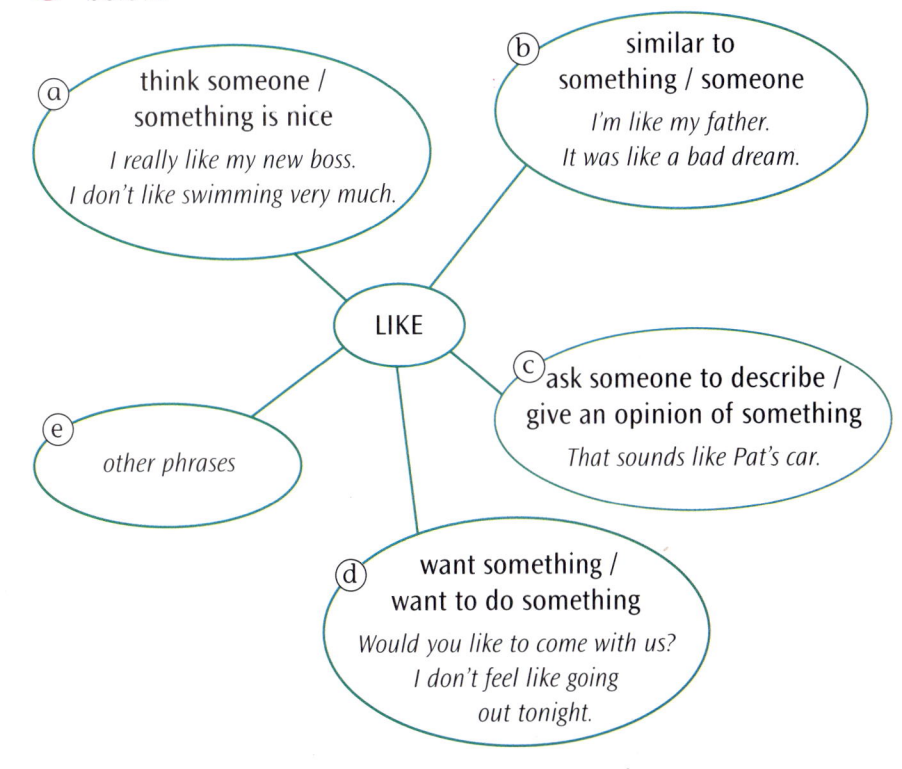

(a) think someone / something is nice
I really like my new boss.
I don't like swimming very much.

(b) similar to something / someone
I'm like my father.
It was like a bad dream.

(c) ask someone to describe / give an opinion of something
That sounds like Pat's car.

(d) want something / want to do something
Would you like to come with us?
I don't feel like going out tonight.

(e) other phrases

LIKE

4 [11.3] You will hear some questions and instructions. Your teacher will stop the recording after each one. Discuss your answers in pairs.

93

module 11 The best things in life ...

Make a list of the most important things in life

Personal vocabulary

Useful language

a   Comparing ideas on the list

"I think ... is more important than ... (because) ..."

"For me ... is particularly important (because) ..."

"Personally, I don't think ... is at all important ..."

"... doesn't really matter to me (because) ..."

"I find it very hard/impossible to choose between these two (because) ..."

b   Comparing opinions with other students

"That's the same for me."

"I agree with you."

"Me too!/Me neither!"

"Well, for me ... is more important ..."

Preparation for task

1 People in several countries were asked, 'What are the most important things in life?' Look at some of their answers. Decide if the statements below are true (T) or false (F).

	France	Germany	Greece	Italy	UK
family	94%	93%	99%	99%	93%
having good friends	94%	93%	98%	85%	98%
having a partner	94%	83%	98%	94%	72%
politics	28%	35%	61%	42%	34%
religion	26%	22%	87%	62%	33%

from *Eurostat 95*

a   For every nationality in the table, family is the most important thing in life.

b   For British people good friends are more important than having a partner.

c   Every nationality believes that religion is more important than politics.

d   There aren't many big differences between any of the nationalities.

2 Is your country in the table?

- If so, is there anything that surprises you?
- If not, what order would you expect for your country? (Not for yourself!)

3 Read the list of important things in life below. Underline any unknown words and check the meaning and pronunciation.

having good friends	having a partner
religion	politics
having children	having a successful career
an interesting job	a good salary
being attractive	being fit and healthy
having a nice home	living in a nice area
having enough money to travel	having enough money for a nice car
having nice clothes	going out a lot
having enough time to relax	having a busy social life

Task

1 a) Work individually. Imagine (for a moment!) you can choose only **one** thing in each pair in *Preparation for task*, Exercise 3. Choose the most important for you.

b) Ask your teacher for any unknown vocabulary.
▶ **Personal vocabulary**

2 Compare answers in small groups.

▶ **Useful language**

3 In groups, make a list of the **eight** most important things in life, using either these ideas or your own. Compare answers with other groups.

4 Did you have different ideas about these things five/ten years ago? Do you think your opinions about these things will be different in ten years' time? Why?

95

module 11 The best things in life ...

Real life

Finding things in common

1 a) Complete the conversations below with the correct phrases. (There is more than one possibility.)

> Neither did I   So am I
> Me neither   So do I
> It's the same for me   ~~Me too~~

a A: I'm bored!
   B: *Me too*. Let's go for a walk.

b A: I think it's really important to keep fit. I go to an aerobics class twice a week.
   B: Oh, really? *So do I*! Where's your class?

c A: He spoke so fast I didn't understand anything. How about you?
   B: *Neither did I*. Let's ask someone else.

d A: I don't know anything about computers.
   B: *Me neither*. I feel I should do a course or something, to learn more about them.

e A: Excuse me, can you help me? I'm lost!
   B: Oh dear! *So am I*! I thought you could help me!

f A: It always takes me hours to get here on the bus. It's a nuisance.
   B: *So do I / It's the same for me*. There's so much traffic!

b) 🔊 [11.4] Listen and check your answers.

Grammar analysis

Answer the questions.
a If you agree with positive sentences (*I like coffee*), do you use *so* or *neither*?
b If you agree with negative sentences (*I don't like tea*), do you use *so* or *neither*?

▶ Language summary C, page 155.

2 The auxiliary verb in the phrases in B matches the one in the original sentence in A. Match the answers in B below with the original sentences in A. (There is only one possibility for each.)

A
a I'm feeling really tired tonight.
b I'm not very hungry, actually.
c I absolutely hate warm milk.
d My husband doesn't like dancing very much.
e I was really ill last week!
f Actually, I wasn't here last lesson.
g We went to Istanbul for our holidays last year.
h We didn't enjoy the film much.

B
That's funny – so was I!
Really? Neither do I, I must say.
No, neither did we.
So do I. It's disgusting, isn't it?
What a coincidence, so did we!
Yes, so am I!
No, neither am I.
No, neither was I, unfortunately.

Pronunciation

1 Notice the stress in these phrases.

   •   •   •   •
   So am I.   Neither am I.

   Practise the stress by mumbling like this:
   MM mm MM > So am I.   MM-mm mm MM > Neither am I.

2 🔊 [11.5] Listen to the conversations in Exercise 2 above and practise them with a partner. Pay attention to the stress.

3 🔊 [11.6] Agree with the statements on the recording. Use any of the phrases from Exercise 2 above.

Consolidation modules 7–11

A Past Continuous, articles

Complete the gaps in the story below. Either put the verb in brackets into the Past Simple or Past Continuous, or put the or Ø (no article) in front of the noun.

A kind old lady (1) _was walking_ (walk) down some steps on her way to town when she (2) _saw_ (see) a little boy who (3) _was sitting_ (sit) at (4) _the_ bottom of the steps. He (5) _was crying_ (cry). 'What is the matter?' she (6) _asked_ (ask). He (7) _stopped_ (stop) crying. 'It's my birthday,' he (8) _said_ (say), 'and my parents (9) _gave_ (give) me a new bicycle and some computer games, and this afternoon we're having a party at (10) _Ø_ home, with (11) _Ø_ ice cream and (12) _Ø_ chocolate biscuits.'
'How strange,' (13) _said_ (say) the old lady, '(14) _Ø_ little boys usually like (15) _Ø_ birthday parties and (16) _Ø_ ice cream. Why (17) _are_ (you/cry)?'
'Because I'm lost!'

B Vocabulary: three things

Work in pairs. The words in the box below are from Modules 7–11. As quickly as possible, find three things:

1. you can play.
2. you can do accidentally.
3. people do with a business.
4. your doctor might tell you to do.
5. people might do with a computer.

take antibiotics	deliver it	hurt yourself	
an instrument	drop something	start it	
replace it	a board game	spill something	
improve it	a role	chat on it	stay in bed
expand it	keep warm		

C Grammar and listening: Present Perfect, future forms, used to, gerunds

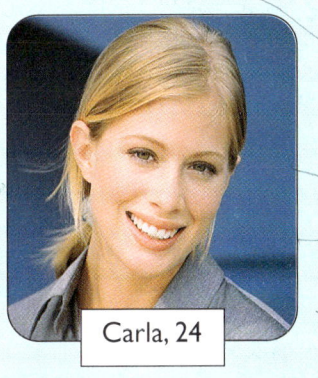

Eliza, 71

Philip, 42

Carla, 24

1 Look at the three people above. Which person do you think:

- enjoys going to parties and meeting people?
- used to earn more than he/she does now?
- would love to have a big family one day?
- has been married four times?
- loves cooking?
- has made over £1 million?
- used to be a film star?
- hasn't had a holiday for three years?
- will probably retire in a few years?
- doesn't like shopping?
- might travel round the world next year?
- spends a lot of time thinking about food?

2 [1] Listen to the three people talking and see how many of your guesses were correct.

3 Listen again and write down two more pieces of information about each person.

D Vocabulary: word search

Work in pairs. Use the clues to help you find words from Modules 7–11 in the square below. (The module number is in brackets.)

Across
1. A very tall building. **(9)**
2. Computers, fax machines, telephones, etc. are all office ... **(9)**
3. Do you think computers will ... teachers one day? **(9)**
4. If you cut yourself, you will probably ... **(10)**
5. What do you want to be when you ... up? **(7)**
6. My brother is a Manchester United ... **(11)**
7. Did you leave a ... for the waiter? **(7)**
8. Mountains, forests, lakes, etc. **(8)**

Down
1. She had a lot of ... after she fell down the stairs. **(10)**
2. If you ... into something, you might be hurt. **(10)**
3. I'd like to live in a country with a hot ... **(8)**
4. Arguments. **(7)**
5. A qualification from university. **(7)**
6. Some people collect them. **(11)**
7. A ... or an obsession? **(11)**
8. Jamaica is one. **(8)**

E Speaking: real life

Work in pairs. Choose a situation from page 145 (who you are, where you are and what you are doing) to act out. Prepare a short conversation, including two of the phrases below. Act out your conversation for other students. They guess what the situation is.

- Do you sell ...?
- Really? So am I!
- Can you explain what ... is?
- Sorry, could you say that again, please?
- No, neither do I.
- Can I pay by ...?
- Where will I find ...?
- What exactly is a ...?
- Can I bring it back if ...?
- Me too.

s	k	y	s	c	r	a	p	e	r	g	t
f	b	h	w	l	p	z	q	v	n	j	r
l	e	q	u	i	p	m	e	n	t	o	s
b	o	b	c	m	q	l	p	r	o	i	l
r	e	p	l	a	c	e	k	s	y	y	a
u	r	t	h	t	y	x	e	p	s	c	n
i	z	b	l	e	e	d	l	d	k	h	d
s	q	u	k	y	g	o	p	e	m	h	f
e	e	m	z	r	b	c	k	g	r	o	w
s	u	p	p	o	r	t	e	r	k	b	c
k	w	m	k	w	q	z	b	e	u	b	t
t	i	p	j	s	c	e	n	e	r	y	u

98

module 12
Must have it!

- ▶ Passive forms (past, present, future)
- ▶ Sentences joined with *that*, *which* and *who*
- ▶ Vocabulary: objects

Task: decide what you need for a trip

Listening and vocabulary

Designer goods

1 What are 'designer goods'? Which famous names can you think of for these products?

clothes and sportswear   accessories (bags, shoes, etc.)
cars and motorbikes   perfume and cosmetics

2 Check the meaning of the phrases in **bold**. Which statements do you agree with? Compare answers.

a "A lot of people in my country want to **own** these **designer goods**."
b "Most people in my country **can't afford** designer labels."
c "Sometimes I **save up for** something really special."
d "People only want these products because of all the **advertising**."
e "Products with a famous name are **better quality** and **last longer**."
f "Products like this are a **waste of money** – you just **pay for** the label. Cheaper things are often **just as good**."
g "People **look better** in designer clothes than in cheaper ones."
h "It worries me that people **spend** so much money on these things, and that they care so much about **possessions**."

3 [12.1] You will hear the people on the left giving their opinions about these things. What do you think they will say? Are they for or against designer goods, or do they have mixed feelings?

4 Listen again, and mark these statements true (T) or false (F).

a Valerie has always spent a lot of money on clothes.
b She always prefers designer products.
c Nicola is worried about how much money people spend on these things.
d She thinks cheaper products are usually just as good.
e Rory thinks people who are obsessed with designer clothes are stupid.
f He thinks all trainers and jeans are cool, and look good.

Valerie, 71
a grandmother

Nicola, 40
her daughter

Rory, 15
Nicola's son

99

module 12 Must have it!

Language focus 1
Passive forms

Match one of the sentences below with the products in the pictures.

Swatch watch

Ray-Ban sunglasses

Porsche sports car

Chanel No. 5 perfume

a More than 10 million bottles are sold every year.
b The design is changed every year.
c They were first built in Germany in the 1940s.
d It was created by clothes designer Coco Chanel in 1925.
e They are often driven in Formula 1 races.
f They were first made in Switzerland in the 1980s.
g They were worn by Will Smith in the film *Men in Black*.
h They are often seen in Hollywood films.

Grammar analysis

1 Look at the difference between an active and a passive sentence.

	subject	verb	object
ACTIVE	They	change	the design every year.

	subject	verb	
PASSIVE	The design	is changed	every year.

In the passive sentence, we are most interested in the design, so this is the subject of the sentence. It is not important who changes the design.

2 We form the passive with *be* + past participle. Look at the sentences a–h opposite.
   a Find four examples of the Present Simple passive, and four examples of the Past Simple passive.
   b Which verbs are singular and which are plural?
   c How do we form the passive with *will*?

3 We can show 'who did it' (the agent), using *by*.

subject	verb	agent
Chanel No. 5	was created	by Coco Chanel in 1925.

▶ *Language summary A, page 155.*

Practice

1 a) Look at the pictures. Which famous company is the text about? What do they make?

b) Complete the sentences with the correct form of the verbs in brackets (past, present or future passive).

Take a look around. How many people in this room are wearing Nike? A large percentage of the training shoes sold in the world during the next year (1)........ (make) by the American company, from Oregon in the USA, which is now the world's biggest sportswear manufacturer. The company (2)........ (name) after the Greek goddess of victory, and (3)........ (start) in the early 1970s. Nike (4)........ (know) for its clever advertising, using the world's best-known sportsmen. In the 1980s, tennis star, John McEnroe, (5)........ (sponsor) by the company, and in the eighties and nineties the basketball star, Michael Jordan, (6)........ (ask) to appear in adverts. In 1997, a $40 million contract (7)........ (sign) with golf star Tiger Woods. He (8)........ (associate) with Nike until the year 2010! The famous Nike tick (9)........ (recognise) all over the world nowadays. It (10)........ (create) by a designer in Oregon in 1971, and he (11)........ (pay) just $35 for his idea!

c) [12.2] Listen and check your answers.

Pronunciation

With passives, the stress is on the past participle. The verb *be* is often weak, or a contraction is used.

The company's named after the Greek goddess of victory.
It was /wəz/ started in the early 1970s.
He'll be /biː/ associated with Nike until the year 2010!

1 [12.3] Listen to the sentences above and practise saying them. Pay attention to the weak forms and contractions.

2 Practise reading the second paragraph of the text (Practice, Exercise 1b) aloud.

2 Passive or active? Complete the sentences with the correct form of the verbs in brackets.

a More cars .... (steal) every year in Britain than in any other European country: about half a million!
b In the next ten years, about 30% of the world's cars .... (manufacture) in Asia.
c Corradino d'Ascenio .... (design) the first Vespa scooter in 1946.
d The Japanese newspaper *Yomiuri Shimbun* .... (read) by over 14 million people every day.
e Australia .... (produce) about 40% of the world's diamonds.
f A book of drawings by Leonardo da Vinci .... (sell) for over $30 million in 1994.
g Surprisingly, the Finns .... (eat) more ice cream than any other people in Europe!
h More than 10 million Sony PlayStations .... (sell) in the next year.
i Georgio Armani .... (start) his successful clothes label in the late 1970s.
j In 1997, 15% of all clothes sold in the world .... (make) by the American company, Levi Strauss.

module 12 Must have it!

Language focus 2

Sentences joined with *that*, *which* and *who*

1 [12.4] Read the rules and then play the game *Definitions*.

Definitions

1 Work in teams.

2 Close your books and listen to some definitions of words. Your teacher will stop the recording after each one.

3 You have twenty seconds to discuss and write down which word was defined.

4 Your team gets two points if you understand the definition and know the word in your own language.

5 Your team gets four points if you know the word in English.

Which team won?

2 Complete the definitions with *who*, *which* or *that*. Listen again to check your answers.

a It's a hat ...which... protects your head from the sun.
b It's a person ...who... designs clothes.
c It's stuff ...that... you use to wash your hands – not water!
d It's a person ...who... sells flowers.
e It's a long leather thing ...which/that... stops your trousers from falling down!
f It's a machine ...which... answers the phone for you when you're busy.
g It's make-up ...that... women (and sometimes men!) wear on their mouths.
h They're a special kind of shoe ...which... you wear in summer.
i It's a person ...who... sells meat.
j They're gold or silver things ...which... people wear in their ears.

Grammar analysis

1 In all the sentences in Language focus 2, Exercise 2 there are two ideas joined together with *who*, *that* or *which*.

It's a hat, ~~It~~ ∧ protects you from the sun.   *which/that*

It's stuff, ∧ You use ~~it~~ to wash your hands.   *which/that*

It's a person, ~~He or she~~ ∧ designs clothes.   *who (that)*

a For **things** we use *which* or *that* (not *what*).
b For **people** we use *who* (or sometimes *that*).

2 Join these short sentences in the same way.
  a A plumber is a person. He mends pipes.
  b A calculator is a small machine. It does arithmetic for you.
  c A kettle is a machine. It heats water.
  d A scarf is a thing. You wear it round your neck.
  e Sun cream is stuff. You put it on your skin when it's very sunny.

▶ Language summary B, page 155.

Practice

1 a) Match the people to the definitions.

antique dealer   car dealer   carpenter   chef
estate agent   greengrocer   jeweller   newsagent

1 person/buy and sell/cars
2 person/make and sell/rings and necklaces
3 person/buy and sell/old furniture
4 person/sell/newspapers, cigarettes, etc.
5 person/cook/meals in a restaurant or hotel
6 person/sell/houses and flats
7 person/make/things from wood
8 person/sell/fruit and vegetables

b) Use the prompts to write sentences like this:

A person who buys and sells cars is called a car dealer.

2

a) Work in pairs. A looks at box A, and B looks at box B. Make questions like this:

What do you call the shorts that men wear for swimming?

A

shorts/men wear for swimming

thing/you make tea in

stuff/makes plates and cups clean

bag/you carry on your back

stuff/you use to clean your teeth

woollen things/keep your hands warm

things/you cut paper with

B

brush/you clean your teeth with

woollen things/keep your feet warm

stuff/makes clothes clean

thing/you use to draw straight lines with

machine/makes coffee

thing/women wear for swimming

big warm bag/you sleep in

b) A looks at the pictures on page 139 and B looks at the pictures on page 145. Use the pictures to answer your partner's questions from Exercise 2a above.

> What do you call the shorts that men wear for swimming?

> swimming trunks

Vocabulary

Objects

1 a) Mark the objects in the box below (✓) if it's a word you know, (?) if you're not sure, (✗) if you don't know.

wallet/purse   corkscrew   diary   keys   plasters   personal stereo
credit card   umbrella   sunglasses   identity card   mobile phone
rubber   address book   tin opener   aspirin   ashtray   tissues
sellotape   lighter   chewing gum   torch   towel
underwear   comb   driving licence

b) Compare with a partner and check any unknown words.

2 Write the words in the best place on the diagram below. Compare your ideas with other students. Can you add any other words to each list?

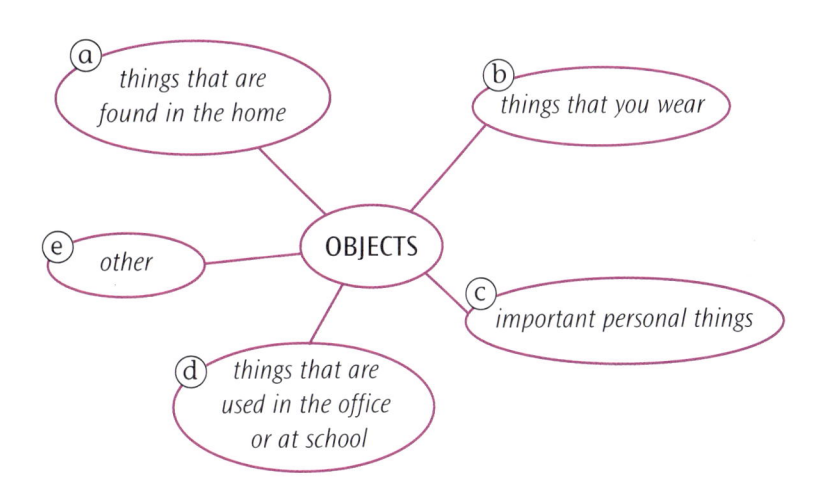

- (a) things that are found in the home
- (b) things that you wear
- (c) important personal things
- (d) things that are used in the office or at school
- (e) other

OBJECTS

3 Answer the following questions individually. Give as many items as you can. Compare answers in pairs and find five things you have in common.

a Which of the things above do you keep:
- in your bedroom?   in the kitchen?   in the bathroom?

b Which of the things above:
- do people often have in their pockets?
- might someone have in their briefcase?
- do you always take with you when you go out?
- do you often forget to take with you?

> I always take my ... with me.

> I never leave the house without my ...

103

module 12 Must have it!

Decide what you need for a trip

Personal vocabulary

Useful language

a Discussing what to take

"We should definitely take ... because ..."

"If ... happens, we'll need ..."

"It might rain/be very hot so ..."

"We could take ..."

"We need a ... to ..."

"Anything else?"

b Suggesting other things to take

"How about ...?"

"Perhaps you should also take ..."

"Have you remembered ...?"

Preparation for task

1 [12.5] Neil and Lucy are going away for a few days. Listen to their phone conversation. Which **two** things from the box below are they **not** taking with them?

toothbrushes	underwear	shorts	T-shirts	pullovers	raincoats
passports	tickets	travellers' cheques	driving licences	camera
guidebook	sun cream	razor	shaving cream	phrasebook

2 Compare answers with a partner. From what Neil and Lucy say, what are the answers to the following questions?

a Are they going to the beach, to the countryside or to a city?
b What are they going to do there?
c What do they think the weather will be like?
d Are they staying in their own country, or going abroad?
e Are they going with anyone else?
f How are they going to travel?

3 Listen again and check your answers.

104

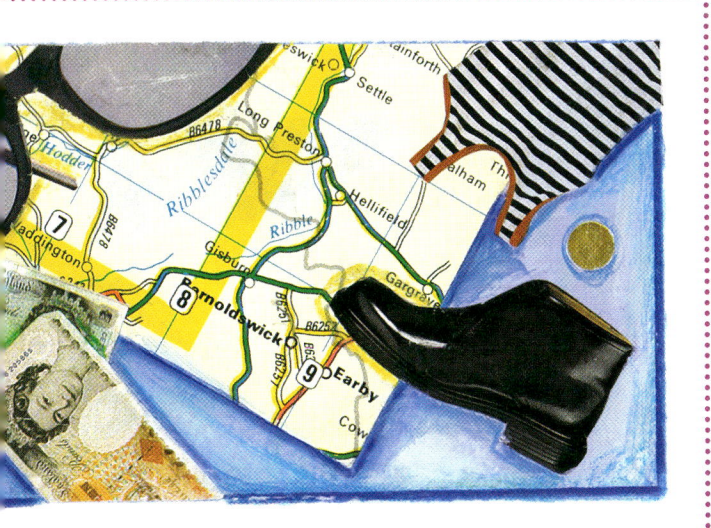

Task

1 a) You are going away and need to make a list of what to take with you. Work in pairs. Your teacher will give each pair a letter, A, B or C. Pair A looks at page 142, Pair B at page 145, and Pair C at page 146.

b) Complete the list of the ten most useful things to take. Ask your teacher for any special vocabulary you need.
▶ *Personal vocabulary*

c) Think about how to explain why you need these things.
▶ *Useful language a)*

2 With your partner, agree on a list of the ten most useful things to take with you and why.

3 Form a new group with people who have planned for a different trip. Tell your partners what you are going to take, but do not tell them what kind of trip it is.

a) Which of these can your new partners guess?

- what kind of place you are going to/what kind of trip it is
- who you are going with
- what kind of weather you are expecting
- how you are travelling

b) Can they think of anything important that you have forgotten?
▶ *Useful language b)*

Real life

Making suggestions

1 Work in pairs. Make sure you know the names of all the objects below.

2 [12.6] Listen to four conversations where people are making suggestions. Answer the following questions for **each** one.

- What is the relationship between the people?
- Where are they?
- Which two objects above are mentioned? Why?

105

3 a) [12.7] Listen to the extracts again, and complete the gaps.

a What .... for dinner tonight?
b Why .... pasta?
c .... my favourite.
d .... this perfume?
e I don't ...., really.
f You .... her a really nice lipstick.
g Yes, maybe I'll ....
h What do you think .... get?
i What .... her a purse?
j Good ....
k Shall .... the assistant for your size in these?
l I .... so.

b) Which phrases are used to:
- ask for a suggestion?
- make a suggestion?
- respond to a suggestion?

Pronunciation

[12.8] Listen again and practise the phrases. Pay attention to the intonation.

4 Choose one of these situations. In pairs, prepare a conversation to act out.

- You are trying to decide what to wear for a special occasion. Your partner makes suggestions.
- You and your partner are going to cook dinner for some friends. You are trying to decide what to cook.
- Your partner is staying with an English family for a month, and wants to take a present. Make suggestions.

106

Do you remember?

1 Discuss the following in pairs. When did you last:
- buy something because of the advertising?
- save up for something special?
- spend a lot of money on a present for someone?
- lose one of your favourite possessions?

2 Match a beginning from A with an ending from B, and a verb from the box. Use a passive form of the verb in the present, past or with *will*.

| use pull down make free replace speak |

A
a) Yoghurt
b) Nelson Mandela
c) The Internet
d) In the future, letters
e) The Berlin Wall
f) Spanish

B
by more than 250 million people.
in 1989.
from milk.
from prison in 1990.
by millions of people every day.
by e-mails.

For example: Yoghurt is made from milk.

3 Three of the sentences below have grammatical mistakes. Can you correct them?
a) People which live in the Netherlands speak Dutch, don't they?
b) I'd like a camera which has an automatic flash.
c) That's the actor who he was in *Die Hard*.
d) Have you got that book what I lent you last week?
e) We've got a new kettle that cleans itself.

4 What do these people buy and/or sell?
- a baker
- a greengrocer
- a newsagent
- an estate agent
- a jeweller
- an antique dealer

5 Put the words in the correct order. In pairs make and respond to the suggestions above.
a) meal/go/a/let's/out/for
b) about/football/a/how/of/game/?
c) see/go/we/a/could/and/film
d) TV/stay/why/we/don't/in/watch/and/?

module 13
The right kind of person

- ▶ Vocabulary and speaking: jobs and personal characteristics
- ▶ Present Perfect Simple and Continuous with the 'unfinished past'
- ▶ *How long ...?, for, since* and *all*
- ▶ Wordspot: *how*
- Task: select a new mayor for Queenstown

Vocabulary and speaking

Jobs and personal characteristics

- learning — primary school teacher
- medicine — doctor
- building/houses — architect
- money — accountant
- hotels and restaurants — waiter
- the arts and media — actor/actress
- transport — taxi driver
- other — lawyer

JOBS

1 Work in pairs. How many more jobs can you add to the diagram? You have three minutes. Compare answers with other students.

2 Divide the jobs into the three categories below. Compare your ideas in pairs.

- I'd really like to be ...
- I wouldn't mind being ...
- I'd hate to be ...

3 a) Check the meaning of the words in **bold** below. Which jobs from Exercise 1 do you think the people are describing?

- 'You need to be **patient** and it's important to have a lot of **experience**.'
- 'You have to be **well-qualified** ... and very **careful** and **accurate**.'
- 'You need to be **good with people**, and you have to be **smart** and **well-mannered**.'
- 'You have to be friendly and **sympathetic**, and you need to know about all the **latest methods**.'
- 'You need lots of **imagination** ... and to know the right people.'
- 'You have to be **good with money and numbers**, and **honest**.'

b) Work in pairs. Take it in turns to describe the qualities you need for one of the jobs in Exercise 1. Your partner guesses which job you are talking about.

107

module 13 The right kind of person

Language focus 1

Present Perfect Simple and Continuous with the 'unfinished past'

1 Work in pairs or small groups. What qualities do people need in these jobs?

- a family doctor
- a driving instructor
- a babysitter

2 Read the texts below. What qualities does each person have? Who would you choose for each job? Explain why.

1 You need a new family doctor.

Pam Hansen is sixty-eight years old, and has been a doctor for over forty years. She doesn't take many patients these days, so she's got plenty of time. She's very kind and interested in her patients, but her methods are a bit old-fashioned.

Matt Gregorio is twenty-nine years old. He hasn't been a doctor for long, but he's very well-qualified, and knows all about the latest methods. He's sympathetic, but very busy because he has lots of patients.

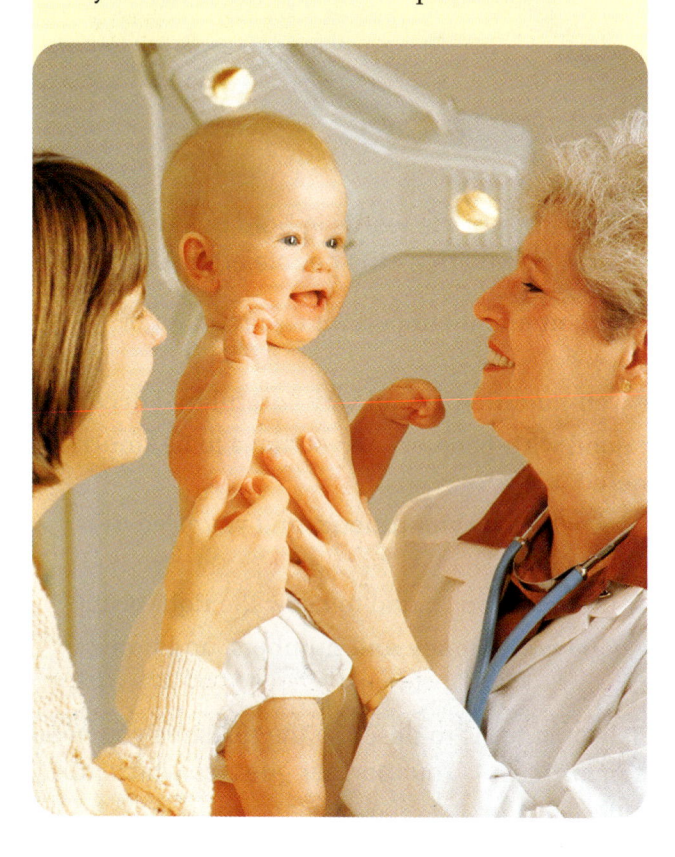

2 You need a driving instructor.

Jim Burrows has been teaching people how to drive for about ten years, and two of your friends passed their driving test first time with him. But they say he's not very patient when you make mistakes.

Angela Dunn hasn't been working as a driving instructor for long, but a friend has recommended her because she is very patient and sympathetic, especially if you are nervous. She charges more than Jim.

3 You need a babysitter three afternoons a week for your children, aged one and seven.

Florence is a twenty-year-old student. She has no experience of working with children, but she has five younger brothers and sisters, who she often looks after. She's kind, good fun, and seems reliable.

Celia is about fifty-five years old, and has been working with children all her adult life. She's kind but seems strict, and has her own way of doing things.

Grammar analysis

1 Look at these examples of the Present Perfect Simple and Present Perfect Continuous.
Is the person still a doctor/driving instructor?
He's been a doctor for forty years.
He's been teaching people how to drive for ten years.

2 **a** Both tenses describe actions that started in the past and continue to the present.

She's been a doctor for forty years

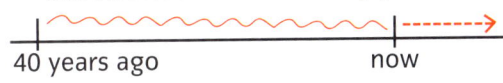

40 years ago — now

He's been teaching for ten years

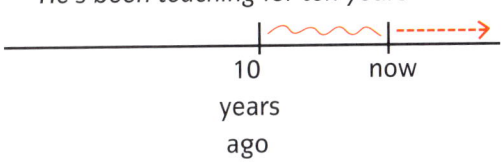

10 years ago — now

b We often choose the Present Perfect Continuous if we want to emphasise the **duration** of the action.
She's been working with children all her adult life.

c But REMEMBER! there are many verbs which we cannot use in the continuous form because they describe states: *be, have, like, know, believe,* etc
She's been a doctor for forty years. (not *She's been being ...*)

▶ Language summary A, pages 155-156.

Practice

1 Complete the conversations with the correct form of the words in brackets. Use the Present Perfect Continuous **when possible**.

a A: You look a bit annoyed.
   B: Yes, well I .... (*wait*) all day for Richard to phone. It's always the same with him!

b A: How long .... (*you/have*) your car now?
   B: Oh, about twelve years! We really need to change it!

c A: Who's P. Pearson? Is it someone in accounts?
   B: I don't know actually, I .... (*not work*) here for very long.

d A: I'm really fed up. It .... (*rain*) all weekend!
   B: I know, it's awful, isn't it.

e A: What do you think of Rosie?
   B: I .... (*not know*) her long, but she seems very nice.

f A: .... (*your parents/live*) in this house long?
   B: No, only about two years.

g A: Poor Tom looks really tired!
   B: Yes, but he .... (*travel*) since seven o'clock this morning, so it's not surprising!

h A: How long .... (*Chris/be*) away?
   B: Nearly three weeks. He's coming back on Friday, I think.

2 [13.1] Listen and check your answers. Write in any contractions (short forms) that you heard.

module 13 The right kind of person

Language focus 2

How long ...?, for, since and *all*

Look at the four examples below. Write a question with *How long ...?* for each, using the words in brackets.

1 A: ....? (*he/travel*)
   B: Since seven o'clock this morning.
2 A: ....? (*she/work with children*)
   B: All her adult life.
3 A: ....? (*she/work as a driving instructor*)
   B: Not for long.
4 A: ....? (*you/have your car*)
   B: For about twelve years.

Grammar analysis

1 To answer the question *How long ...?* with the Present Perfect Simple and Continuous:
   a we use *for* with a **period** of time.
   b we use *since* with a **point** in time.

   for 5 years
   since 1996   now

2 Change the following phrases with *for* to phrases with *since*, without changing the meaning.
   for two years   for three days   for five hours
   for six months

3 Notice that there are many phrases with *all* which we can use with the Present Perfect Simple and Continuous. For example:
   all my life   all day   all summer

   Can you think of two more?

   ▶ *Language summary B, page 156.*

Practice

1 [13.2] Listen and write the time phrases below. Add *for, since* or *all* as necessary.

a for ten years   e ....   i ....
b ....   f ....   j ....
c ....   g ....   k ....
d ....   h ....   l ....

Pronunciation

1 [13.3] Listen to these examples. Notice the contractions and weak forms we use in the middle of sentences.

   /bɪn/
   I**'ve been** waiting since nine o'clock.
   /bɪn/
   She**'s been** working here since May.
   /hævənt/   /fə/
   I **haven't** known her for long.
   /bɪn/   /fə/
   They**'ve been** living with us for two years.
   /həv/
   How long **have** you had your car?
   /həz/
   How long **has** he been waiting?

2 Practise the sentences. Pay attention to weak forms and contractions.

2 You are going to interview other students using the questionnaire below. First, spend a few minutes thinking about the questions.

How long?	Student A
1 occupation work/study? How long ...? *Do you work or study?* *How long have you been working/studying there?*	
2 learning English How long ...?	6 years
3 your home How long/this town? How long/your house?	14 yers
4 organisations member of any clubs How long ...?	
5 sports/music play any sports/musical instruments? How long ...?	
6 relationships married/partner/best friend? How long/know ...?	
7 possessions got car/bicycle/motorbike/computer/pet? How long/have ...?	4 yers

110

3 a) Find three students to interview. Ask each one at least five questions, and write their answers in columns A, B and C in the questionnaire.

For example:

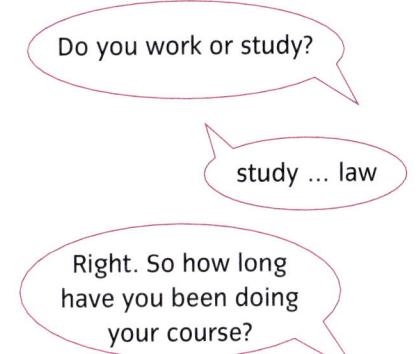

- Do you work or study?
- study ... law
- Right. So how long have you been doing your course?

b) Read out some information about one of the students to the class, but don't say the student's name. The rest of the class guesses who it is.

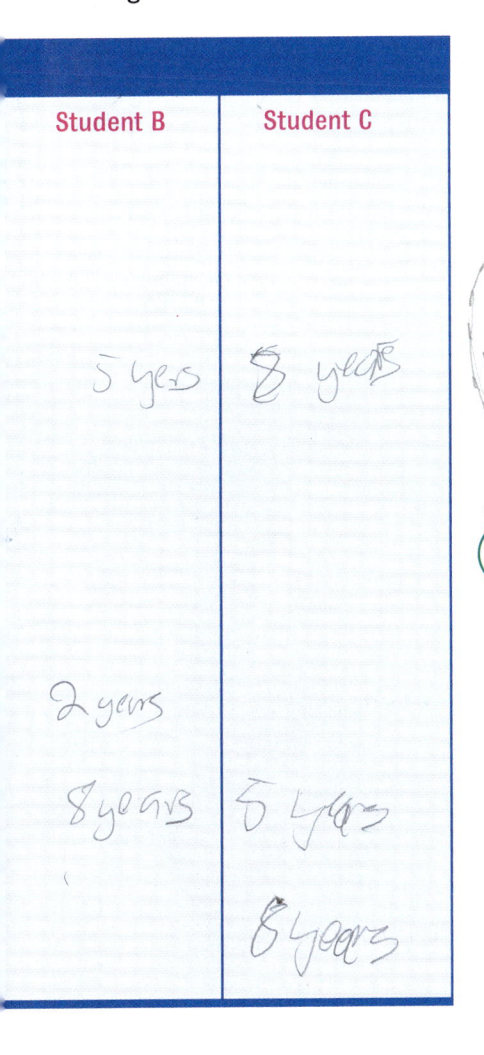

Student B	Student C
5 yes	8 years
2 years	
8 years	5 years
	8 years

Wordspot

how

1 Complete the questions with *how* with a word from the box. Add the phrases to the diagram below.

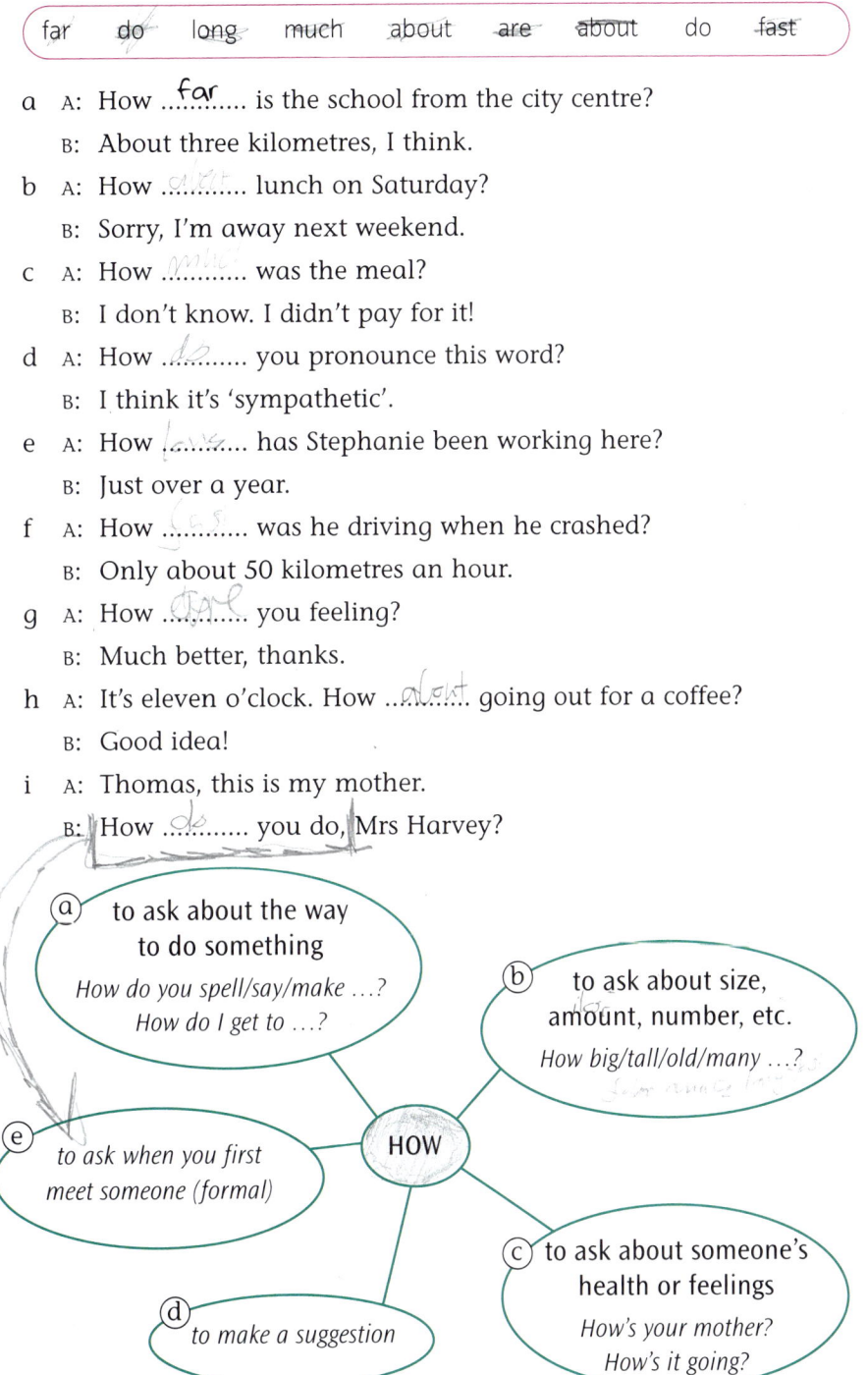

~~far~~ ~~do~~ ~~long~~ much about are about ~~fast~~

a A: How ...**far**... is the school from the city centre?
  B: About three kilometres, I think.
b A: How .... lunch on Saturday?
  B: Sorry, I'm away next weekend.
c A: How .... was the meal?
  B: I don't know. I didn't pay for it!
d A: How ...**do**... you pronounce this word?
  B: I think it's 'sympathetic'.
e A: How .... has Stephanie been working here?
  B: Just over a year.
f A: How .... was he driving when he crashed?
  B: Only about 50 kilometres an hour.
g A: How .... you feeling?
  B: Much better, thanks.
h A: It's eleven o'clock. How ...**about**... going out for a coffee?
  B: Good idea!
i A: Thomas, this is my mother.
  B: How ...**do**... you do, Mrs Harvey?

(a) **to ask about the way to do something**
How do you spell/say/make ...?
How do I get to ...?

(b) **to ask about size, amount, number, etc.**
How big/tall/old/many ...?

(e) **to ask when you first meet someone (formal)**

HOW

(c) **to ask about someone's health or feelings**
How's your mother?
How's it going?

(d) **to make a suggestion**

2 a) Work in pairs. A looks at page 143 and B looks at page 147. Complete the questions on your card.

b) Read the questions to your partner. He/She guesses the correct answer.

111

module 13 The right kind of person

Select a new mayor for Queenstown

Personal vocabulary

Preparation for task

1 a) Does your town have a mayor? How is he/she chosen? What are the duties of a mayor?

b) Read about the election for the mayor of Queenstown.

> The city of Queenstown (population 100,000, main industries tourism and peanut farming), on the island of St Helena, needs a new mayor. The current mayor, Mr Tony Bolleri, is going to retire after five years in the job. There are four candidates to replace him.

2 [13.4] Here is some information about two of the candidates to be mayor. Read the information. Check the meaning and pronunciation of any unknown words, then listen and complete the gaps.

ZELDA MARKOVITCH

Since her first appearance on TV at the age of (1)............ (in an advertisement for soap!), Zelda (2)............ in television for nearly twenty-five years. She is now the country's most popular TV presenter, thanks to her Saturday night game show 'Your Money Or Your Life'. She moved to Queenstown (3)............ and says it is her favourite city. Although she has (4)............ of politics, she promises to use her fame to bring more tourists to Queenstown. Her slogan is: 'Queenstown – first for fun, first for sun!'

Useful language

a Saying who you prefer

"I think ... will do more for the economy/for ordinary people/for young people."

"I prefer (Zelda) ... to ... because ..."

b Explaining your reasons

"... has more experience of ..."

"... knows more about ..."

"... is too (young/old). ..."

"... isn't suitable because ..."

c Agreeing and disagreeing

"I agree ..."

"I don't agree ..."

"Yes, but what about ...?"

112

MAX ROBERTSON

A successful peanut farmer for the last (1) .... years, Max Robertson has lived in Queenstown (2) .... and is a popular local politician. He entered politics (3) .... years ago, and is now deputy mayor to Mr Tony Bolleri. He promises to improve the local economy, but he thinks tourism is bad for the town. He wants to make Queenstown the peanut capital of the world. Now (4) .... years old, his campaign slogan is 'Peace, Prosperity and Peanuts'.

Task

1 You are going to find out about the other two candidates. Work in pairs, A and B.

A reads the information about Jack Novak on page 142, and completes the fact file below.

B reads the information about Cristina Scarlatti on page 146, and completes the fact file below.

JACK NOVAK: FACT FILE

Job:
How long:
How long/living in Queenstown:
Campaign slogan:
Good points:
Bad points:

CRISTINA SCARLATTI: FACT FILE

Job:
How long:
How long/living in Queenstown:
Campaign slogan:
Good points:
Bad points:

2 Ask your partner questions to complete the fourth fact file. First, spend a few minutes thinking about the questions.

3 Complete the voting form below. Number the candidates from 1–4. How will you explain your choice?
▶ *Useful language a) and b)*
▶ *Personal vocabulary*

ZELDA MARKOVITCH	3
MAX ROBERTSON	4
JACK NOVAK	1
CRISTINA SCARLATTI	2

4 Compare your answers in groups of three or four. Explain why you put the candidates in that order. Did you agree or not?
▶ *Useful language c)*

3 What are the positive and negative points about each candidate? Discuss with a partner.

module 13 The right kind of person

Writing and real life

An application for a job

1 Read about *Work Canada*. What is it?

Work Canada is an organisation helping young people (aged 18–27) to find work within the tourist industry in Canada. Jobs include hotel and restaurant work, child day care, sports instructors, activity leaders, tour guides for foreign visitors, etc.

WORK CANADA APPLICATION FORM

First name .... Iris .... Last name .... Hauptmann ....
male ☐ female ☒ (tick)
Address .... Borgfelder Strasse 11 .... Postcode ....
City/Country .... Hamburg, Germany ....
Tel (include town & country code) (home) .... 0049 40-332309 ....
Tel (work) .... Fax ....
e-mail ....
Best time to reach me is .... after 6 o'clock ....
Date of birth .... 28.6.79 ....
Earliest travel date (year/month) .... June 2000 ....
Driving licence yes ☒ no ☐ learning ☐
Languages spoken .... German, Spanish, English ....
Present occupation or studies .... Hamburg University ....
Which of these work areas interests you? (tick at least one box)
hotel ☐   restaurant ☒   child care ☐   tour guide ☒
sports instructor ☒   activity leader ☐
Describe any relevant experience you have .... driving licence, experience as a .... worked in various restaurants, tennis coach, with people ....

How did you hear about Work Canada?
newspaper ☐   website ☐   personal recommendation ☒
other ....

Borgfelder Strasse 11
Hamburg 20537
Germany
(0049) 40 - 33 23 09

12 March 2000

Dear Sir/Madam,

I have heard about your organisation from a friend, and am writing to apply for work with you this summer. I am interested in any jobs you may have, either as a tour guide, a sports coach or possibly restaurant work.

I am a twenty-year-old student (date of birth 12th July 1979), in my third year of a four year language course at Hamburg University. I speak three languages fluently (German, English and Spanish) and have had a full driving licence for a year. I have had no experience as a tour guide, but have worked in various restaurants in Hamburg, and I am good at working with people. I am also a member of my university tennis team, and have been working as a tennis coach with children aged 12-14 for the last three years.

Please note that my university course finishes on 10th June, so I will be available from then. If you want to phone me, you can contact me at home after six o'clock. Unfortunately I don't have a fax number or e-mail address.

I look forward to hearing from you soon.

Yours faithfully,
Iris Hauptmann

Iris is a student from Hamburg in Germany. She wants to apply for a job with Work Canada.

2 Iris wrote a letter of application to *Work Canada*. They sent back a form for her to complete instead. Use her letter to complete the form.

3 a) Work in pairs. Student A is the interviewer and Student B is Iris. Student A prepares questions and Student B prepares answers. Think about:

- more information about Iris' occupation
- why Iris is interested in particular work areas
- Iris' other interests and hobbies

Why are you interested in …?

How long have you been …?

b) Interview your partner. Would you give him/her the job?

Do you remember?

1 Choose an adjective from the box for the perfect:
- teacher
- friend
- waiter

honest   well-mannered   smart   sympathetic
good with people   honest   strict

2 Complete the gaps in the article with the correct form (Present Perfect Simple or Continuous).

Julia Molina (1)............ (play) the piano since she was five, but she (2)............ (never/play) professionally. That will change on Monday, when Julia makes her first CD for a big recording company. For the last two weeks Julia, from Bristol, (3)............ (stay) in a hotel in London, and (4)............ (practise) for ten hours a day. 'It's really strange,' she said, 'I (5)............ (eat) in the hotel restaurant every day, and I (6)............ (only/leave) the hotel two or three times!' Julia is very excited: 'This is my big chance – I (7)............ (wait) for something like this all my life.' Her mother is not so happy. She is so busy that she (8)............ (not/have) time to phone her!

3 Finish the following sentences so they are true for you. Compare your answers with a partner.

a) I've been in this lesson since …
b) I've been wearing these shoes for …
c) I've known the person next to me for …
d) I've been studying the Present Perfect since …
e) I've had my … for a long time.
f) I've been … all my life.

4 Match a word from A with one from B to make jobs.

A	B
1 tour	editor
2 TV	instructor
3 taxi	presenter
4 newspaper	guide
5 sports	driver

5 Work in pairs. Think of a job. Your partner asks questions to find out the job. You can only answer *Yes* or *No*.

115

module 14
Building your dreams

- *Some*, *any* and quantifiers
- Vocabulary: describing houses and apartments
- Describing where things are
- Task: describe a favourite room

Language focus 1

Some, *any* and quantifiers

1 Discuss with other students.

- Do you live in a city, village or in the country?
- Are you happy with this or not?

2 a) [14.1] What do you think people are talking about in extracts 1–7? Listen and write:

- C for life in a big city.
- V for life in a small village.
- ? for not sure/it could be either.

b) Listen again. Is each opinion positive (+) or negative (–)?

Grammar analysis

Answer the questions about the following examples.

1. a *There are some lovely old houses.*
   b *There aren't any modern buildings.*
   Why do we use *some* in a) and *any* in b)? Which do we usually use in questions?

2. a *There are no clothes shops near here.*
   b *There aren't any clothes shops near here.*
   c *There are any clothes shops near here.*
   Which of these sentences is wrong? Can you correct it?

3. a *There are a lot of old people.*
   b *There aren't many young people.*
   A lot of and *many* mean 'a large number of'. Which do we use in a positive sentence and which in a negative sentence?

4. a *There aren't many shops.*
   b *There isn't much nightlife.*
   Why do we use *many* in a) and *much* in b)?

5. a *There are a lot of cafés and restaurants.*
   b *There are too many cafés and restaurants.*
   c *There aren't enough cafés and restaurants.*
   In which two sentences is the speaker unhappy about the bars and clubs? Which words tell you this?

6. a *There are **a few** nice restaurants.*
   b *There are **some** lovely old houses.*
   Look at the words in **bold**. Which means 'a small number of'? Which means 'an indefinite number of'?

▶ *Language summary A, page 156.*

Pronunciation

[14.2] Listen to these examples. Notice the links between the words. Practise saying the phrases.

there's a good baker's   there isn't much nightlife

there are no clothes shops   there aren't many young people

Practice

1 Complete the sentences with the correct quantifier.

a Be careful on the road. There's *many/much/a lot of* traffic at this time of day.

b My flat's got a nice view, but there really isn't *many/enough/no* space.

c Unfortunately, there aren't *many/much/some* young people around here.

d I can't go out tonight, I've got *any/no/many* money.

e The city's mainly modern, but there are *any/much/some* old buildings.

f We're very lucky, there are *a lot of/much/too many* parks where we live.

g There aren't *any/no/much* shops around here. You have to go into the town centre.

h There are *no/a few/any* places for young people to go, but not enough, really.

2 a) Choose a place to visit. Think of reasons to go there. Use some of these ideas.

old buildings   hotels   parks
museums   scenery   people
tourists   cinemas/theatres
nightlife   shops   restaurants

b) Work in pairs. Persuade your partner to go to the place.

> Let's go to Paris. There are a lot of fantastic shops and ...

> Oh, but there are too many tourists.

module 14 Building your dreams

Vocabulary
Describing houses and apartments

1 Read the three extracts below. What kind of building does each one describe? Which comes from:

- a brochure for holiday homes?
- a letter?
- a story?

(a) ...finally found somewhere to live! It's on the fifth floor of this lovely old apartment block, right in the city centre. It's very spacious and there's lots of light, but the best thing is that it has a wonderful view of the river. If you look out you can actually see the parliament building ...

(b) ...this **three-storey** house with a charming **balcony** is situated **in a small village** on the west coast of the island.

Set in its own **private garden** with a large **swimming pool**, it has 6 **bedrooms**, 3 **bathrooms**, a **modern kitchen** and an **attractive living room**. There are tennis courts within a few minutes drive, and bars and supermarkets nearby.

(c) ... the address was **in the suburbs, at the end of a quiet street**. Sylvia went up the **path**, unlocked the front door, and walked in. Inside, the rooms were small and **rather dark**. As she looked round the living room, she noticed some wood next to the **fireplace** and the vase of fresh flowers by the window. The **old-fashioned furniture** was **simple** but **elegant** and there were **colourful rugs** on the **wooden floor**. At the back of the house there was a small, **sunny courtyard** with some plants in pots. Sylvia smiled. It was perfect.

2 Check the meaning of the words and phrases in **bold**, and add them to categories a) to e) below.

a where things are on the fifth floor, in a small village, in the suburbs
b types of building an apartment block, three storey house,
c phrases to describe buildings and places spacious
d things buildings have 6 bedrooms, 3 bathrooms, inside,
e things rooms have old-fashioned furniture, colourful rugs

3 Use these questions to interview your partner about where he/she lives. How similar are your homes?

- Do you live in a flat or a house? Where is it?
- Which floor is it on?/How many storeys does your house have?
- How many bedrooms/bathrooms are there?
- Does it have a nice view/garden/balcony?
- What other important features does it have?

Language focus 2
Describing where things are

Look at the pictures on page 119 and choose the correct preposition or phrase to complete sentences a) – m) below.

behind	between	under
in front of	below	near
on top of	opposite	above
next to	inside	outside

a A is ...behind... B.
b A is .... B.
c A is ...opposite... B.
d A is ...between... B and C.
e A is ...next to... B.
f A is ...near... B.
g A is ...inside... B.
h A is ...outside... B.
i A is ...above... B.
j A is ...below... B.
k A is ...under... B.
l A is ...on top of... B.

Grammar analysis

1 Which phrases start with:
- at?
- in?
- on?

2 Which phrases are followed by:
- to?
- of?

▶ **Language summary B, page 156.**

118

Practice

1 Look around you now. Who/What is:

- above the teacher's desk?
- on top of the teacher's desk?
- behind you?
- between you and the door?
- sitting next to you?
- opposite the window?
- outside the door?
- under your bag?
- below your classroom?
- inside your purse/wallet?
- sitting near you?
- in front of you?

2 Work in pairs. A looks at the picture on page 143. B looks at the picture on page 147. Find ten differences between the two pictures.

Real life and writing

Giving directions

1 Mark and Lola have invited some friends to a party at their home. Read the invitation and directions they sent to their guests. Complete the gaps with these words or phrases.

cross	past	opposite	Get off	along
take	it takes	towards	about	turn
on the left	the train			

Mark and Lola invite you
to a barbecue in their garden
at: 5 New Road, Banfield
on Saturday 21st June. 2 p.m. till?!
Bring a friend, and good weather!

How to get to Mark and Lola's flat.

From LIVERPOOL STREET STATION take (1)............ which goes to STANSTED AIRPORT. (2)............ at BANFIELD HILL (9th stop – (3)............ about 25 minutes).
When you come out of the station, (4)............ the road and (5)............ right. Walk (6)............ BUSH HILL ROAD (7)............ BANFIELD. Go up the hill and (8)............ the garage.
New Road is the third road (9)............
No. 5 is the big house (10)............ the school. (Just press the bell marked, Bottom Flat.)
OR
(11)............ the Underground (Blue Line) to HALETON JUNCTION. Then take a number 351 bus to Enfield Lock Station (it takes (12)............ 45 minutes).
351 bus stop is opposite the main exit.

See you there!

Mark and Lola

119

module 14 Building your dreams

2 a) [14.3] Jeff is driving Cindy to the party. She calls him to ask for directions to his house. Listen and put a X on the map where Jeff's house is.

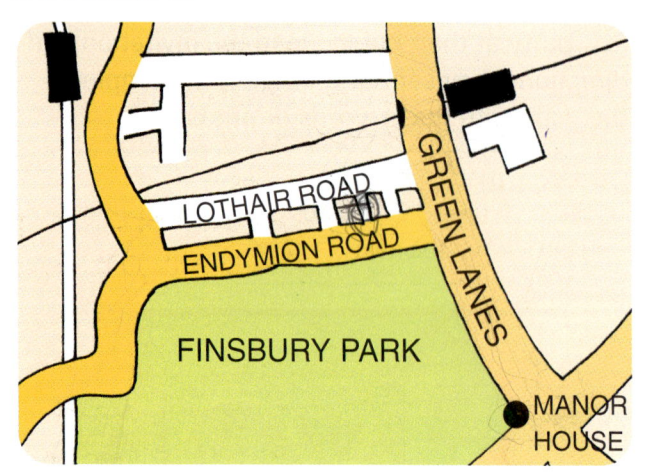

b) Listen again. Circle the word or phrase you hear in the instructions below.

1 When you *come to/come out of* Manor House station, take the Finsbury Park *exit/road* and *go straight on/turn left*. Then go *down/up* Green Lanes with Finsbury Park on your *left/right*.

2 You go *across/past* the park and there's a bridge *in front of/next to* you. Keep going towards the bridge and *cross/take* the road on the left just *before/after* you get to the bridge.

3 Then my road's the *first/second* turning on the *left/right*.

4 My house is at the *beginning/end* of the road. It's number four, the second house on your *left/right*.

5 It takes about *ten/twenty* minutes.

3 a) Draw a map of the area near your house, and mark the nearest station or bus stop. Do **not** mark your house.

b) Work in pairs. Give the map to your partner and direct him/her from the station/bus stop to your house. Your partner marks your house on the map.

4 You are having a party at your house. Write a similar note to Mark and Lola's in Exercise 1 on page 119.

Reading

Elvis Presley's home - Graceland

Bill Gates' home by Lake Washington

Aaron Spelling's Hollywood home

Justo Gallego's cathedral in Majorda del Campo

Building your dream ...

① For most people, a dream home is just that ... a dream. But for those people who have the right combination of money and imagination, building that dream can become reality and the results can be rather strange!

② A Frenchman named François Labbé built the world's first revolving house in the village of Saint-Isidore, near Nice. Made of metal, it can turn to the sun at the press of a button. A Spanish ex-priest named Justo Gallego spent nearly thirty years building his own personal cathedral in Majorada del Campo, a small town 25 kilometres east of Madrid. The strange building looks like a castle with its two 55-metre towers. The roof is made of zinc and its entrance is similar to that of the White House in Washington DC.

③ Not surprisingly, perhaps, it's in the United States that the idea of dream homes seems strongest. Jim Onan, of Illinois, USA, built his own five-storey golden pyramid. The pyramid is surrounded by water – and just to make sure there are no unwanted visitors, there are sharks swimming around in it! The pyramid has five bedrooms, six bathrooms and an observatory on the top floor so Jim can watch the stars in peace.

④ But that's tiny compared to the Hollywood home of TV producer Aaron Spelling: the house itself occupies 3,390 square metres, and contains four bars, three kitchens, eight garages, a doll museum and a special room for wrapping presents!

⑤ And if it's technology you're interested in, computer billionaire Bill Gates spent over $50 million on his state-of-the-art home by Lake Washington. Everyone who enters receives an electronic pin which controls lights, services and even turns off the TV when you leave the room!

⑥ Perhaps America's most famous dream home is a white-columned mansion in Memphis, Tennessee, which now attracts 700,000 visitors a year. Graceland, Elvis Presley's 'rock 'n' roll palace' was decorated in his favourite bright colours – red, orange and green – and is filled with velvet, gold, wall-sized mirrors, and enormous statues. Elvis lived at Graceland with his family from 1957 – but became more and more lonely there. He died alone in an upstairs bathroom in 1977.

1 Look at the four places in the pictures on page 120. Who lives/lived in each one? Which one looks:

- the biggest?
- the most interesting?
- the most attractive?

2 Read the text. Which of the places in the pictures:

a is near Madrid?
b cost over $25 million?
c has a toy museum inside?
d looks like the White House when you walk in?
e has enormous mirrors on the walls?
f is full of large statues?
g has a special room for wrapping presents?
h has a special system to operate the lights and television?

3 Two other houses are described in the text.

a What is special about François Labbé's house near Nice?
b Read the description of Jim Onan's house in Illinois. Using your mini-dictionary to help you, draw a rough sketch of the house.

4 a) Which of the houses in the text would you most like to visit/live in? Why?

b) Do you have an idea of your dream home? Describe it to other students. (Draw a picture too, if you want to.)

module 14 Building your dreams

Describe a favourite room

Personal vocabulary

Useful language

a Where the room is/was and why you go/went there

"It's/It was in/on/near …"

"I go/I used to go there to …"

"I spend/I used to spend a lot of time … (read)-ing there."

b Describing the room

"It's got/It had a … view of …"

"It's/It was quite/very …"

"There is/There was …"

"There are/There were a lot of …"

"It's got/It had a(n) … atmosphere."

c Why you like/liked the room

"I like/liked the room because …"

"I love/I used to love the …"

"I always feel/I felt … there."

Preparation for task

1 In a room, which of the following is the most/least important for you? Tell your partner.

the furniture and decoration (colours, etc.)   the size
the atmosphere   things like books, plants, ornaments, etc.   the view

2 [14.4] Sandra and Tom are talking about a favourite room. Listen and complete the table below.

	Sandra	Tom
Where it is/was and what he/she does/did there		
Description of the room: furniture, view, etc.		
Why he/she likes/liked the room		

Do you remember?

1 Put these words into three groups:

- places to live
- things in a house
- words to describe a room

> suburbs   balcony   village   modern   attractive
> furniture   spacious   elegant   building   fireplace
> wonderful   private   courtyard   apartment

2 Work in pairs. Discuss the following questions.

a) Would you prefer to live:
- in the city centre or in a small village?
- in an apartment block or in a house?
- in a place with lots of nightlife or lots of parks?

b) Would you prefer to have a house with:
- a wonderful view or lots of light?
- a private garden or a swimming pool?
- a balcony or a courtyard?

3 A word is missing from four of the following sentences. Can you think of the right word and put it in the right place?

a) There isn't space for the piano. Can you move that sofa?
b) There are some people at the door. Can you see what they want?
c) Oh dear, I think I put much salt in this soup.
d) Are you ready? The taxi will be here in few minutes.
e) There's a lot noise next door. Are they having a party?
f) There's no milk in the fridge. I'll go and get some.

4 Look at the pictures and descriptions below. Which information is not true, in each case? Can you correct it?

(a)
1. The cat is sitting above the table, behind the fish bowl.
2. The fish is at the bottom of the bowl.
3. There's a mouse near the table.

(b)
1. The dog is lying in front of the fire.
2. There's a bone between the dog and the fire.
3. The cat is inside the house.
4. There's a mouse in the corner of the room.

Task

1 You are going to give a short talk about a favourite room, like those you heard in Preparation for task, Exercise 2. Make notes under the following headings.

- Where the room is/was and what you do/did there
- Description of the room
- Why you like/liked the room

Ask your teacher for any words or phrases you need
▶ *Personal vocabulary*
▶ *Useful language*

2 a) Work in groups. Talk about your room and answer any questions other students have.

b) Listen to the other students' talks and decide which room would be a good place for:

- a meal with a few friends.
- relaxing and reading.
- a party.
- studying.

module 15
Money, money, money

- Vocabulary: verb phrases to do with money
- Past Perfect
- Reported speech
- Wordspot: *make*

Task: find the differences between two stories

Vocabulary

Verb phrases to do with money

1 a) Check the meaning of the verbs and phrases in **bold**.

- **can't afford** something
- **save** money
- **borrow** money from
- **waste** money
- **lend** someone money
- **pay** money back
- **lose** money
- **earn** money
- **spend** money on
- **win** money
- **invest** money in
- **owe** money
- **bet** money on

b) Which five places can you see in the pictures? Which verbs above relate to these places?

For example:

People save money in the bank.

2 Complete each of the statements below so they are true for you. Then compare your answers with a partner. What are the most important differences between you?

a Two of the things I spend most money on are … and …
b I think too many people waste money on …
c If I borrow money from …, I always/usually/never pay it back.
d I sometimes/never forget about money people lend me.
e I find it easy/difficult/impossible to save money.
f The person who earns the most money in my family is …
g The most money I've ever lost/won was …
h One person who owes me money is …
i I'd like to buy a(n) …, but I can't afford it.
j It's not a good idea to invest money in …
k In my country, people often bet money on …

124

Language focus 1

Past Perfect

Read about how the Hoens lost all their money and explain the connection between the pictures below. What was Ilona's 'expensive mistake'?

AN EXPENSIVE MISTAKE

Dutch housewife Ilona Hoens made an expensive mistake when she threw away a pair of her husband's old shoes: her husband had hidden £15,000 of savings inside them. When her husband found out what had happened, the couple rushed to the rubbish tip in Amsterdam. The people there listened sympathetically, but explained that they had burned all that day's rubbish several hours before.

Grammar analysis

1 Look at the example below.

... she **threw away** a pair of her husband's old shoes: her husband **had hidden** £15,000 of savings in them.

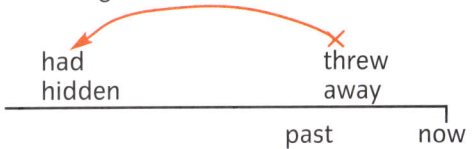

```
had                    threw
hidden                 away
_____
                past            now
```

a How many past actions are there?
b Which action happened first: hiding the money or throwing away the shoes?
c What tense is *threw*? What tense is *had hidden*?

2 Find two other examples of the Past Perfect in the text.

▶ Language summary A, page 157.

Practice

1 Match a beginning from A with an ending from B. Put the verbs in brackets into the Past Perfect.

A

a She couldn't afford the shoes because ...
b By the time George retired ...
c Hilda and Jerry bought a new car ...
d Kate needed some advice ...
e When Grandma died, nobody knew that ...

B

1 ... with the money they (*win*) in a competition.
2 ... because she (*never/invest*) money before.
3 ... she (*spend*) all her money on presents for her family.
4 ... she (*save*) thousands of pounds in a box.
5 ... he (*earn*) enough money to buy a holiday home.

125

module 15 **Money, money, money**

2 a) Read about Justine Klaus. What did she do with her money when she died?

When Swiss millionairess Justine Klaus (1)......... (die) in Geneva at the age of 79, most of her family (2)......... (come) to hear the details of her will, hoping the old lady (3)......... (remember) them. Instead they (4)......... (get) a real shock. Justine (5)......... (live) alone for many years, and most of her family (6)......... (not see) her for several years. The family (7)......... (be) amazed when they (8)......... (hear) that the old lady (9)......... (leave) £370,000 to her favourite house plant! Justine said that the plant (10)......... (be) her best and only friend. In contrast, her family only (11)......... (receive) £100 each!

b) Complete the sentences with the Past Simple or the Past Perfect.

c) Justine also gave £170,000 to a man in his forties called Willi. Why? Think of two possible reasons.

(Maybe he'd ...)

(... or perhaps he was ... and he'd ...)

Look at the answer on page 141. Did anyone guess correctly?

Language focus 2

Reported speech

1 Look at the pictures below. What do you think happened? Discuss in pairs.

2 [15.1] Listen to the story. Is it the same as yours?

Grammar analysis

1 Look at the sentences below. How does the verb form change:
   • in the Present Simple?   • in the Past Simple?
   • with *will*?

Direct speech	Reported speech
'You **look** just like my daughter.'	The old lady told my sister that she **looked** just like her daughter.
'She **died** a year ago.'	She said that her daughter **had died** a year ago.
'My daughter **will pay**.'	She said that you **would pay**.

2 Which of the alternatives below is wrong?
   She told me/She said me/She said that her name was Mary.

▶ Language summary B, page 157.

126

Practice

1 Complete the sentences below about yourself. Some should be true, and some false.

a I love …
b I don't like …
c I bought a new … at the weekend.
d I'm planning to … next weekend.
e I'll probably … after this lesson.
f I never spend money on …
g In 19… I won … in a competition.
h I can't …
i I'll be … tomorrow morning.
j I saw … yesterday.

2 Read your sentences to a partner. Your partner makes a note of your answers, and decides which are true/false.

3 Tell each other which sentences you think were false, like this:

> You said you loved tea, but I don't believe you, because you always drink coffee.

> You're right, it's false!

> You told me you'd be at home tomorrow morning, but I think you'll be at work.

> No, it's true. I've got the day off tomorrow!

Wordspot

make

1 [15.2] Complete the gaps with a word from the box. Then listen and check your answers.

> dinner   noise   a mess   a cup of tea   profit
> a phone call   feel   angry   cry   friends

a Wait a minute – I need to make …………… before we go.
b This company has made a big …………… again this year.
c Are you hungry? I'm going to make …………… in a minute.
d Stella's already made lots of …………… at her new school. I think she's really happy there.
e That washing machine's making a very strange …………… .
f You look really tired. Sit down and I'll make you …………… .
g Our Maths teacher's horrible – he made Lucy …………… today.
h Andrew really makes me …………… . He's always late!
i Can I have a party here, Mum? We won't make …………… .
j I hate flying – it makes me …………… ill.

2 Underline the phrases with *make* in the sentences above and add them to the diagram.

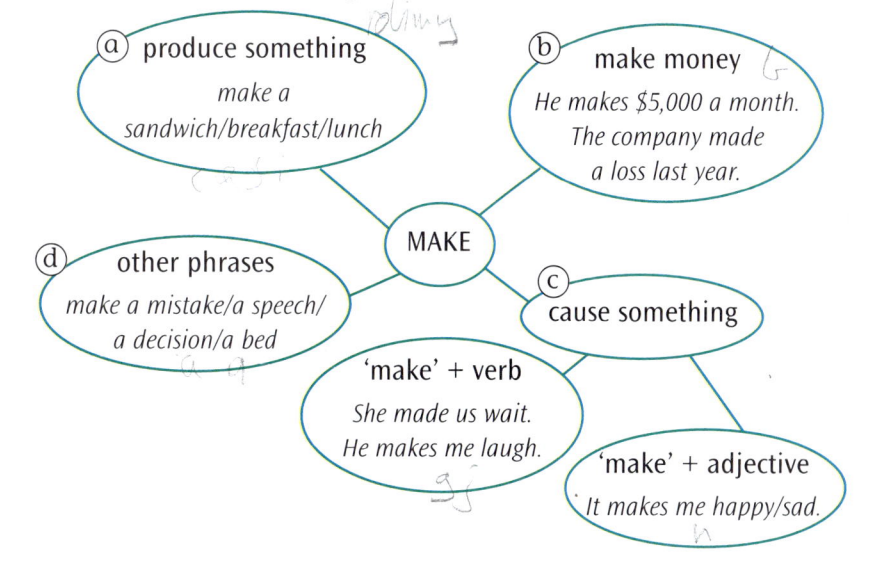

- (a) **produce something** — *make a sandwich/breakfast/lunch*
- (b) **make money** — *He makes $5,000 a month. The company made a loss last year.*
- (c) **cause something**
  - *'make' + verb* — *She made us wait. He makes me laugh.*
  - *'make' + adjective* — *It makes me happy/sad.*
- (d) **other phrases** — *make a mistake/a speech/a decision/a bed*

MAKE

3 Discuss with a partner. Think of two:

- things that make you angry.
- things that make a lot of noise.
- reasons why people make speeches.
- things that are made in Scotland.
- things that you can make with eggs.
- mistakes that you often make in English.

127

module 15 Money, money, money

Find the differences between two stories

Useful language

Checking information

"What did he say about …?"

"I didn't understand the part about …"

"How many differences did you find?"

"I've got … differences."

"That's the same in both versions."

Describing the differences

"The first/second/third thing that's different is …"

"On the recording he said that …/but in the article it says that …"

"Another difference is that …"

"Are you sure that's different?"

IS THIS MAN BRITAIN'S UNLUCKIEST CRIMINAL?

Local businessman, Edward Carson, stole clients' money

Everybody in the small town of Thornaby, in the north-east of England, had always thought that local businessman Edward Carson was an honest man. But when Carson lost all his money after a series of bad investments, he decided it was time to do something …

Carson stole £60,000 of his clients' money and took an aeroplane to Monte Carlo, in the south of France, where he planned to get back the money he had lost by playing roulette. However, the casinos became suspicious of a man with so much cash and did not accept his bets. Carson returned to England.

Still thinking that gambling was the answer to his problems, he went to Doncaster races, put £10,000 on a horse called Lucky Seven. Sadly, the horse was certainly not lucky, and finished last in the race!

The casino in Monte Carlo where Carson tried to win back the money

Preparation for task

1 Read the first paragraph of the article above and answer the questions.

a Who was Edward Carson, and was he honest?
b What was his problem?
c Can you guess what he decided to do?

2 Read the rest of the article and find:

- three ways in which he tried to make money.
- three ways in which he was unlucky.

Doncaster races – not lucky for Edward Carson

Carson then invested the rest of his money in a travel company ... a few days later the company collapsed. Carson had lost everything.

He used his last £1,000 to buy a second-hand car. He had decided to kill himself by driving off the cliffs near his home town. Just before he reached the cliffs, a police officer stopped him for speeding. It was enough to make Carson think that perhaps he wasn't so unlucky after all. He told the police officer everything, and Carson was arrested.

At his trial, the judge gave him just one month in prison: he said Carson had probably suffered enough already.

The car in which Carson tried to kill himself – the police stopped him

Task

1 [15.3] After he left prison, Carson gave an interview about what happened. There are at least ten differences between the article and what **he** says happened. Make a note of any differences you hear.

2 Work in a group. Make a list of the differences between the article and Carson's version of what happened.
▶ *Useful language*

3 [15.4] Listen and check to see if you identified all the differences correctly.

Real life

Dealing with money

1 Where are the people in the pictures? In which places might they:

a   change money?
b   ask if they can pay by credit card?
c   ask about the exchange rate?
d   leave a tip?
e   ask for change?
f   ask if service is included?
g   ask the price of something?
h   pay in cash?
i   find some pound coins?
j   open a bank account?

2 [15.5] You will hear five conversations. Match the conversations with the pictures above.

129

3 Listen to the conversations again and complete the information below.

a The person wants to change $............ into pesos. The exchange rate is .... to the dollar. She receives ....
b The person needs £............ for the machine. Her friend gives her .... pound coins and .... fifty pence coins.
c The girl would like to buy some earrings. The larger ones cost .... , and the smaller ones cost ....
She decides to buy .... She pays by credit card/in cash.
d Which documents does the young man need to open a bank account?
e What food and drinks did they have? How much did they cost? How much did they pay in total?

4 Look at these sentences. In each case, cross out the incorrect/unnecessary word.

a What's the exchange rate for the US dollars?
b I'd like to change this money into pesos, please. It's 200 of American dollars.
c Have you got any change for £5?
d Excuse me. How much are these earrings cost?
e OK, I'll be take this pair.
f Can I pay by my credit card?
g What the documents do I need?
h Can we to have the bill, please?
i Is the service included?
j Do you think we should to leave a tip?

Pronunciation

[15.6] Listen to the correct sentences from Exercise 4 and repeat them. Copy the intonation.

5 Look back at the pictures on page 129. Invent **three** conversations of your own for these situations. Use some of the phrases in Exercise 4 above.

Do you remember?

1 When he died, a millionaire left his money to his three children: Lucky Luke, Clever Clare, and Unfortunate Fred. What do you think they did with the money? *For example:*
Clever Clare invested some money in a computer company and made a profit.
a) ... lost some money in a game of cards.
b) ... saved some money in the bank.
c) ... spent money on a lottery ticket and won.
d) ... lent money to a friend who never paid it back.
e) ... bet on a horse which won all its races.

2 What is the difference in meaning between the following pairs of verbs?
a) He **earns** much more than me.
I never **win** any money in the competitions.
b) I think we need to **borrow** some more money.
I can **lend** you £50, but that's all.
c) She never **spends** any money on clothes.
You **waste** too much money on CDs.

3 Think of two reasons for each of these situations. Use the Past Perfect. Why:
a) did Freda have a plaster on her hand?
Because she had burnt her hand on the cooker.
b) didn't Jim telephone his wife?
c) did Martin crash his car?
d) was Robert sitting in the bath in his clothes?
e) did Jake run up and down the road shouting?

4 Put the sentences below into a logical order to make a story. What were Rita's actual words in a, b, d, e and g?
a) You said you'd never leave me.
b) You said your name was Rita.
c) I met you in a cocktail bar.
d) One day you said you loved another man.
e) You said I had a nice smile.
f) Then you left me.
g) You said you loved me.

module 16
Imagine ...

- Conditional sentences with *would*
- *Will* and *would*

Task: choose people to start a space colony

Reading and vocabulary

1 John Lennon and Martin Luther King were famous in the 1960s. In pairs, discuss the following questions. Who:

- was a pop star?
- was a civil rights leader?
- won a Nobel Prize?
- was married to a Japanese woman?
- received an award from the British Queen?
- was a Christian minister?

John Lennon
1940–1980, British singer and songwriter

'... imagine all the people, sharing all the world ...'

Martin Luther King
1929–1968, Christian minister and Black American civil rights leader

'I have a dream ... that all God's children, black and white, Catholic and Protestant, will join hands and sing "Free at last! Thank God we are free at last!"'

131

module 16 Imagine...

2 Work in two groups. **Group A** reads the text about John Lennon. **Group B** reads the text on page 142 about Martin Luther King. Answer the appropriate questions below with other students in your group.

The Decade of Dreamers
John Lennon

A In 1969 ... many people were shocked to open their newspapers and see photographs of the Beatle, John Lennon, and his new Japanese wife, Yoko Ono, sitting in bed in their hotel room in the Amsterdam Hilton as a 'peace protest'.

Lennon, the writer of songs like All you need is love and Give peace a chance, put into words many young people's hopes for a new and better world. A world of freedom and peace, without wars, religion, governments and even countries.

John Lennon had become more and more interested in these ideas in the late 1960s. In 1968 he travelled to India with the other Beatles to study meditation with the Maharishi and in the same year he returned his MBE, a special award from the British Queen, as a protest against Britain's part in the wars in Nigeria and Vietnam. In 1971 he wrote perhaps his most famous song, Imagine, which expresses his ideas of the perfect world. It is particularly tragic that a man who believed so strongly in peace was to die so violently, less than ten years later, when he was shot in front of his New York apartment building by a crazy fan, Mark Chapman.

A Questions about John Lennon

a What did John Lennon and Yoko Ono do in 1969, as a peace protest?
b Which of John Lennon's songs were about changing the world?
c Why did he return an award to the British Queen? When?
d When did he write Imagine? What was it about?
e How did John Lennon die?
f Where did he die and who killed him?

B Questions about Martin Luther King

a What happened in Washington in 1963?
b Who was speaking, and what famous words did he say?
c How many people joined the demonstration?
d Was the demonstration peaceful or violent?
e Which two things happened the next year?
f How and when did Martin Luther King die?

3 Ask and answer questions with a member of the other group. Student A asks the questions about Martin Luther King and Student B asks about John Lennon.

4 Discuss the following questions in groups.

- In what way were Martin Luther King and John Lennon 'dreamers'?
- Who did more to change the world?
- Can you think of any other famous dreamers? What did they do? What did they believe in?

5 Complete the gaps in the table using your mini-dictionary if necessary. Be careful with the spelling of the adverbs.

	noun	adjective	adverb
a	peace	peaceful	peacefully
b	violence	violent	violently
c	power	powerful	powerfully
d	freedom	free	freely
e	religion	religious	✗
f	tragedy	tragic	tragicly
g	strength	strong	strongly

Pronunciation

[16.1] Listen to the pronunciation of the nouns and adjectives in Exercise 5 above. Listen and mark the stress on words of more than one syllable. Practise saying the words.

Listening and vocabulary

Imagine

1 Look at the pairs of phrases below and mark them **S** if they have the same meaning and **D** if they are different.

a peace/war   D
b above us/below us
c it's easy/it isn't hard
d heaven/hell
e heaven/the sky
f to kill/to die
g to imagine/to wonder
h a dreamer/a madman
i possessions/things people own
j greed/hunger
k to share/to join

2 [16.2] Listen to the song and write in the phrases you hear. Compare answers with a partner.

3 a) Tick (✓) the things below that John Lennon thought were good. Write a cross (✗) next to the ones he thought were bad.

living in peace ✓	heaven
hell ✗	countries	brotherhood
living for today	possessions
greed	hunger	dreamers

b) Which of his ideas do you agree with? Which do you disagree with?

IMAGINE

Imagine there's no (1) ....
(2) .... if you try
No hell (3) ....
(4) .... only (5) ....
Imagine all the people
Living for today

Imagine there's no countries
(6) .... to do
Nothing to kill or (7) .... for
And no religion too
Imagine all the people
Living life in (8) ....

You may say I'm (9) ....
But I'm not the only one
I hope some day you'll
(10) .... us
And the world will live as one

Imagine no (11) ....
I (12) .... if you can
No need for (13) .... or (14) ....
A brotherhood of man
Imagine all the people
(15) .... all the world

You may say I'm a (16) ....
But I'm not the only one
I hope some day you'll (17) .... us
And the world will live as one

module 16 Imagine...

Language focus 1

Conditional sentences with *would*

Underline the endings to the sentences **you** think are true. (You can underline both endings if you want.) Compare answers with a partner.

1 If there were no countries,
  - the world would be a better place.
  - life wouldn't be so interesting.

2 If people didn't have possessions,
  - people would share everything equally.
  - some people would still try to become rich and powerful.

3 If there weren't any wars,
  - we would all have a much better life.
  - people would soon get bored.

4 If everyone lived only 'for today',
  - we would enjoy life much more!
  - there would be chaos!

Grammar analysis

1 Answer the questions below.
  a Are the sentences above about:
    • *real* situations?
    • *imaginary* situations?
  b Which verb form comes after *if*?
  c Which verb form can we find in the other part (the main clause) of the sentences?
  d Are the sentences about the past/about the present/general?

2 a What are the negative and question forms of *would*?
  b Notice the contractions with *would*.
    I'd enjoy life more. I wouldn't enjoy life.
    What are the forms for *you, he, she, it, we* and *they*?

▶ Language summary A, page 157.

Practice

1 Complete the sentences with the correct form of the words in brackets.

a If there (*be*) .... no countries, there (*not be*) .... any governments or laws either.

b We (*not need*) .... policemen or prisons if we (*not have*) .... any laws.

c If countries (*not exist*) .... , people (*not have*) .... passports, and they (*can live*) .... anywhere in the world they liked.

d If there (*not be*) .... any countries, everyone (*speak*) .... the same language, in the end.

e If people (*not have*) .... possessions, nobody (*need*) .... money any more.

f Without money, we (*not have*) .... shops.

g Many people (*lose*) .... their jobs if we (*not have*) shops ....

h If we (*not own*) .... anything, what (*people/wear*) ....? Where (*they/sleep*) ....

2 a) If **you** were the prime minister or president of your country, what would you do? Look at the ideas below.

> build better hospitals/schools
> pay teachers/politicians more
> open more universities/cinemas
> make the weekend four days long/the working day shorter
> make the army bigger/smaller
> build more roads/shopping malls
> clean up cities/rivers
> give more money to old people/the unemployed

b) Compare answers with other students. Tell your partner about anything else that you would do, if you were president.

I would definitely build better ...

I think I'd pay teachers more.

134

Language focus 2

Will and *would*

1 Look at the picture. What is happening?

2 a) Match the words/thoughts below with the people in the picture.

"… and I promise that if I become president, I will open *more* schools and employ *more* teachers than ever before …"

"If I was president, I'd close all the schools and there would be *no* teachers!"

b) Who says/thinks:

'schools will work longer hours'
'there wouldn't be any homework'
'school holidays would be longer'
'all children will do a minimum of two hours' homework a day'

Grammar analysis

1 Which person in the picture
   a might **really** become president?
   b is only imagining?

2 Look at these examples:
   If I become president, I'll open more schools.
   If I was President, I'd close all the schools.

   a Which verb form is used after *if* in each type of sentence?
   b Which verb form is used in the other part of the sentence (the main clause)?

▶ *Language summary B, page 157.*

Practice

Complete the sentences below with your own ideas using *will* or *would*. Compare answers with a partner.

1 If I learn to speak English well, …
2 If I could live anywhere in the world, …
3 If I have time this week, …
4 If I could change places with a celebrity, …
5 If I go out tonight, …
6 If I were invisible, …
7 If I'm up early tomorrow, …
8 If I could turn back time, …
9 If I live to be eighty, …
10 If I were very rich, …

Pronunciation

[16.3] Listen to the phrases below and write *'ll* or *'d* in the gaps.

1 I ………… see you later.
2 I ………… have a look.
3 I ………… love to.
4 I ………… think about it.
5 You ………… like him.
6 That ………… be great.
7 We ………… be back soon.
8 I ………… prefer not to.

135

module 16 Imagine...

Choose people to start a space colony

Preparation for task

1 Do you believe that there is life on other planets? Do you think that humans will ever go and live on other planets?

2 Read about the new planet Hero, and answer the questions. Compare your answers with a partner.

a Why do scientists think that humans will be able to live on Hero?
b Are there any aliens on Hero?
c How many people will they send to Hero, and why?
d When will these people come back to Earth?
e Will other people join the space colony later?
f What will the volunteers take with them?
g How long will it take to travel to Hero?
h How many people have volunteered to go?

Useful language

Explaining why people are suitable

"He/She would be very useful because …"

"He/She knows a lot about …"

"He/She has experience of …"

"He/She can have children …"

"We need someone who can …"

"He/She could …"

Explaining why people are not suitable

"There might be problems with …"

"He/She's too old to …/too young to …"

"If … happened, perhaps he/she would …"

THE NEW PLANET HERO

Scientists have discovered a new planet, Hero. They are very confident that human beings will be able to live there, as it has water, light, oxygen and the temperature and air are similar to those on Earth. They have done tests and know that plants can grow there. They have not seen any alien life there, but they cannot be sure that it doesn't exist.

They have decided to send a spaceship of people there from Earth, to start a space colony, and a new human society. But there is space for only **six** people. These people will have to stay there for the rest of their lives. No one else will be able to join the space colony for at least a hundred years. They will take enough food tablets for five years, together with four guns to protect themselves, and blankets, space-tents, etc. The spaceship will be controlled from Earth, so there will not be a pilot. The journey to Hero will last about ten weeks.

The organisers have asked for volunteers, but unfortunately only ten people have volunteered. The spaceship must leave in two days' time so there is no time to find new volunteers.

Ten Candidates

Natalya Boreva, 38, from Moscow. University lecturer in Ancient Greek Literature. Unmarried, no children. Very good health.

Jake Green, 42, from New York, U.S.A. Engineer. Recently divorced after eighteen-year marriage. No children. Had cancer two years ago, but doctors say he is now clear.

René Bernard, 76, from Lyon, France. Retired doctor. Widower with seven adult children. Has travelled all his life and has been to every corner of the world. Lived alone on a Pacific island for three years. In very good health.

Claudette Parkin, 22, from Ohio, USA. Factory worker (married to Brandon below). Six months pregnant. Health OK, but heavy smoker.

Brandon Parkin, 25, also from Ohio, USA. Unemployed (married to Claudette above). As a teenager, he went to prison for a violent crime and because of this cannot get a job. Very loving husband to Claudette. Excellent health and very strong physically.

Gheeta Singh, 29, from Birmingham, UK. Nurse. Unmarried, no children.

Rashid Bengherbia, 56, from Algiers, Algeria. A judge in his own country. Has travelled the world and worked for many years as a United Nations representative. Widower with adult daughter. Good health.

Luciana DeSouza, 17, from Rio de Janeiro, Brazil. School student. Unmarried, no children. A very good singer. Wanted to become an opera singer before she heard about this mission. Parents have given permission for her to go. Excellent health.

Roberto Fratelli, 31, from Naples, Italy. Policeman. Divorced with three children. Won a special award from the Naples police for bravery last year. Very good health.

Lourdes Lagraña, 43, from Malaga, Spain. Agricultural scientist. Divorced with one adult child. Has worked in difficult conditions all over the world. History of health problems, but now says that these are finished.

Task

1 Work individually. Spend five minutes choosing the six best candidates, in your opinion.
▶ *Useful language*

2 **a)** Work in pairs. Compare the reasons for your choices. Try to agree on the six best candidates.

b) Discuss and compare answers in larger groups or with the class. Can you agree on the six final candidates?

3 Do you think a space mission like this will ever happen? Would you volunteer? Why/Why not?

Creative writing

You are one of the people travelling to Hero. You have just landed on the new planet. Write a letter to a friend back on Earth. Describe:

- the planet.
- the journey there.
- what you think of the other people you are with.
- how you feel at the moment.

3 Read about the ten candidates. Underline like this (_____) the reasons that make them suitable to travel, and like this (_ _ _) the reasons that make them unsuitable.

Consolidation modules 12–16

A Vocabulary: connections

Work in small groups. Take it in turns to choose a word from each box below and explain the connection between them. For example:

- scarf/velvet You can have a scarf which is made of velvet.
- chef/waiter A chef and a waiter both work with food.

If the other students think your explanation is convincing, you win a point.
You can use each word more than once.

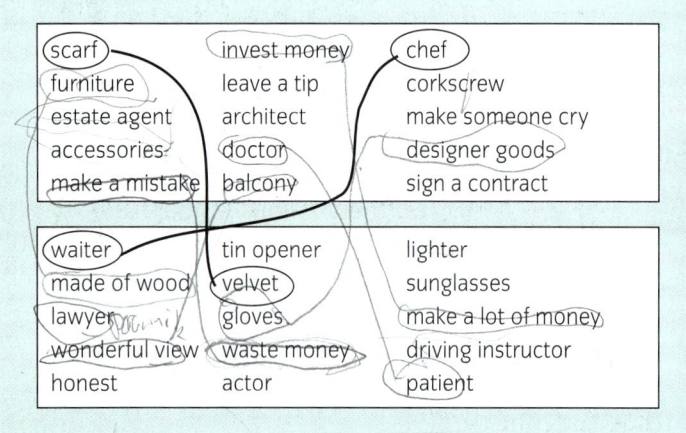

scarf	invest money	chef
furniture	leave a tip	corkscrew
estate agent	architect	make someone cry
accessories	doctor	designer goods
make a mistake	balcony	sign a contract

waiter	tin opener	lighter
made of wood	velvet	sunglasses
lawyer	gloves	make a lot of money
wonderful view	waste money	driving instructor
honest	actor	patient

B Speaking: real life

Work in pairs. Act out the following situations.

1
A A friend from another country is coming to stay in your city for a few days. You are not sure about the best places to go/things to see. Ask B for some suggestions.

B Give A some suggestions about the best things to do/places to go with a visitor from another country.

2
A You are standing near the main entrance of your school. B is a new student. Answer his/her questions.

B Ask A where the nearest telephone is. You also need some coins for the telephone.

3
A You have lost your bag and you are upset. Tell B.

B Try to calm A down and help him/her to find the bag.

4
A You are talking to a travel agent about a holiday. Ask about the place you want to go to, the hotel, price, etc.

B You are a travel agent. Answer B's questions about the place he/she wants to go to.

C Speaking and listening

1 Work in pairs. The sentences below come from conversations. Read them and decide:

- who the speakers are.
- where they are.
- what the situation is.

a Yes, all the bedrooms are cleaned every morning, madam.
b Then he said he never wanted to see me again!
c If you gave me £10,000, I wouldn't go there again.
d I saw that someone had broken the kitchen window.
e I've been working on it all day, but I haven't finished it yet.

2 Choose a sentence and expand it into a conversation. Act it out for the other students like this:

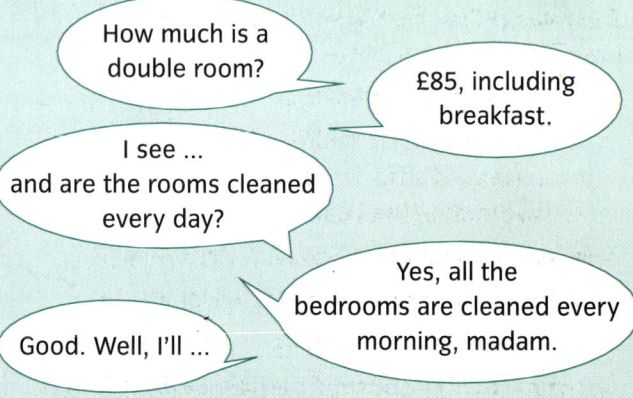

- How much is a double room?
- £85, including breakfast.
- I see ... and are the rooms cleaned every day?
- Yes, all the bedrooms are cleaned every morning, madam.
- Good. Well, I'll ...

3 [1] Listen to the conversations. Were yours very similar/different?

Communication activities

Module 1: Exercise 2, page 11

Group A

HOW ENERGETIC ARE YOU?
1 .... usually get up as soon as you wake up?
2 .... slow getting ready in the morning, or .... usually leave the house quickly?
3 .... walk to school or work, or .... usually go by car or bus?
4 How often .... run upstairs?
5 .... often sleepy after lunch?
6 energetic when you come home in the evening, or usually tired?
7 How often .... stay up very late or all night?

Module 2: Exercise 2, page 16

Student A

Make these into complete questions and answers.

1 Which/was/first country/introduce/a driving test?

   a France   b Germany   c Switzerland

Answer: France (*be*) the first country to introduce a driving test, in 1899.

2 Where/people/first/use/paper money?

   a China   b India   c Japan

Answer: People first (*use*) paper money in China nearly 1,500 years ago.

3 What/Louis Réard/design/1946?

   a the world's first bikini
   b the world's first mini-skirt
   c the world's first jeans

Answer: He (*design*) the world's first bikini.

4 Where/first World Cup final/take place?

   a Argentina   b Brazil   c Uruguay

Answer: The first World Cup final (*take*) place in Montevideo, Uruguay, in 1930. The home team (*win*) 4–2.

Module 2: Exercise 1, page 16

1 The first woman to graduate from university was Italian. Her name was Elena Cornaro, and she received a doctorate of philosophy from the University of Padova on 25th June 1678 – nearly two hundred years before the first woman received a degree in the United States.

2 The world's first vending machine was at an Underground railway station in London. It sold postcards.

3 The first McDonald's restaurant opened in December 1955, in Des Plaines, Illinois. Today there are over 26,000.

4 The first space flight took place at the end of 1951 when four monkeys named Albert 1, Albert 2, Albert 3 and Albert 4 flew into the stratosphere from White Sands, New Mexico, USA. They all returned to Earth safely.

Module 11: Exercise 4, Page 90

Answer: Obsession

Module 12: Practice, Exercise 2, page 103

Student A

[Image showing labelled items: sleeping bag, coffee machine, swimsuit, toothbrush, socks, ruler, washing powder]

Communication activities

Module 5: Task, Exercise 2, page 45

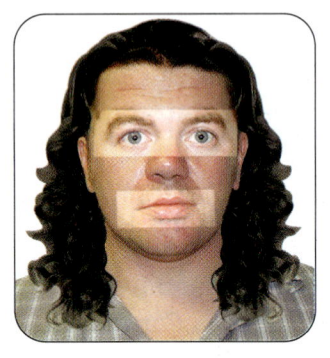

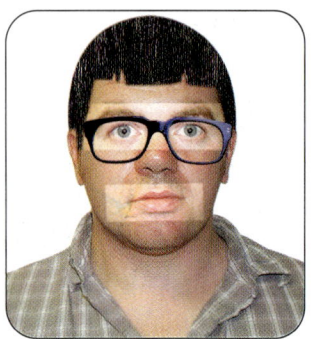

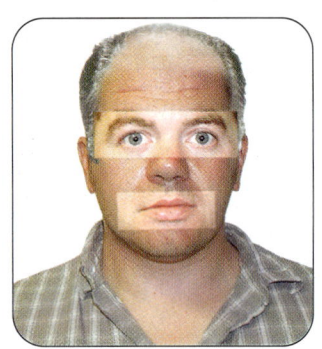

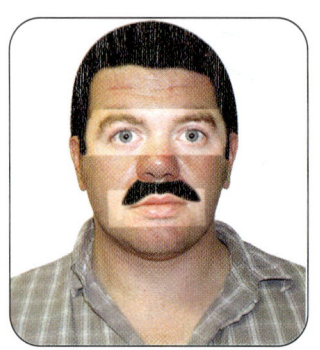

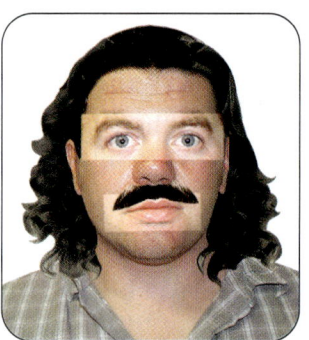

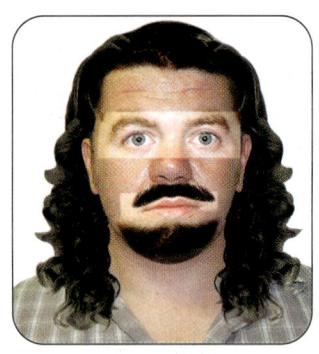

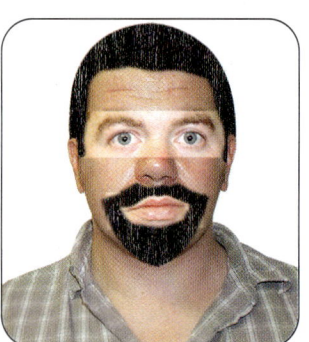

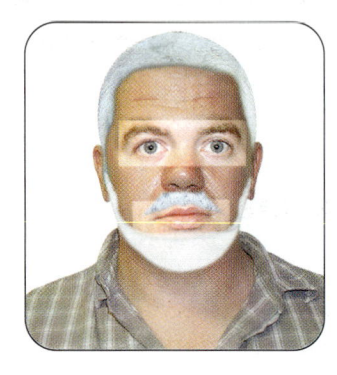

Module 7: Wordspot (*know*), Exercise 3, page 61

Student A

1 What do you know about the weather in England?
2 Do you know how to say 'I love you' in more than three languages?
3 Think of a place you know well – tell me three things about it.
4 How long have you known your best friend?
5 Do you know what to do if you spill red wine on your clothes?
6 Do you know the words of any English songs?

Module 6: Task, Exercise 2, page 53

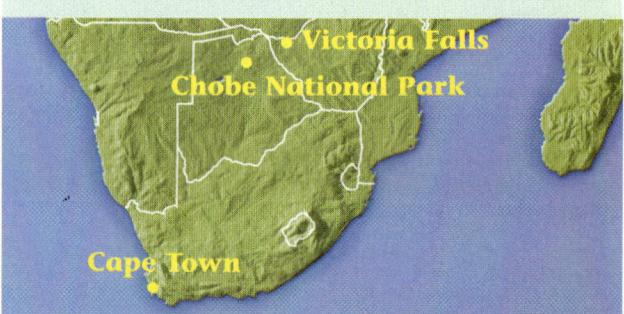

African Wildlife Safari: Fact File

Main places to visit: The tour begins in Cape Town, South Africa's oldest and most elegant city. We then fly to Zimbabwe, where we see one of the natural Wonders of the World – the Victoria Falls. From there we cross the border into Botswana, where we hope to find lions, rhinos and elephants in the world-famous Chobe National Park.

How many days? 14
Accommodation: In Cape Town and at the Victoria Falls you will stay in comfortable four-star hotels. On our visit to Chobe, you can camp out under the African stars, or stay in one of our simple but comfortable safari lodges.

When to go? The dry season is the best time to see the animals (June to October – temperatures 25–40°C). The temperatures are highest in October (36–40°C).

Optional excursions: You can choose three of the following optional excursions.
- A visit to an ostrich farm. You can ride on an ostrich!
- A visit to the vineyard region of Stellenbosch.
- A relaxing cruise along the River Zambezi.
- A chance to bungee-jump at Victoria Falls.
- A visit to a Zulu village to see traditional Zulu dancing.

Communication activities

Complete the table to design your dream holiday.

Main places to visit	1
	2
	3
Number of days	
Accommodation in each place	
Best time to go and why	
Optional excursions you prefer	1
	2
	3

Module 8: Task, page 69

Student A

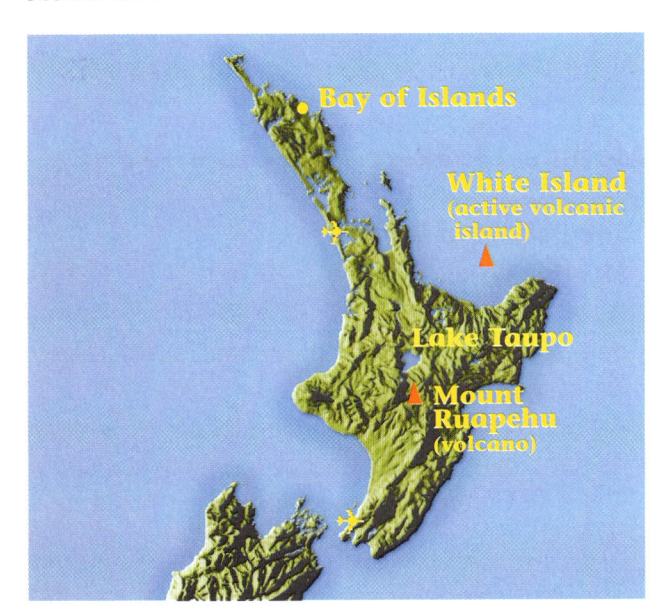

[Map of New Zealand's North Island showing: Bay of Islands, White Island (active volcanic island), Lake Taupo, Mount Ruapehu (volcano)]

Module 11: Practice, Exercise 1, page 93

Student A

1 Do/Would you like (live) in the United States? Why/Why not?
2 Do/Would you like (own) a dog? What kind?
3 What kind of music do/would you most like (listen to)?
4 Which country in the world do/would you most like (visit)?
5 Do/Would you like (cook)? If yes, what's your speciality?

Module 10: Task, page 87

Group A

Shirley Yeats: on holiday on cruiseship/ sail/near Malaysia

one day/go back to her cabin/could smell burning/look around/see smoke

immediately telephone the captain/then go up to help/soon fire out of control/captain decide to leave ship

Shirley help passengers get into lifeboats/give first aid to other passengers/one of the last to leave/1,100 passengers get off safely

Module 15: Practice, Exercise 2, page 126

Answer: Willi was the owner of the shop where Justine had bought the house plant.

Communication activities

Module 10: Exercise 1, page 85

Module 12: Task, page 105

Student A

> You are going camping in the mountains by a small lake for the weekend, with your friend. You will be ten kilometres from the nearest village – the weather forecast is quite warm, but it may rain. You are travelling by bicycle.
> List • tent

Module 13: Task, page 113

Student A

> ### JACK NOVAK
> Probably the richest man in the whole of St Helena, 70-year-old Jack Novak has been the owner of the biggest national newspaper, the St Helena Times, since 1994. He moved to Queenstown a month ago. Police have been investigating his connections with the local mafia for more than a year, but so far they have not found any reason to arrest him. He promises to reduce taxes and spend a lot of money improving facilities in the city (for example, a new swimming pool and sports centre). His slogan is, 'With Jack Novak, everyone will be better off.'

Module 16: Exercise 2, page 132

> **The Decade of Dreamers**
> **Martin Luther King**
>
> **B** In 1963 more than 200,000 people demonstrated in Washington. Black Americans walked with show business stars like Marlon Brando, Judy Garland and Bob Dylan, demanding civil rights for everyone, black and white. But most of all, people had come to hear Martin Luther King, the most exciting of the young black leaders. It was a time when, in many states of the USA, African Americans could not go to the same schools, ride on the same buses or eat in the same restaurants as whites. The Washington police were very worried about so many thousands of people demonstrating in their city, but the day passed peacefully: King, a Christian minister, believed in non-violent action, and the crowd listened quietly as King gave his famous speech beginning "I have a dream…"
>
> The next year in 1964, the law in the USA was changed to give black people civil rights, and Martin Luther King won the Nobel Prize for Peace. But he continued his work until his death, always fighting for 'shared power'. On the day of his assassination in April 1968, he was, as always, speaking out against violence.

Communication activities

Module 13: Exercise 2, page 111

Student A

1 .... did Johnny Dell Folley, from Texas, USA, throw an egg in 1978 without breaking it?
   a 9 m   **b 98 m**   c 980 m

2 .... wives did the English King Henry VIII have?
   a one   **b six**   c ten

3 What is the best answer to the question, 'How ....?'
   a I am very well, thank you. And you?
   b Good idea!   c I'm going home.

4 .... is Hollywood star Danny De Vito?
   a 1.52 m   b 1.72 m   c 1.92 m

5 .... was Princess Diana when she died in 1997?
   a 26   b 30   **c 36**

6 Brazil is the biggest country in South America. .... is it?
   a 8.5 million square kilometres
   b 20.5 million square kilometres
   c 65 million square kilometres

Module 2: Exercise 2, page 16

Student B

Make these into complete questions and answers.

1 What/was/first programme/satellite TV?
   a a boxing match   b a football match
   c a tennis match

Answer: The first programme on satellite TV (*be*) a boxing match between Muhammad Ali and Joe Frazier in 1975.

2 When/the world's first Disney theme park/open?
   a October 1961   b October 1971
   c October 1981

Answer: Disney World (*open*) in October 1971. It (*be*) in Florida, in the USA.

3 Where/people/first/play/chess?
   a Africa   b Asia   c Europe

Answer: People first (*play*) chess in what is now Pakistan, Asia, about 4,500 years ago.

4 When/the first *Star Wars* film/appear?
   a 1967   b 1977   c 1987

Answer: The first *Star Wars* film (*appear*) in 1977.

Module 8: Vocabulary, Exercise 1, page 66

1 the Nile   2 Italy, Germany
3 Switzerland, Hungary, Austria
4 Greece   5 Venice   6 Algeria, Egypt, Libya
7 Spain, Italy, Switzerland, Germany   8 Tripoli
9 Barcelona   10 Rome, Athens
11 Egypt, Morocco, Tunisia, Libya, Algeria
12 Italy   13 Switzerland

Module 14: Exercise 2, page 119

Student A

Communication activities

Module 6: Task, Exercise 2, page 53

The Florida Experience: Fact File

Complete the table to design your dream holiday.

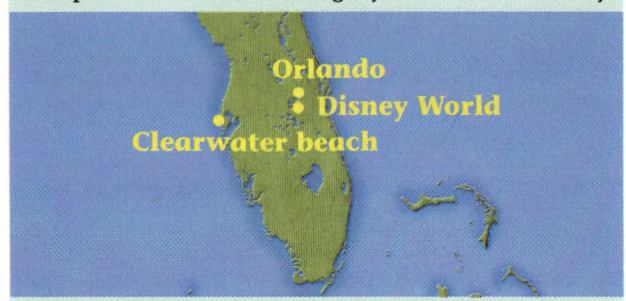

Main places to visit: Your holiday begins in the city of Orlando – the world's theme park capital. From Orlando, it's a short trip to Disney World, where you can choose between a number of theme parks, such as Disney's Animal Kingdom, Disney's Water Park or Disney's Wide World of Sport. Finally, you will spend a week relaxing in the sunshine at Clearwater Beach on Florida's Gulf Coast.

How many days? 14

Accommodation: You can choose between accommodation in self-catering homes (most have their own swimming pool) and comfortable motels just outside Orlando.

When to go? Temperatures in Florida are high all year round, from 20–25°C in winter to 35°C or more in summer (June–August).

Optional excursions: You can choose three of the following optional excursions.
- A visit to the Kennedy Space Center.
- A visit to SeaWorld Adventure Park to feed the dolphins and see the whales.
- A visit to Fort Lauderdale – the 'Venice of America'. Perfect for cruising.
- A visit to Miami, with its exciting mixture of American, Caribbean and Hispanic cultures.
- A visit to Universal Studios to see the magic of the movies come to life.

Main places to visit	1
	2
	3
Number of days	
Accommodation in each place	
Best time to go and why	
Optional excursions you prefer	1
	2
	3

Module 7: Wordspot (*know*), Exercise 3, page 61

Student B

1 What do you know about the food in the USA?
2 Do you know how to spell 'disappointed'?
3 Think of a person you know well – tell me three things about him or her.
4 How long have you known the other people in this class?
5 Do you know what to say if someone says 'Cheers!'?
6 Do you know the difference between the Present Perfect and the Past Simple?

Module 8: Task, page 69

Student B

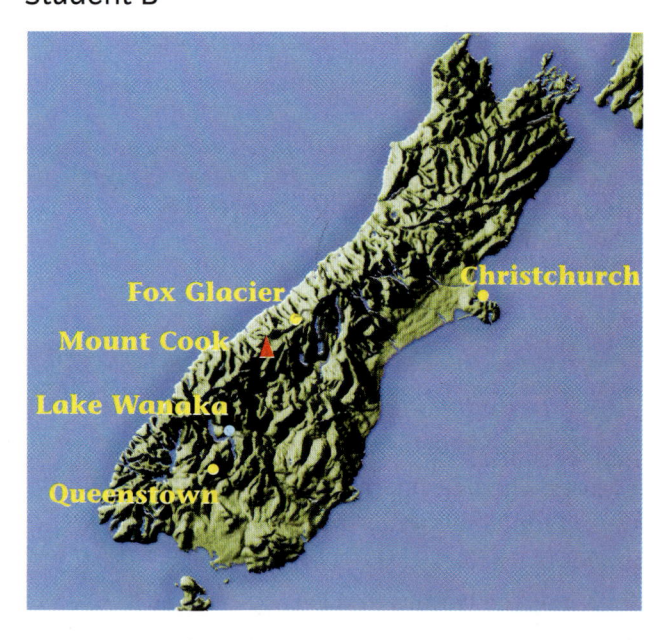

Module 11: Practice, Exercise 1, page 93

Student B

1 Do/Would you like (watch) sport? Which one(s)?
2 Do/Would you like (speak) any other languages (apart from English!)?
3 Where do/would you like (go) next summer holidays?
4 Do/Would you like (travel) by plane? Why/Why not?
5 Do/Would you like (go) to bed early? Why/Why not?

Communication activities

Module 10: Task, page 87

Group B

Simon Roland/10 years old/one day play on the beach near home/young man jump into water

a few minutes later/hear shouts/the young man drown/Simon decide to help

Simon swim 100 m/reach young man/young man unconscious/Simon pull him back to the beach

later/young man recover/ambulance take him to hospital/thank Simon for saving his life

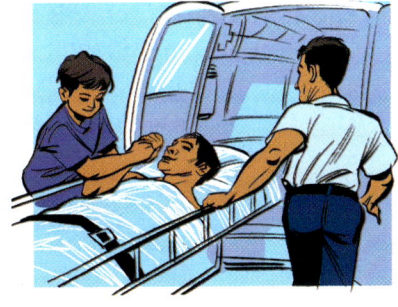

Consolidation Modules 7–11: Speaking, page 98

Situations for speaking.

- two people in the doctor's waiting room
- someone buying an unusual birthday present
- someone's first day in a new office
- someone trying to book a holiday
- someone in a foreign country trying to buy a train ticket
- someone reporting a crime at a police station

Module 12: Practice, Exercise 2, page 103

Student B

- ruck sack
- toothpaste
- swimming trunks
- scissors
- gloves
- tea pot
- washing-up liquid

Module 12: Task, page 105

Student B

You are taking three nephews and nieces (aged 4, 6 and 8) to a nearby city for the day. You are going to a science museum in the morning and to a zoo in the afternoon. It is an hour each way by train. It is autumn and the weather forecast says it might rain.

List • umbrellas

Module 1: Exercise 2, page 11

Group B

HOW HEALTHY ARE YOU?

1. How many hours' sleep .... normally have?
2. .... normally sleep well or .... often awake in the middle of the night?
3. .... usually have a good breakfast in the morning?
4. How many cups of coffee .... normally drink every day?
5. .... smoke? If yes, ... a heavy smoker?
6. How often .... drink alcohol?
7. .... play any sports regularly?
8. In your own opinion, ... very fit and healthy, OK or unfit?

145

Communication activities

Module 6: Task, Exercise 2, page 53

European City Tour: Fact File

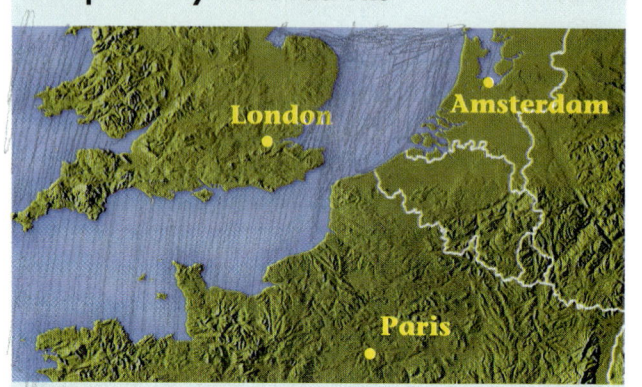

Main places to visit: Your holiday begins in **London**, famous for its history and tradition. You can visit Buckingham Palace, and the Houses of Parliament, and of course many excellent theatres and shops. From there, we travel by high-speed Eurostar train to **Paris**. Take a romantic walk by the river Seine and visit Notre Dame, the Louvre and many other famous places. Finally, we move on to the canals, museums and cafés of **Amsterdam**.

How many days? 10. Either 3 days in each city or 6 days in one city (you choose) and 2 days in the others.

Accommodation: In all three cities, accommodation is in three-star or four-star hotels in the city centre.

When to go? July and August are the warmest months (average 18–20°C), but there are fewer tourists in May–June (average 14–16°C) and in September (average 16–18°C).

Optional excursions: You can choose three of the following optional excursions.

London
- Visit the Millennium Dome in Greenwich.
- Take a day trip to the historic city of Cambridge.

Paris
- Enjoy a family day out at Disneyland, Paris.
- Day trip to the beautiful seventeenth-century palace of Versailles.

Amsterdam
- Visit the Keukenhof Gardens, the world's greatest flower show.
- Take a canal trip to the historic town of Arnhem.

Complete the table to design your dream holiday.

Main places to visit	1
	2
	3
Number of days	
Accommodation in each place	
Best time to go and why	
Optional excursions you prefer	1
	2
	3

Module 13: Task, page 113

Student B

CRISTINA SCARLATTI

A well-known student politician, Cristina Scarlatti was born in Queenstown and was a student at the university. After leaving university she travelled overseas doing voluntary work for three years. Now 25 years old, she has been editor of the student newspaper Young Voice for two years. An excellent speaker, she is very popular with the young people of Queenstown. Her main promise is to stop corruption, and to spend more money on schools and hospitals. Her slogan is, 'Queenstown: Time for a Change.'

Module 5: Exercise 2, page 44

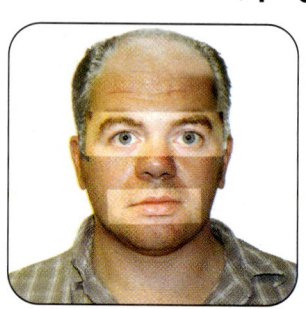

Communication activities

Module 13: Exercise 2, page 111

Student B

1 .... the word 'height'?
   a H-E-I-G-H-T   b H-I-G-H-T   c H-I-T-E
2 .... did US President Bill Clinton pay for a haircut in at Los Angeles airport in 1993?
   a $8   b $830   c $83,000
3 What's the best answer to the suggestion '.......... going to see a film tonight?'
   a Yes, good idea.   b Yes, I will.
   c Yes, I'd like.
4 .... have East and West Germany been reunited?
   a since 1945   b since 1985
   c since 1990
5 What is the best answer to the question, 'How do you do?'
   a Fine thanks, and you?
   b How do you do?   c Not bad.
6 .... did world record holder Fred Rompelberg ride his bicycle in October 1995?
   a 26 km an hour   b 159 km an hour
   c 268 km an hour

Module 12: Task, page 105

Student C

> You are going with a group of friends for a picnic in the country by a river. It is the middle of summer and the weather forecast for the day is very hot. You are travelling by bus and the journey is two hours each way.
> List • plastic plates and cups

Module 14: Exercise 2, page 119

Student B

147

Irregular verbs

Verb	Past Simple	Past Participle
be	was / were	been
beat	beat	beaten
become	became	become
begin	began	begun
break	broke	broken
bring	brought	brought
build	built	built
burn	burned / burnt	burned / burnt
buy	bought	bought
can	could	been able
catch	caught	caught
choose	chose	chosen
come	came	come
cost	cost	cost
cut	cut	cut
do	did	done
draw	drew	drawn
dream	dreamed / dreamt	dreamed / dreamt
drink	drank	drunk
drive	drove	driven
eat	ate	eaten
fall	fell	fallen
feed	fed	fed
feel	felt	felt
fight	fought	fought
find	found	found
fly	flew	flown
forget	forgot	forgotten
get	got	got
give	gave	given
go	went	gone / been
have	had	had
hear	heard	heard
hide	hid	hidden
hit	hit	hit
hurt	hurt	hurt
keep	kept	kept
know	knew	known
lead	led	led
learn	learned / learnt	learned / learnt
leave	left	left

Verb	Past Simple	Past Participle
lend	lent	lent
let	let	let
lie	lay	lain
light	lit	lit
lose	lost	lost
make	made	made
mean	meant	meant
meet	met	met
must	had to	had to
pay	paid	paid
put	put	put
read / ri:d /	read / red /	read / red /
ring	rang	rung
run	ran	run
say	said	said
see	saw	seen
sell	sold	sold
send	sent	sent
set	set	set
shoot	shot	shot
show	showed	shown
shut	shut	shut
sing	sang	sung
sit	sat	sat
sleep	slept	slept
smell	smelled / smelt	smelled / smelt
speak	spoke	spoken
spend	spent	spent
spill	spilled / spilt	spilled / spilt
stand	stood	stood
steal	stole	stolen
swim	swam	swum
take	took	taken
teach	taught	taught
tell	told	told
think	thought	thought
understand	understood	understood
wake	woke	woken
wear	wore	worn
win	won	won
write	wrote	written

Language summary

Module 1

A Question words

To ask about:	We use:
a thing	**What**'s that under the table? **Which** coat is yours?
a time	**When**'s your next holiday?
a place	**Where** do you go at Christmas?
a reason	**Why** do you always wear blue?
a person	**Who**'s your favourite film star?
the way you do something	**How** do you remember their names?
a period of time	**How long** does the programme last?
the number of times you do something	**How often** do you see Maria?
the cost of something	**How much** is this?

1 We use **what** if there are many possible answers.
What's your name?

2 We use **which** if there are only a few possible answers.
Which girls' names begin with J and end with E?

Some other expressions with *what* and *which*.

What sort of computer have you got?
Which countries do you want to visit?
What time does the newsagent's open?
Which part of Poland is Wroclaw in?
What colour are his eyes?
What size are your shoes?

B Word order in questions

1 With the verb *be* we put the subject after the verb.
They are in the kitchen. – Are they in the kitchen?
You were late for class. – Were you late for class?

2 With the Present Simple, we put the auxiliary *do* or *does* before the subject.
You like skiing. – Do you like skiing?
Jamie works in that office. – Does Jamie work in that office?

3 If *who* or *what* asks about the **subject**, the word order is the same as in a statement.
Who lives in that strange house?
What happens at midnight on 31st December?

4 If *who* or *what* asks about the **object**, we put the auxiliary *do* or *does* before the subject.
Who do you (= subject) know in the class?
What does Gina (= subject) wear to the gym?

C Present Simple

	I / you / we / they	he / she / it
+	know	knows
?	Do you know?	Does he know?
–	I don't (= do not) know.	She doesn't (= does not) know.

We use the Present Simple for:
a habits. *He goes for a run before breakfast.*
b things that are generally / always true. *They live in a small village.*

These are the spelling rules for *he / she / it*.

Verb	Rule	Example
ends in a consonant + -y (fly)	change -y to -ies	This airline **flies** to Malawi.
ends in -s (miss) -x (fix) -ch (catch) -sh (wash)	add -es	She **misses** him. He **fixes** old cars. She **catches** the 6.30 train. She **washes** her hair in beer.
do and go	add -es	He **does** all the cooking.
all other verbs	add -s	My sister **speaks** German.

D Showing how often things happen

1 Adverbs

never   sometimes   often   usually / generally   always
0%   100%

a With most verbs, we put the adverb before the main verb.
We never drink wine at lunchtime.

b With the verb *be*, we put the adverb after the verb.
He's always late.

2 Other phrases

every	day
once / twice / X times a	week month

a We usually put these phrases at the end of the sentence.
We go swimming every week.
She cleans her teeth twice a day.

b But we can also put them at the beginning of the sentence.
Every day I go for a short walk in the park.
Once a month we go out for a really nice meal.

Language summary

Module 2

A Past Simple

Regular Past Simple forms end in *-ed* in the positive form.
But many verbs have an **irregular** past form (see list on page 148).

+	I / you / he / she / it / we / they	liked (reg) saw (irreg)	the film.
–	I / you / he / she / it / we / they	didn't like / see	the film.
?	Did	I / you / he / she / it / we / they	like / see	the film?

1 We use the Past Simple to talk about a finished action or state in the past. It can be something that happened once or many times. We often say **when** it happened.
He **died** in 1970. (= single action)
My dad **took** me to school every morning. (= repeated action)
We **lived** in a very small house in those days. (= state)

2 For regular verbs, we add *-ed* (watch**ed**, start**ed**). But there are some exceptions.

Verb	Rule	Example
ends in one *-e* (*hate*)	add *-d*	I hat**ed** spinach.
has one syllable and ends in vowel + 1 consonant (*stop*)	double the final consonant	They **stopped** for lunch.
ends in consonant + *-y* (*carry*)	change *-y* to *-ied*	He **carried** the bags all the way home.
has two syllables and ends in one vowel + *-l* (*travel*)	double the *-l*	We **travelled** with three friends.

3 The past of *be* is *was/were*.

+	I / he / she / it **was** late	we / you / they **were** late
–	I / he / she / it **wasn't** (= was not) late	we / you / they **weren't** (were not) late
?	**Was** I / he / she / it late?	**Were** we / you / they late?

B Time phrases often used in the past

1 In, on, at

These time phrases can also be used in the present and future.
a *at* + time   at 9.30
              2/3 days   at the weekend   at Christmas
b *on* + day, date   on Wednesday, 10th July
              day + part of day on Wednesday morning
c *in* + month   in June
              season   in the winter   year   in 1993
              part of day in the afternoon decade in the 1960s

2 Ago

Ago means *before now*. We use it to show how far in the past something happened.
I first met Jackie two years **ago**.
We do not use *ago* after specific time periods with *the*.
I met him ~~ago~~ the summer ~~ago~~. (in)

3 No preposition

We do not need *in*, *on* or *at* **last**, **yesterday**, **this**
I saw him yesterday / last Thursday / this morning.

Module 3

A Can, can't, have to, don't have to

1 Can, can't

+	I / you / he / she / we / they **can**	speak English.
–	I / you / he / she / we / they **can't** (= cannot)	speak English.
?	**Can** I / you / he / she / we / they	speak English?

We use *can* and *can't* to talk about what is or isn't possible.
a ability
   Sue **can dance** quite well but she **can't sing**.
b permission
   You **can't come** in here.
   Can we **go** home now?

2 Have to, don't have to

	I / you / we / they	he / she / it
+	have to go now	has to go now
–	don't have to go now	doesn't have to go now
?	Do I have to go now?	Does he have to go now?

a We use *have to* if something is necessary (or very important).
   In my country you **have to stay** at school until you are fifteen.
b *Have to* is very similar to *must*.
   We **must go** now.   (= it's necessary)
   We **have to** go now.   (= it's necessary)
c We use *don't have to* if something is not necessary or important.
   We **don't have to wear** a uniform at my new school.

> **REMEMBER!**
> Don't have to is **not** the same as mustn't.
>
> You **mustn't** take any photographs. (= you can't, it's prohibited)
> You **don't have to** take any photographs. (= it's not necessary)

B Should / Shouldn't

+	I / you / he / she / we / they should buy a dictionary.
–	I / you / he / she / we / they shouldn't worry about the exam.
?	Should I / you / he / she / we / they come in now?

1 We use *should* to say that something is a good idea, or the right thing to do. We use *shouldn't* to say that something is not a good idea or not the right thing to do.
You **should try** to learn three new words every day.
Those CDs **shouldn't be** on the floor!

150

Language summary

2 *Should* is less strong than *have to*.
We **have to leave** now or we'll be late.   (= this is necessary)
We **should leave** now or we'll be tired for work tomorrow.   (= this is a good idea)

Module 4

A Present Continuous

+	–	?
I'm going.	I'm not going.	Am I going?
You / We / They're going.	You / We / They aren't going.	Are you / we / they going?
He / She's going.	He / She isn't going.	Is he / she going?

1 We use the Present Continuous for: something happening at this moment or something happening in the present period, but perhaps not at this moment.
Sue**'s phoning** her boyfriend.
We**'re studying** French this term.

2 For *–ing* forms with most verbs, we add *-ing* (star**ting**, go**ing**, buy**ing**). But there are some exceptions.

Verb	Rule	Example
ends in one *-e* (*make*)	take away *-e*	What are you **making**?
has one syllable and ends in vowel + 1 consonant (*stop*)	double the final consonant	Why is the train **stopping**?
ends in *-ie* (*lie*)	change *-ie* to *-y*	He's **lying** in bed.
has two syllables, ends in vowel + 1 consonant, stress on the last syllable (*begin*)	double the final consonant	I'm **beginning** my new course today.
has two syllables and ends in 'l' (*travel*)	double the *-l*	They're **travelling** in Peru this month.

3 We do not usually use some verbs in the continuous form. These verbs describe states (things which stay the same): *believe, know, like, love, own, remember, understand, want*.
I **believe** what she said.   (not I'm believing what she said.)

B Present Continuous for future arrangements

1 We use the Present Continuous to talk about what we have arranged to do in the future.
A: What **are** you **doing** next weekend? (= what have you arranged?)
B: **I'm taking** my little sister to the zoo on Saturday afternoon, then **I'm cooking** lunch for some friends on Sunday. (= I've arranged to take my sister to the zoo, and I've invited my friends to lunch)

2 When we use the Present Continuous like this, we either give a future time (for example *next weekend*), or we know from the situation that we are talking about the future.

Module 5

A Comparative and superlative adjectives

1 One-syllable adjectives and two-syllable adjectives ending in *-y*

Adjective	Comparative	Superlative	Spelling rule
cheap	cheap**er**	**the** cheap**est**	most adjectives: + *-er*, *the -est*
dark	dark**er**	**the** dark**est**	
nice	nic**er**	**the** nic**est**	adjective ends in *-e*: + *-r*, *the -st*
large	larg**er**	**the** larg**est**	
thin	thin**ner**	**the** thin**nest**	1 vowel + 1 consonant: double the consonant
big	big**ger**	**the** big**gest**	
happy	happ**ier**	**the** happ**iest**	change *-y* to *-i*

2 Other two-syllable adjectives and longer adjectives

famous	**more** famous	**the most** famous
attractive	**more** attractive	**the most** attractive

But we usually use *-er* and *the -est* with: *clever, quiet, simple, gentle*.

3 Irregular forms

good	better	the best
bad	worse	the worst
far	farther / further	the farthest / furthest

4 Prepositions in comparative phrases
I think he's **more attractive than** his brother.
Your eyes are very **similar to** your mother's.
Are these glasses **different from** your old ones?
Do you think he **looks like** his father?
No, I'm sure they're not **the same as** mine.
My little sister's **the tallest in** the family! (not *of* the family)

5 Making comparisons with nouns
Julie spends **more time** at the gym than anyone I know.
Our team won **the most games** last year.

B Describing what people look like

1 We use questions with *have got* to ask about features, for example *nose, mouth, eyes, beard, moustache, glasses*.

Has he got a beard (noun)?   No, he hasn't.
Has she got big eyes (noun)?   Yes, very big!

2 We use the verb *be* in these questions.

Is he tall or short (adjective)?   He's very tall.
How old (adjective) is she?   She's about 35.
How tall (adjective) is he?   He's about average height.
What colour (noun) is her hair?   It's darkish. (= quite dark)
What size (noun) are her feet?   Size 38, I think.

3 We use the question *What does he / she look like?* to ask about appearance in general.
A: What **does** your boyfriend **look like**?
B: He's tall and quite good-looking, and he's got long hair.

151

Language summary

4 We use the question *What is / are* (noun) ... *like?* when we mean *Tell me about ...*, *Describe ...* or *Give me your opinion about ...* It is used for character, as well as appearance.
   A: What**'s** your piano teacher (noun) **like**?
   B: Oh, he's lovely. He's very old and grey, and patient with me.

> **REMEMBER**
> We do not use *like* in the answer.   He's ~~like~~ lovely.
> We do not use *How ...?* to ask about appearance or character.
> We use *How ...? to ask about things that change, for example health, work.*
> A: **How** are you this morning?   B: I'm fine, thanks.
> A: **How** was school today?   B: Really good, I got 'A' for English!

Module 6

A Intentions and wishes

1 Going to, planning to

+	I'm You / We / They're He / She's	going to planning to	buy a car.
−	I'm not You / We / They're not He / She's not	going to planning to	buy a car.
?	Am I Are you / we / they Is he / she	going to planning to	buy a car?

a We use *going to* to talk about what we intend to do in the future. It can be the near future or the more distant future.
   I**'m going to be** a famous actor.
   Are you **going to see** him again?

b We normally use *planning to* when we have thought carefully about the plan and decided how to do it.
   What **are** you **planning to say** at the meeting?
   I**'m planning to leave** this company next year.

2 Would like to, would prefer to

+	I / You / He / She / We / They	would like to have a holiday. would prefer to go by train.
−	I / You / He / She / We / They	wouldn't like to miss the plane.* wouldn't prefer to sit at the back.*
?	Would I / you / he / she / we / they	like to stay in a hotel? prefer to pay by credit card?

* These negative forms exist but we do not use them very often.

a We use *would like to* to say what we want to do.
   I**'d like to travel** round the world.
   It is less direct than *want to* and we often use it to be polite.
   I**'d like to change** some money, please.

b We use *would prefer to* to say we want to do something more than something else.
   I**'d prefer to go** on a cycling holiday. Beach holidays are boring.
   Would you **prefer to have** a view of the sea or the mountains?

B Will for predictions

+	I / You / He / She / We / They	**'ll be** here at six.
−	I / You / He / She / We / They	**won't see** him next week.
?	**Will** I / you / he / she / we / they	**have** time to phone them?

1 We use *will* to say what we **expect** to happen. We use it when there is **no** particular plan or intention.
   The weather **will be** *lovely in June.*   (= this is what I expect)
   Will *there* **be** *a lot of people?*   (= what do you expect?)

   Notice the difference between *will* and *going to* here.
   We're **going to visit** *the National Gallery today.*   (= this is what we intend / plan)
   It'll probably be really busy and we'll have to queue.   (= this is what I expect, but it's **not** a plan)

2 We often use *will* with *I think* or *I don't think*.
   *Do you think we***'ll win**?
   *I don't think she***'ll be** *very pleased about this.*

3 Notice the *will* forms of *can* and *have to / must*.
   *You***'ll be able to see** *the mountains from your hotel room.*
   London's terribly expensive! You **won't be able to buy** *anything.*
   *If you go to Warsaw in March, you***'ll have to take** *a warm coat.*

Module 7

A Present Perfect

We form the Present Perfect with *have / has* + past participle.
Regular past participles end in *-ed* in the positive form.
Many verbs have an **irregular** past participle (see list on page 148).

+	I / you / we / they've finished / won	he / she / it's finished / won
−	I / you / we / they haven't finished / won	he / she / it hasn't finished / won
?	Have I / you / we / they finished / won?	Has he / she / it finished / won?

We use the Present Perfect to talk about the past and present together. The Present Perfect tells us something about the present.
   I**'ve met** *your new boss before.*   (= I know something about her now)
   *They***'ve left** *the country.*   (= they are not in the country now)

B Present Perfect and Past Simple with *for*

1 We use the Present Perfect with *for* to talk about an action or state which continues from the past to the present.
   *My dad***'s worked** *at the post office* **for** *fifteen years.*

2 We use the Past Simple with *for* to talk about a past action or state in a period of time which is finished.
   We **had** *our dog* **for** *two years and then he ran away.*

152

Language summary

C Present Perfect and Past Simple with other time words

1 To talk about actions or states in a period of time that is finished, we use the **Past Simple** with:
a days, dates, times, years.
They arrived **on Saturday, at about four o'clock.**
I started college **in 1998.**

b *last* and *ago*.
Did you see the football match **last** night?
They moved away two or three years **ago**.

c questions and statements with *when*.
She got married **when** she was seventeen.
When did you get home?

2 To talk about actions or states in a period of time which continues from the past to the present, we use the **Present Perfect** with:
a no time reference.
He's lived in lots of different countries.

b adverbs such as *never, already, just, recently, lately, yet*.
I've **never** liked eggs.   (= not at any time)
He's **already** gone.   (= before now, maybe before you expected)
Mum's **just** made a cake.   (= a short time before now)
She's **recently** got married.   (= not long ago)
They've had a lot of problems **lately**.   (= like recently, but goes at the end of the sentence)
Have you finished **yet**? I haven't had time **yet**.   (= before now, not used in the positive form)

c *this*.
I haven't seen Marco **this morning**.   (= the morning isn't finished)

d *times*.
I've told him to clean his room **three times!**

Module 8

A Using articles

1 We use *a* or *an* the first time we mention something. When we mention it again, we use *the*.
I saw **a** beautiful vase in **an** antique shop a few days ago. When I went back to **the** shop yesterday, **the** vase wasn't there any more!

2 We do **not** use *the*:
a to make general statements about a group of things or people.
Dogs make very good pets.
American people eat a lot of fast food.

b with many place names.

continents	Africa, Asia	countries	Spain, Poland
cities	Madrid, Sydney	lakes	Lake Como
islands	Sicily, Jersey	hills	Primrose Hill
mountains	Mount Fuji	streets	Oxford Street
roads	Camden Road		

3 We use *the*:
a with some place names.

oceans and seas	the Arctic Ocean, the Tasman Sea
rivers	the Danube, the Thames
mountain ranges	the Alps, the Himalayas
countries which are republics or unions	the UK, the Czech Republic
groups of countries and islands	the Netherlands, the West Indies

b with superlative forms.
the longest river in the world

c when there is only one and we see it as unique.
the Sun, **the** Earth, **the** Moon, **the** Sky, **the** Pope

B Phrases with and without *the*

a with *the*
on the left, on the right, in the middle, in the centre
in the east, in the west, in the south, in the north
on the floor, on the wall, on the ceiling
on the coast, on the border
at the top, at the bottom
in the morning, in the afternoon, in the evening

b without *the*
at home, at work, at school, at university, at college
in bed, in hospital, in prison
at night, at sunset
on holiday

Module 9

A *May, might, will, definitely / probably* etc., for making predictions

	will definitely	win the game. (= you are sure this will happen)
	will probably may (not)	win the game. (= you are less sure)
I / You / He / She / We / They	might (not)	win the game. (= you think it's possible)
	probably won't	win the game. (= you think it's less possible)
	definitely won't	win the game. (= you are sure this won't happen)

Notice that *definitely* and *probably* come after *will* but before *won't*.

153

Language summary

B Present tense after *if*, *when*, *before* and other time words

Look at these examples, which talk about the future.
I'll go to the bank *if I* **have** time.
(not *I'll* go to the bank *if I* ~~will~~ have time.)
When Clarke arrives, *I'll* ask him about the money.
(not **When** Clarke ~~will~~ arrive, *I'll* ask him about the money.)

1 We are talking about the **future**, but we use a **present** tense:
a *if / when*
If Sandra phones, I'll tell her. (= you think Sandra might phone)
When Sandra phones, I'll tell her. (= you know Sandra will phone)

b *when / as soon as*
As soon as John arrives, we'll have lunch. (= you want to have lunch immediately)
When John arrives, we'll have lunch. (= it is not so urgent)

2 In the other part of the sentence (the main clause), we use:
a a future verb form.
Next time I see you, **I'll be** married!
I **won't see** the children before I leave.
When the rain stops, **I'm going to take** the dog for a walk.
As soon as I finish work on Friday, **I'm flying** to New York.

b other modal verbs.
Before you go out, you **should do** your homework.
If you're good, I **might buy** you an ice cream.
If Sue comes on Saturday, she **may bring** her new boyfriend.
When François gets here, we **can start** the meeting.
After you finish that, you **must go** to bed.

Module 10

A Used to

+	I / You / He / She / We / They	used to	walk to school.
–	I / You / He / She / We / They	didn't use to	have a car.
?	Did I / you / he / she / we / they	use to	go by train?

1 We use *used to*:
a for actions that happened more than once in the past.
He **used to wait** for me at the school gates.

b for past states.
They **used to live** in a house by the river.

Notice that the action or state may **not** be true now.
We **used to have** two dogs. (= we don't have the dogs now)
Or it may be true now.
I **didn't use to** like Maths at school. (= and I still don't like it)

2 We can always use the Past Simple instead of *used to*.
We **had** a dog called Tilly. I **didn't like** Maths.

3 We do **not** use *used to* for actions that happened only once.
I went skiing last Christmas. (not I ~~used to~~ go)

B Past Continuous

+	I / He / She was looking	We / You / They were looking
–	I / He / She wasn't looking	We / You / They weren't looking
?	Was I / he / she looking?	Were we / you / they looking?

1 We use the Past Continuous to talk about actions in progress:
a at a certain time in the past.
I **was driving** home at 6.30 this evening.
The action started some time **before** 6.30.

b when another (completed) action happened.
I **was cooking** dinner when she came home.
The Past Continuous action started first.

2 We often use the Past Continuous to describe the background situation in a story. The main events are in the Past Simple.
I **was sitting** in my car, **listening** to the radio, when suddenly that idiot **crashed** into me!

3 Sometimes the other action interrupts the Past Continuous.
She **was crossing** the road when she **slipped** on some ice.
(= she stopped crossing the road)

4 When two actions happen one after the other, we use the Past Simple.
When I **heard** the crash, I **ran** to the end of the street.

> **REMEMBER!**
> State verbs are not used in the continuous form.
> knew
> I ~~was knowing~~ / her when we were children.

5 We use *when*, *while* and *as* to join Past Continuous and Past Simple parts of a sentence.
I saw Karl **when / while / as** I was getting off the train.

We do not use *while* with a single completed action in the Past Simple.
The sun was shining **when / ~~while~~ / as** we got to the top of the hill.

Module 11

A Gerunds (-*ing* forms)

We use gerunds (-*ing* forms) in the same way as nouns / pronouns:
a as the subject of the sentence.
Learning English is very important for my career.
Going to the gym regularly is very good for you.

b after certain verbs that express likes and dislikes, for example *like, love, enjoy, hate, don't mind, can't stand, feel like*.
I always **enjoy** see**ing** my grandchildren.
I **don't mind** cook**ing** dinner, if you're tired.

> **REMEMBER!**
> A large number of other verbs are also followed by the gerund, for example suggest, finish, give up, go on, spend time, imagine.
>
> Mary suggested **having** a break, and the others agreed.
> I finished **writing** that report at 2 a.m.

c after prepositions.
Do you feel OK **about** stay**ing** here on your own?
Did you know Ferdie's frightened **of** fly**ing**?

Language summary

B Like versus would like to

1 We use *like* when we talk about things in general that we enjoy.
   *My little brother **likes** horror films.*
   If we put another verb after *like*, we use the *-ing* form.
   *I **like** stay**ing** in bed late.   He **doesn't like** ly**ing** on the beach.*

2 We use *would like* when we talk about things we want to happen in the future. (We often use it to be more polite.)
   *I'**d like** a new tennis racket for my birthday.*
   If we put another verb after *would like*, we use *to* + verb.
   *We'**d like to speak** to the manager, please.*

> **REMEMBER!**
> We often use *Would you like …?* for an offer or an invitation.
>
> **Would you like** a coffee before you go?
> **Would you like to have** lunch with me?
>
> Notice that the answer is:
> Yes, I would. or Yes, I'd love to. (not Yes, ~~I'd like.~~ or Yes, ~~I'd love.~~)

3 Other verbs with gerunds / infinitives follow a similar pattern.
a Verbs which express general likes / dislikes **+ gerund**.
   *She **loves** horse-riding.*
b Verbs that express particular wishes for the future **+ infinitive**.
   *I'**d love to go** somewhere hot for our holidays this year.*
   *She **hopes to become** a ballerina one day.*

C So and neither

To agree with a positive sentence we use *so*, to agree with a negative sentence we use *neither*:

| Positive: | I love pizza. | – **So** do I. |
| Negative: | I'm not ready | – **Neither** am I |

The verb after *so* and *neither* 'agrees' with the verb in the first sentence. Notice the order of the subject and verb:

   1   2   1 2.
   I **was** ill yesterday.   – So **was** I.

With the Present and Past Simple we need to use *do* or *did*:
   I **know** the answer.   – So **do** I.
   I **slept** badly.   – So **did** I.

Module 12

A Passive forms

We form the passive with the subject + *be* + past participle. Regular past participles end in *-ed*. Many verbs have an **irregular** past participle (see list on page 148).

	+	–	?
Present Simple	It's / They're made	It isn't / They aren't made	Is it / Are they made?
Past Simple	It was / They were made	It wasn't / They weren't made	Was it / Were they made?
Will	It'll / They'll be made	It won't / They won't be made	Will it / Will they be made?

1 We use the passive when the person who does the action is not important or not known.
   *This chocolate **is made** in Switzerland.*
   (= where it is made is more important than who makes it)

   *Hundreds of cars **are stolen** every week.*
   (= we do not know who steals them)

2 When we want to say who or what is the 'doer' of the action (the agent), we use *by*.
   *All her clothes are designed **by** Armani.*
   *The boy's bicycle was hit **by** a black car.*

3 Active or passive? Compare the following examples:
a *Martine **posted** the letter last week*   (= active)
b *The letter **was posted** last week.*   (= passive)

In example a, we use the active because we are interested in **who** posted the letter, so Martine is the subject of the sentence. In example b, we use the passive because we are most interested in **the letter**, not in who posted it. The letter is the subject of the sentence.
We use the passive when we are speaking formally, or writing letters or reports. We often find the passive in news reports.
*More than 3,000 people **were killed** by the hurricane.*

B Sentences joined with *that*, *which* and *who*

That, *which* and *who* are relative pronouns. We use them instead of *it*, *he*, *she* or *they* to join two parts of a sentence.

1 We use *that* or *which* for **things**.
   *Gloves are woollen things **which** keep your hands warm.*
   *Washing powder is stuff **that** makes your clothes clean.*

Notice that we cannot use *what* here.
                              which / that
   Did you read the letter ^ ~~what~~ arrived this morning?

2 We use *who* or *that* for **people**.
   *A carpenter is a person **who** makes things from wood.*
   *I saw a girl in town **that** went to the same school as me.*

Notice that *who* is more usual than *that*.

> **REMEMBER!**
> We do **not** use *he, she, it* or *they* with a relative pronoun.
>
> A person who ~~he~~ sells houses and flats is an estate agent.
> What do you call the thing which ~~it~~ takes telephone messages?

3 We can leave out *that*, *which* or *who* when it is the object.
   It's a hat which you wear in the sun.
   OR
   It's a hat you wear in the sun.
   Hat is the object of the verb *wear*, so we can leave it out.
   BUT
   It's a hat which protects you from the sun.
   Hat is the subject of the verb *protect*, so we cannot leave it out.

Module 13

A Present Perfect Simple and Continuous with the 'unfinished past'

	Present Perfect Simple	Present Perfect Continuous
+	I / We / They've read it. He / She's read it.	I / We / They've been reading. He / She's been reading.
–	I etc. haven't read it. He etc. hasn't read it.	I etc. haven't been reading. He etc. hasn't been reading.
?	Have you etc. read it? Has he / she read it?	Have you etc. been reading? Has he / she been reading?

155

Language summary

1 Sometimes we want to talk about an action that started in the past and continues up to the present. We can call this the 'unfinished past'. We can use both the Present Perfect Simple and the Present Perfect Continuous.
I**'ve worked** here since I was twenty-two.
I**'ve been reading** all afternoon.

We often use the Present Perfect Continuous here, because continuous forms show **duration**.

2 But if a verb describes a **state** (for example, *like, love, be, have, see, know*, etc.) we cannot put it in the continuous form.
I've known her all my life. (not I've ~~been knowing~~)
We've had this car for ages. (not We've ~~been having~~)

3 The following time phrases are often used to describe 'the unfinished past'.
How long have you been waiting?
I've been trying to speak to him **all morning / all day** etc.

B *For* and *since*

The use of *for* and *since* is similar, but *for* is used with periods of time.
She's been on the phone **for hours**.
I haven't seen her **for about three weeks**.

Since is used with points in time.
He's been off work **since last Friday**.
We've been living here **since about 1995**.

2 We usually use **any** in:
a sentences with a negative meaning.
There aren't **any** cinemas where I live.
b questions, when the answer can be 'yes' or 'no'.
Are there **any** shops near your house?

3 **No** means the same as *not any*.
There's **no** bread left.
Notice that the verb is positive. We do **not** say:
~~There isn't no~~ bread left.

4 **A few** means 'a small number of'. We usually use it in positive sentences.
I've got **a few** minutes now, if you want to speak to me.

5 We usually use **a lot of** (also **lots of**) in positive sentences, meaning 'a large number of'.
There are **a lot of** nice places to eat round here.

6 We usually use **many** and **much** in negative sentences or in questions.
I haven't got **much** money at the moment.
Are there **many** tourists at this time of year?

7 **Too much** and **too many** have a negative meaning. We use them when we mean 'more than the right amount'.
I can't work here – there's **too much** noise.
We've got **too many** things in this room – it's impossible to move.

8 **Not enough** has a negative meaning. We use it when we mean 'less than the right amount'.
There are**n't enough** places for children to play.

Module 14

A *Some, any* and quantifiers

With plural nouns		With uncountable nouns	
(not) many too many a few	minutes pounds	(not) much too much	time money

With plural nouns and uncountable nouns	
some (not) any no a lot of (also 'lots of') not enough	minutes pounds time money

> **REMEMBER!**
> We do not use *some, any* and other quantifiers with singular countable nouns.
> Would you like ~~some~~ a piece of cake?

1 **Some** means 'an indefinite number of'. We usually use it in positive sentences.
There are **some** beautiful pictures in the museum.

We can also use *some* to make questions more positive, for example if you expect the answer 'yes'.
Would you like **some** more wine? (= an offer)
Could you get me **some** milk? (= a request)

B Describing where things are

1 A is **in front of** B.
B is **behind** A.

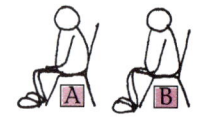

2 A is **next to** C.
B is **near** A and C.

3 A is **above** B.
B is **below** A.

4 A is **between** B **and** C.

5 A is **opposite** B.

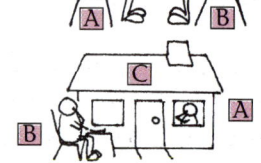

6 A is **inside** C.
B is **outside** C.

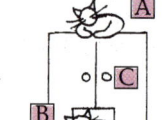

7 A is **on top of** C.
B is **at the bottom of** C.

Language summary

Module 15

A Past Perfect

We form the Past Perfect with *had* + past participle. Regular past participles end in *-ed*. Many verbs have an **irregular** past participle (see list on page 148).

+	I / You / He / She / We / They 'd gone
–	I / You / He / She / We / They hadn't gone
?	Had I / you / he / she / we / they gone?

1 We use the Past Perfect to show that one action happened before another in the past, and that the first action finished before the second action started.
 When I **looked** out of the window the rain **had stopped**.

2 We often use the Past Perfect with *because* to explain a past situation.
 Patrick **felt** ill because **he'd eaten** all the chocolates.

3 To show that two actions happened at the same time, we use the Past Simple.
 He **woke up** when the telephone **rang**.

4 If the sequence of actions is clear from the context, we do not use the Past Perfect.
 I **left** the house and **went** to the station. (not I had left the house and went to the station.)

B Reported speech

	Direct speech (someone's actual words)	Reported speech (reporting what someone said)
	Before we went on holiday, the travel agent said:	
Present Simple	'The hotel **is** near the sea.'	… (that) the hotel **was** near the sea.
Past Simple	'Everyone **enjoyed** the holiday last year.'	… (that) everyone **had enjoyed** the holiday last year / the year before.
Will	'The weather **will be** lovely.'	… (that) the weather **would** be lovely.

1 The verb forms change because what the travel agent said is now in the past.
Notice that:
a we can leave out *that* in reported speech.
 She said the hotel was very cheap.

b we can change *last year* to *the year before* and *yesterday* to *the day before*.

c we sometimes need to change the possessive adjective.
 '**My** son lives in Monte Carlo,' she said.
 She said (that) **her** son lived in Monte Carlo.

2 *Say* and *tell*
 He **said** (that) he was a film star.   He said me …
 He **told me** (that) he was a film star.   He told (that) he …

3 If what the person said is still true, we do not need to use reported speech.
 'Australia's really beautiful.'
 He said (that) Australia's really beautiful.

Module 16

A Conditional sentences with *would*

If + Past Simple + *would (n't)* + infinitive without *to*

If I **became** president,   I **would build** more roads.
  I **wouldn't pay** politicians more.
  would you **vote** for me?

We use conditional sentences with *would* to talk about imaginary situations. The verb after *if* is in the past tense, but we are **not** talking about the past. We are talking about a general present time.
 If I **had** a ticket, I'**d come** with you.   (= the speaker hasn't got a ticket)
 If you **lived** in the country, you'**d get** bored.   (= the person doesn't live in the country)

Notice that:
1 we can change the order of the two clauses.
 You'd get bored if you lived in the country.

2 we can use *were* instead of *was* after *I / he / she / it*.
 If he **were** here now, he'**d tell** you the truth.

 we often use *If I were you, I'd …* to give advice.
 If I **were** you, I'**d forget** all about it.

3 we can use *might* or *could* instead of *would*.
 If you **worked** hard, you **might** pass the exam.
 If I **borrowed** Mum's car, I **could** give you a lift.

B *Will* and *would*

If + present + *will (won't)* + infinitive without *to*

If the weather'**s** nice tomorrow, I'**ll phone** you.
  I **won't go** to work.
  will you **go** swimming?

1 We use *will* to talk about real possibilities in the future.
 If Frank **phones**, I'**ll tell** him you want to see him.

2 We use *would* to talk about imaginary situations.
 If I **were** taller, I'**d buy** that suit.

3 The choice of *will* or *would* sometimes depends on how we see a situation. Look at these examples:
 If I **get** the job, I'**ll take** you out for a meal.
 If I **got** the job, I'**d earn** a lot more money.

In the first sentence, the speaker thinks it is a real possibility that he will get the job. In the second sentence, the speaker thinks it is unlikely that he will get the job (the situation is 'imaginary' for him).

157

Tapescripts

Module 1

Recording 1
a   The Winter Olympics are held every four years, just the same as the main Olympics.
b   The Barcelona Olympics were in 1992.
c   A 100 metres race normally starts when someone fires a gun.
d   Judo originated in Japan, but it is now popular all over the world.
e   An ice hockey match has three periods of twenty minutes. That's sixty minutes in all.
f   A rugby ball is similar to the type used in ordinary football, but there is one important difference, the shape, which is oval or egg-shaped.
g   Baseball is the national sport in the USA.
h   There are 21 spots on a dice.
i   The white player always starts in a game of chess.
j   The three most important sports in which players use a racket are tennis, badminton, and squash.
k   The referee tosses a coin to decide which way the two teams will play.
l   They play extra time until someone scores a goal. If there are no goals after thirty minutes, there is a penalty competition.

Recording 3
a   When do you usually play football?
b   Who do you play with?
c   Where do you usually play?
d   Why do you play?
e   How often do you have English lessons?
f   How long are the lessons?
g   Which days are the lessons on?
h   How many teachers do you have?

Recording 4
Toshi, a nineteen-year-old, form Nagasaki, in Japan, wants to become a sumo wrestler. Toshi, who weighs over 175 kilos, and is 1 metre 95 tall, lives in a special training camp, called a Heya, with thirty other sumo wrestlers. Their training is very hard. Even before breakfast, they normally practise for four and a half hours! It is important that Toshi doesn't lose weight, so he always has a large lunch of rice, meat, fish and vegetables with lots of beer, and sometimes he eats extra pizzas and burgers. After lunch he goes to sleep for a few hours. One day, Toshi hopes to be famous – and rich – but at the moment he doesn't earn much money, so each month his parents send him money to help him.

Ania, who comes from Lublin in Poland, is a champion gymnast. She's seventeen years old and lives in a small apartment with her mother. She trains very hard – usually about eight hours every day, except Sunday, when she rests. She normally gets up at about seven in the morning and practises for three or four hours. Then she rests in the afternoon, before practising for another four hours in the early evening. Like most gymnasts Ania is very small – only about 1 metre 50, and she weighs very little too – around 40 kilos.
This is very important for a gymnast, so she doesn't eat very much – although her mother makes sure she has a healthy diet! Ania doesn't earn very much money, but she enjoys her lifestyle very much.

Dan, from Bucharest in Romania, is a professional footballer with a big Italian football club. He lives with his Italian girlfriend in a large villa in the mountains near Milan. Although he's only twenty-three years old, he earns around $50,000 a week. He spends his money on fast cars, Italian designer clothes and goes to all the best restaurants and clubs in Milan. But Dan has to live a healthy life – he never smokes and only occasionally drinks alcohol, and most days he lives on a special diet of pasta and vegetables. Most mornings, before he goes to train with the rest of the team, he runs about eight kilometres.

Recording 5
1
WAITER: **Can I help you**, madam?
WOMAN: Yes, **where are the toilets, please**?
WAITER: Over there, next to the bar.
WOMAN: Thanks. And then **can we have the bill, please**?
WAITER: Certainly madam.
2
A: Excuse me. **Do you speak English?**
B: A little bit.
A: **Where's the nearest** underground station – do you know?
B: Over there, next to the cinema. Can you see it?
A: Oh yes. Thank you.
B: **Where are you from?**
A: Ontario, Canada.
B: That's a long way. What are you doing in Warsaw?
A: Oh, I'm just here on business.
B: And **how long are you going to stay**?
A: Just a week, but I'm having a great time!
B: Oh well, good luck and enjoy your stay.
A: Thanks, bye.
3
A: Excuse me. **How much does this cost?**
B: Twelve ninety-nine.
A: OK, right … I'll take it then.
B: **Anything else?**
A: No, that's it thank you
B: How do you want to pay?
A: By credit card, if that's OK.
B: Sure …

Recording 6
Where are you **from**?
What **time** is it?
What's your **date** of **birth**?
How long have you been in England?
How long are you going to **stay**?
How do you **spell** your **name**?
How much does this **cost**?
Where's the nearest **bank**?

Module 2

Recording 3
a   When's your birthday?
b   What time does this lesson finish?
c   What time did it start?
d   When did you last watch TV?
e   Which month does it usually start to get hot in your country?
f   What time do you usually go to bed?
g   In which year were you born?
h   In which decade did your parents grow up?
i   When did your grandparents get married?
j   When is your next holiday?

158

Tapescripts

Recording 4
nervous excited disappointed worried bored surprised guilty frightened angry relaxed in a good mood embarrassed fed up

Recording 7
DAVID: OK well, I remember the first time I went abroad … I was eleven years old at the time, and we had a trip, a school trip to Paris. So to get to Paris we took a coach to London airport, to catch the plane, and it was about a three-hour drive, down the motorway, and about half way we stopped at a service station and had lunch. And then we got back on the coach and continued our journey to the airport and we were nearly in London, nearly at the airport, when the teacher suddenly said, 'Oh my God! I've left the passports in the service station, the place where we stopped for lunch.' So we went all the way back to the service station, collected the passports, drove all the way back to the airport, .finally, finally we got on the plane, arrived in Paris. And the other thing I remember is when I got to Paris, I bought some cakes, some cream cakes. They were so good, I ate, oh I don't know four, five cream cakes … and I was sick, I was so sick. I didn't get out of bed for three days … I was so ill …

JAYNE: I remember very clearly how I met my boyfriend. I had a job, in a shop which sold sandwiches, … I was about nineteen … and when someone asked for a sandwich, we had to cut up the bread with a big, big knife and make the sandwich. So one day, a really gorgeous-looking guy came in and I thought, 'Oh, he's lovely!' and, well, I felt a bit nervous … and he asked for a cheese sandwich 'No problem!' I said. So there were a lot of people in the shop, it was very busy, so very quickly I cut up the bread, made the sandwich, gave the sandwich to this young man … with a big smile on my face … and he looked at the sandwich and went 'Argh!' and I saw the sandwich was all red, it was covered in blood. I'd cut my hand making the sandwich because I was so nervous … and well, there was a silence and then everyone laughed. And I felt so stupid … but anyway, when the shop closed at six o'clock … he came back and asked me out for a pizza, and we started going out!

Module 3

Recording 1
Ildiko
I think for any Hungarian person, learning another language is really important. Most foreigners can't speak Hungarian, of course, so if you want to meet and talk to people from other countries, you have to learn English . . . and of course it's also very important if you want to get a good job!

Karina
It's very important for me to learn Greek, because I'm married to a Greek man! He can speak Danish, of course, so I don't have to speak Greek at home, but when we go to Greece in the summer, I can't talk to my husband's parents or any of the older people in the family, and I think that's really sad.

Dorothy
For me learning Italian is just a hobby. I don't have to study it for a special reason, I just like the language and I like going to my evening classes – it's something to do in the winter. And, of course I love Italy . . . I always go to Italy for my holidays, so then I can practice what I learn . . .

Daniel
My reasons are very simple – I have to learn English for my university exams. At my university, if we don't pass, we can't continue into the second year, and we have to do the first year again! If we pass, we can take another course instead of English – economics or other things – but I want to continue with English, it might be useful one day.

Recording 2 (missing words / phrases only)
a can, have to   b can   c can't
d have to   e don't have to   f can't
g can   h don't have to, have to

Recording 4
ELLEN: There are a lot of laws in Britain about what pupils can and can't study. For example all students at **both primary school and secondary school have to study RE and PE at least once a week**, and all **primary school pupils have to do at least one hour of Maths every day, and one hour of English**. But later in secondary school, students actually have a lot of choice about what they study. **After the age of fourteen** they can stop studying quite a lot of subjects. For example, **they don't have to study Geography or History** if they don't want to. By law, **everyone has to stay at school until they're sixteen** in Britain, but if they choose to stay at school after the age of sixteen, pupils can study what they want to. They have a free choice, depending on what courses the school can offer, of course. For example, you can't study subjects like philosophy or psychology in many secondary schools, but you can easily study these at university if you want to. There is one important rule for entering university though … **if you want to study any subject at all, you have to pass Maths GCSE**. If you don't pass it, you can't go to university. So sometimes if people are really bad at Maths they have to take it three or four times, or they can't go!

Recording 5
KRISTINA: We think it's very important for the teacher to use English as much as possible and only to use the students' language when it's really necessary so the students can hear as much English as possible. The teacher should always give homework. After every lesson there is some homework, but not too much, something quite short, and, of course, I have to correct the homework and give it back quickly so it's good for me if there isn't too much homework! Of course, the teacher should always try to make the lessons interesting. Sometimes it's not so easy, but it's important always to make the effort! Yes, we think that the teacher should always try to answer the students' questions, but it can happen that you don't know, so the teacher shouldn't be afraid to say, 'Sorry I don't know but I'll try to find out for you and I'll tell you next lesson.' You should use the course book, but maybe not every lesson. It's a good idea to bring in other materials from time to time. About correcting mistakes, well, some students say the teacher should always correct all the mistakes, but in fact, if you do that, the students never get to the end of their sentence! I think the teacher should just correct the important mistakes myself.

Recording 6 (missing words / phrases only)
1 could you speak more …, Thank
2 … is it OK if I leave …, go ahead, telling me
3 Can I borrow it …, … here you are
4 Do you mind if I …, What's the problem

159

Tapescripts

Module 4

Recording 1

1. Chinese New Year is either at the end of January or the beginning of February.
2. St Valentine's Day is on the fourteenth February.
3. In Britain, Mother's Day is at the beginning of March, usually the first Sunday in March.
4. Easter is usually between the end of March and the middle of April.
5. May Day is on the first of May. In some countries this is called Labour Day.
6. In Britain, Father's Day is in the middle of June.
7. American Independence Day is on the fourth of July.
8. Halloween is on the thirty-first of October.
9. Christmas Day is on the twenty-fifth of December.
10. New Year's Eve is on the 31st of December.

Recording 4

1. What did you do the day before yesterday?
2. Which weekday begins with T-H?
3. Write the name of someone you talk to every day.
4. Write one reason why people have a day off.
5. What will the date be in three days time?
6. Write the name of a daily newspaper in your country.
7. What are you doing the day after tomorrow?
8. Write the name of a place you would like to go for a day out.
9. Write the name of a singer who is popular in your country nowadays.
10. When did you last stay in bed all day?

Recording 5

K = Karen J = Johnny

K: So what happens at New Year in Hong Kong, Johnny?
J: Well, most importantly for Chinese people, we eat a lot and we also eat special food with special meanings. So for example, we eat Chinese mushrooms and oysters, because they bring us good luck and also lots of money!
K: Aahh.
J: What about in Scotland?
K: Well in Scotland we have special food, as well, but the food is very sweet. We have special cakes with lots of fruit in them and that brings us good luck and lots of money.
J: Mmm, we also wear, we also wear our new clothes, again to bring good luck, so … because it's New Year, so we wear all our new clothes.
K: Really? In … in Scotland, another thing we do to bring good luck is to clean the house. So before the stroke of midnight on the thirty-first of December you have to clean everything in the house, and then you open the front door and the back door, so that the good luck can come in the front door and the old year can go out of the back door.
J: Mmm. Now, your New Year is on December the thirty-first (Yeah) … or the first as well now in Hong Kong, Chinese New Year is different, because sometimes it's at the end of January, and sometimes it's at the beginning of February, because we have a special Chinese calendar, which follows the moon, and all special festivals and special days follow that calendar, so every year it's different, so sometimes I don't remember when New Year is!
K: Really? So how do you find out, is it shown on the calendar?
J: My mother knows everything. She has a special calendar.
K: Yes, mothers are like that. Do you do anything special – do people do anything special at New Year?
J: Oh yes, New Year's particularly lovely for children because they get little red envelopes, with money in them, and red is a lucky colour. And…what they do is, they go to adults, and they say, 'Happy New Year' in Chinese, and the adults give them little red envelopes of money.
K: Sounds good.
J: It is. It is very good, because I still get little red envelopes of money, because I'm not married … so I'm still a child!
K: In Scotland the children don't really play much of a part in New Year. It's mostly for adults because everything takes place in the middle of the night. Oh yes, at twelve o'clock on New Year the first person to come to your door brings you your good luck for the year. We call them your 'first foot', and it's very important who your 'first foot' is.

Recording 7

J = Jackie D = David I = Interviewer

J: January … yes … I put January 11th because that's the day when I took my driving test this year. I was very nervous before, but it was OK. I passed. It was the first time. I was really, really happy when I got my licence.
D: February, well, in February obviously the most important day is the 14th.
I: Valentine's Day.
D: Valentine's Day, yes.
I: Do you ever send a card? Or have you ever sent one?
D: No, I don't think I have, no …
I: Really? Not very romantic.
D: Well I receive lots of them though …
I: Of course.
D: Well, for May, I've got my sister's birthday, it's my younger sister. It's important that I remember. I can forget my other brothers and sisters, but my little sister, she gets very angry with me if I don't phone her up or anything. So I always do that wherever I am, I always phone her up and sing Happy Birthday to her over the phone …
I: How old is your sister?
D: Thirty-five! No, she's sixteen, sixteen next birthday …
J: Because I come from Malta, I chose 2nd June, because that's when we have the festa in my town, which is Rabat. It's like a special day, or five days, for the saint of each town or village and there are fireworks. It's like a big party in the street. There is a big parade to the church. Everybody enjoys themselves, it's really good fun, and this year, the festa in Rabat is starting on 2nd June.
September. For September I've got September the twenty-first, which is Independence Day in my country. We became an independent country in 1964 so it's a holiday now.
D: October, which is this month, my important day is the twenty-third. It's next week, because I've got a friend coming. My friend Glen is coming from New Zealand and he's arriving at the airport on Sunday evening, so I have to meet him.
I: Is he an old friend?
D: Quite old. I met him in New Zealand when I was working there.
J: December 1st is my parents' wedding anniversary and this year is their twenty-fifth anniversary, so we're having a big family party.

Recording 9

a. Well, it's happened! I'm 30 years old … today.
b. I've got some news for you. James and I are getting married!
c. Well, I think that's everything … a beer for you, André, and a glass of wine for you, Elisa.
d. And I bought this for you Leonardo. I hope you like it. I made it myself.
e. (Sound of bell striking twelve. Sounds of a party.)
f. I'd better go now. I've got my exam tomorrow morning.
g. … anyway, I've decided not to come out tonight. I've got a really awful cold, and I just want to go home to bed!
h. Ben, we've got to go now, but thanks for a lovely party.

Module 5

Recording 1

I'm pretty tall actually, around 5 foot 8, about 1 metre 75, and the only time I feel small is when I'm with my sisters – they're both taller than me. Kath is the youngest, and the tallest, although you can't see it in the photo, then comes Sophie. People say Sophie and I look very similar and that we both look like my father. We both have fairer hair than Kath, and high foreheads like Dad. Actually, we all have our Dad's blue eyes, but Kath looks more like my mother.
In personality, I think I'm very different from my sisters. They're both more organised than me! Kath always has to phone me to remind me of family birthdays and things like that. The truth is, I'm really the oldest in age only!

Recording 2

a My mother's older than my father.
b I'm very different from my sister.
c Her hair's very similar to mine.
d She's the nicest person I know.
e His nose is the same as mine.

Recording 5

a
A: Morning!
B: Oh, morning! How are you?
A: I'm fine, I'm fine. Nice day, isn't it?
B: Yes, it's lovely.
A: So, have you got any plans for today?
B: No, nothing special. We might go to the park later, what do you think?
C: Yes, Mummy.
B: How about you?
A: Well, my grand-daughter's coming over later …
B: Oh, that's nice.
A: Yeah, well she's just come back from …
C: Mummy …
B: Yes, darling, I'm just talking.
C: Mummy can we go to the park now?
B: Listen, I'd better get on. I hope you have a nice day.
b
A: Hello dear.
B: Hello, Laura. Are you feeling better now?
A: Yes, I'm much better thanks. I had to take a couple of days off, it's my back again.
B: Oh dear.
A: Yeah, I'm just… it's because I'm sitting here all day.
B: Mmm.
A: Anyway, I went to see the doctor, and he gave me something for it so I'm going back next week.
B: Mmm. How's the family?
A: Oh, they're all right. Yes, they're all fine.
B: The children are back at school now are they?
A: Oh yes, they're back. That's £8.26, please.
c
A: Afternoon.
B: Good afternoon.
C: Hi there.
B: Where are you going?
A: It's the, er, Caledonian Hotel, please, it's in. Princes Street.
B: Caledonian Hotel, I know it, all right So are you here on holiday?
A: Right yeah. We're here on holiday. How did you know?
B: Oh I can always tell. Where are you from, America is it?
C: No, we're Canadian. We're from Toronto.
B: Canada, eh? Well, well, that's a long way to come. Is this your first time in Edinburgh?
A: Yes, it's our first time here, but I have family here.
B: Is that right?
A: Yes, my family came from near here. They moved to Canada.
d
A: Hi.
B: Hello there
A: Did you have a good weekend?
B: Yeah, it was OK. I didn't do much, really, just sat at home relaxing, y'know. How about you?
A: Yeah, oh I had a fantastic weekend, great yeah.
B: Oh really. What did you do?
A: Oh well, nothing really.
B: Oh right. Like me then.
A: Yeah, I suppose so.
B: Did you see the football on Sunday?
A: Oh, yeah, fantastic, wasn't it? That goal was brilliant!
B: Did you think so? I wanted United to win, actually. I thought they were a bit unlucky.
A: What do you mean unlucky! They were lucky they only lost 1–0, and that was definitely a penalty …
B: Nah! He just fell over.

Recording 7

Nice day, isn't it?
So, have you got any plans for today?
Are you feeling better now?
How's the family?
Is this your first time in Edinburgh?
Did you have a good weekend?
Did you see the football on Sunday?

Module 6

Recording 1

a I'm planning to have a party for my birthday.
b I'm going to see my grandparents at the weekend.
c I'd like to go to Dublin in the summer.
d I'd prefer to travel with a group of friends.

Recording 2
Part 1
R = Rosa   M = Mark
R: So anyway, we decided to have a really good holiday – a 'dream holiday' in the Caribbean, because we'd always wanted to go there. So we saved our money up for months and months, and booked this holiday in a place called San Antonio. It cost over a thousand pounds each, but we wanted to do something really special so we booked it for two weeks in May, because all the brochures said that the weather's beautiful there in May …
M: We were flying from Gatwick airport, and the flight was overnight … leaving Gatwick late at night, and arriving in San Antonio the next morning, or that was the idea, anyway! But when we arrived at the airport they told us that because of bad weather in the Caribbean, the flight was delayed until the next morning. So we had to spend the night at the airport, sleeping on the floor, and we finally got on the plane the next morning twelve hours late!
R: But that was just the beginning. On the plane they told us that the bad weather over the Caribbean was actually a hurricane – Hurricane George – and that we couldn't fly to San Antonio. We had to go to the capital city instead, and stay in a hotel there for the night, until the hurricane passed. Anyway, we weren't too worried, we thought – well it's only one night … and they told us that we were going to a five-star hotel, next to the beach, with a swimming pool, so we were quite happy at that point...

Tapescripts

Part 2

M: Anyway, we arrived at the hotel, the Hotel Paradiso it was called, what a joke! They said it was a five-star hotel, but I wouldn't give it one star! It was just awful.. I don't know how to describe it ... it was an awful building, yes, it was next to the sea, but it wasn't a beach! Just a few rocks, and the sea was so dirty you couldn't swim in it. There were big ships travelling past, and the sea was all polluted and brown, it looked horrible.

R: So we went to look at the swimming pool, but that was no better. It wasn't a nice blue colour, like you'd expect. It was a sort of greeny-black colour and as we looked at it we could see things moving about in it, and we looked more closely and we realised it was full of frogs. There were hundreds and hundreds of frogs in it. So after that obviously we didn't use it.

M: And then there was the food. Do you remember the food?

R: I'll never forget it! The first morning, we went downstairs for breakfast, expecting to have you know, the usual things you get in hotels, bread, marmalade, fruit, coffee, and we were very surprised instead to see lots of different types of vegetables, carrots, peas, cabbage and a big bowl of lettuce! But anyway, I was really, really hungry so I decided to have some of the lettuce until I saw that it was moving! The leaves of lettuce were slowly moving around the bowl, and I looked a bit more closely and saw that the lettuce bowl was full of ants, hundreds of them, and there were so many that they were actually moving the lettuce leaves! After that, we didn't eat in the hotel again. We didn't want to.

M: The worst part though, was when the hurricane arrived. That was really frightening. It was a fifteen-storey hotel so you felt really terrified with all that wind, and rain, and the windows banging, and the trees crashing outside.. It was terrible.

R: And then they told us that because of the hurricane, there were no flights to San Antonio, and that we had to stay there for another three days, three more days in that place! There was nothing to do! Nowhere to go! We couldn't eat the food! It was noisy and dirty. We just couldn't believe that it could happen.

M: So when we finally arrived in San Antonio, we were five days late. And the worst thing was that Hurricane George had never arrived there. The weather had been perfect in San Antonio all the time!

Recording 3 *(missing words / phrases only)*
a You'll   b You'll   c There'll   d It'll   e It'll

Module 7

Recording 1
a I've had my car for about six months. .
b I've been a student for two years.
c I've been at secondary school for six years.
d Before that, I went to primary school.
e I've lived in London for ten years.
f I've known Anna for about eight years.
g My grandparents have been married for over fifty years.
h My mother has worked as a doctor for twenty years.
i Helen has been a teacher for three years.
j Before that she was a translator for two years.

Recording 2 *(missing words/phrases only)*
a Could you say that again, please?/What exactly is a warranty agreement?
b I'm sorry, I don't understand./What does 'or Dover' mean?/And can you explain what Bay Yin Tar Vey Zee is?
c Sorry, what was that?/How do you spell it?/What do you mean exactly?

Module 8

Recording 1
1 No, that's a myth, I'm afraid. It's actually <u>very</u> unusual to see a man in a bowler hat.
2 Well, if you go to the south, I think it's true. We always start our main meal with a pasta dish.
3 Yes, that's true. I saw it in London a lot. Japanese people were always carrying a camera.
4 Yes, that's seventy per cent true if you live in Paris. Paris is the fashion capital. But people in the street are not always well dressed, you know.
5 That's not really true any more. It <u>was</u> often foggy years ago. You read about it in Sherlock Holmes stories, don't you?
6 Oh yes, it's true. I think it's in the blood, it's in the air, it's in the spirit, it's in Brazil!
7 No, not true. Very few men actually wear kilts as everyday clothes, but a lot of people wear kilts when they go to weddings, or to special parties, like New Year celebrations.
8 No, that's false. It depends on where you are and when: for example, don't go to Harlem at night.
9 Well, that's true for older people, but now young people prefer to eat bread or cereal or fruit. We've become much more westernised.
10 Oh no, that's a complete myth…just for tourists! Most people are leaving work to go home at five o'clock!
11 That's not really true, no. In the north, in particular in winter, it rains, but not a lot. In the south it rains less, very occasionally.
12 That's certainly true….because of the nice weather, we can eat outside a lot – even at Christmas, in fact.

Recording 2
Sentence one is true.
Sentence two is false. The river Nile is, of course in Africa. The longest river in Asia is the Yangtze or Chang Jiang river in China.
Sentence three is true, and so is **sentence four**.
Sentence five is false. Hawaii and Tahiti are both in the Pacific Ocean, but Madagascar is in the Indian Ocean, near the coast of Africa.
Sentence six is false too. Lake Superior is the second largest lake in the world. Despite its name, the Caspian Sea in central Asia, is the largest lake in the world.
And **number seven** is also false. The river Danube, which runs through Germany, Austria and many other European countries is twice as long as the River Rhine.

Recording 4
New Zealand is in the South Pacific, about one thousand two hundred miles south-east of Australia. It's not a very big country, about the same size as Great Britain, or Japan but it has a much smaller population, only 3.5 million. There are two official languages, English and Maori.
I suppose when most people think of New Zealand they think of New Zealand lamb or butter and it's true that a lot of the country is farmland. There are a lot of sheep and cows! But there's a lot more to it than that. There are people who say that it's the most beautiful, unspoilt country in the world. I don't know about that, but it's certainly an amazing place to visit. There are so many different types of scenery and climate. We have almost everything. In the north there are fantastic beaches, mountains, volcanoes, even a small area of

desert, and the climate is pleasant and warm, usually around twenty-five degrees in the summer, while in the south of the country the temperatures are lower, especially in winter, and the scenery is almost like Norway or Canada. There are glaciers, fjords, and lots of snow-covered mountains where you can go skiing. There are so many different things to see and do.

Recording 5

New Zealand is divided into two main islands, North Island and South Island. Then to the south of South Island there's a much smaller island called Stewart Island, but anyway, the most important islands are North and South Island, and between them there's a small sea called the Cook Straits. Most people live on the North Island, and that's where the two biggest cities are, Wellington the capital city, and Auckland which is actually the biggest city in terms of population: over one million people live there. Wellington is on the south coast of North Island, on the Cook Straits to the west side. It's a very nice place with a beautiful harbour. Auckland is in the north east of North Island, on the coast too, people call it 'the city of sails' because of all the sailing boats there, and all the region to the north of Auckland is known as Northland. It's the hottest part of the country with lots and lots of beaches, very popular for holidays.
Both North and South Island are very mountainous. There are several volcanoes on North Island, and South Island is really divided into two halves by a big range of mountains that runs from north to south, called the Southern Alps. They're very, very beautiful, with lots of lakes and fjords in the south. That's the area where most people go skiing, or do other adventure sports such as climbing or bungee jumping ...

Module 9

Recording 1 *(missing words / phrases only)*
(1) definitely won't do (2) probably buy (3) might stop
(4) definitely be (5) may not disappear
(6) probably won't replace (7) will probably use

Recording 4 *(missing words / phrases only)*
a ... this programme finishes
b ... the weather's not too bad
c ... I get dressed
d ... I can find something else
e ... I get back
f ... we have enough money

Recording 5

a Our office is just uncomfortable in every way. For one thing it's terribly hot in summer, and terribly noisy in the street outside, so the first thing I'd like to do is put in air-conditioning so that we don't have to open all the windows in summer, and have that awful noise. The office chairs are also really uncomfortable, so the next thing I'd like to do is get some good quality comfortable chairs. Oh, and the worst thing is that we're on the fifth and sixth floors of our building, so I'd love to put in some lifts. Just one little lift would make our lives so much easier!

b What I'd most like to have in our school is a little cafeteria and next to it a nice lounge for students to spend their breaks in, with comfortable chairs and a drinks machine, and newspapers and magazines in English for them to read. At the moment people have to stand in the corridor, or even outside in the street and there's nowhere to buy a drink or snack, or read the paper, so people don't stay in school for long after the lessons finish. I think it would be completely different if they had somewhere to sit and relax.

c Our school is in quite a nice building, and in a nice part of the city, but unfortunately we haven't got much equipment, so I'd really like to have a special computer room with the Internet available on every computer, and a library of CD-ROMs. I think students can learn so much this way and they can do it whenever they have time. Oh, and I'd like to put videos in every classroom instead of cassette players. Videos are so much more interesting for learning a language, I think, but unfortunately they're very expensive.

d Really I'm very lucky with my office. It's a very, very big company, and we have a nice modern building, and nice furniture, and very good facilities and everything, but there is one thing I would really love – a gym. We're right in the middle of a big city and the traffic's very busy and everything, so I find it very difficult to get out to the gym at lunchtime, and we work very long hours, so it's hard after work. It would be good for the company too, if more people went to the gym and did some exercise. They'd probably work harder!

Recording 7

a Is there a restaurant in here?
b Have you got this in black, please?
c Where's the escalator, please?
d Excuse me, where will I find the toy department?
e Can I bring it back if he doesn't like it?
f Excuse me, can I pay by cheque?
g Do you sell swimming trunks?

Module 10

Recording 1

OK well **if you burn your hand**, you should put it under the cold tap, for at least twenty minutes. I know it sounds like a long time, but for it to work, that's what you need to do. It's not a good idea to put a plaster on it, because you could damage the skin when you take it off, you know ...
For **a temperature**, well I know people often think they should keep warm, but actually you need to let your body get cool, so really the best thing is to open the windows, or even get in a bath of, well, warm water to start with, then add cold water to it, to make the water cooler and to bring the temperature down. You can take something like paracetamol, too. That will help.
Now, if you've got **a bad cold**, you certainly shouldn't go to the doctor. There's really nothing we can do for you. No, all you can do is go to bed, have lots of hot drinks, and just allow it to get better by itself. That's all, I'm afraid!
OK now, **to lose weight** people often think that you shouldn't eat potatoes, bread, pasta, things like that, but it depends how much of them you eat and how you cook them. I mean, you certainly shouldn't have fried potatoes, but that's because of the fat. It's really fat and sugar that you should eat less of and then you should combine this with taking more exercise. And make sure you have regular exercise.
Taking antibiotics, well the important thing is that you finish the prescription, because if you don't, your body could become resistant to the the organism. As far as alcohol is concerned, though, with most antibiotics nowadays, you can have alcohol, obviously not too much, but quite a small amount is OK, yes.
Now the thing about **backache** is that ideas have changed. It certainly used to be true in the old days that you had to go to bed and lie still, but of course that's not going to help your muscles. You'll find it even more difficult to move if you don't use them at all, so now we recommend that you keep moving, gently, of course. We don't want you to go and lift heavy boxes or anything like that!

Tapescripts

Recording 2

medicine plaster aspirin antibiotics exercise headache
healthy prescription temperature

Recording 5

a One motorist was listening to loud music.
b Other people were looking at him angrily.
c Several people were waiting at the bus stop.
d They weren't watching the accident.
e A woman was putting on her make-up.
f A man was reading the newspaper.

Module 11

Recording 1

HELENA: I know everyone thinks I'm really strange, but I really hate icecream. I've never liked it. Even when I was a child I always hated it. It's so cold and horrible. My mother used to think I was very strange.

OLIVER: I think spiders are really sweet. I'd really like to get a tarantula for a pet. They're lovely and furry, and they're really easy to look after, and they can live for ages. I could keep it in my bedroom. The only trouble is my mum can't stand them. She says if a spider moves in, she's moving out!

DAVID: I know a lot of people think it's strange, but I really enjoy spending my birthday on my own, I do it every year. It's my own choice. My sister always invites me to her house with her and her children, and my parents, but to be honest, spending my birthday with my family isn't really my idea of fun. At home, in my own flat, I can eat my birthday cake, I read my birthday cards, and I watch my favourite video!

MELISSA: People always think it's a bit strange, but I actually really enjoy washing up! I don't know why, really, I just find it quite relaxing after a meal. Whenever I go to friends for dinner I always get up immediately after the meal and start washing up. I suppose I just hate sitting at the table looking at dirty plates. I feel much better when it's all clean again!

JULIA: A lot of people can't understand this, but I really hate chocolates. It's not just that I don't like them much, I absolutely loathe them. It's very embarrassing if I am given them for a present or I am offered them at the end of a meal at someone's house. I don't mind other kinds of sweets, and I love cakes and biscuits, but I can't stand chocolate. Ugh! It's disgusting!

Recording 3

a Would you like to travel back in time? Why/Why not?
b Which famous person would you most like to meet and why?
c You want to invite someone to the cinema. What do you say?
d What was the weather like yesterday?
e What does snow taste like?
f Think of two kinds of food you don't like very much.
g Think of two friends who are like you, and say why they are like you.

Recording 5

a A: I'm feeling really tired tonight.
   B: Yes, so am I!
b A: I'm not very hungry, actually.
   B: No, neither am I.
c A: I absolutely hate whisky.
   B: So do I. It's disgusting, isn't it?
d A: My boyfriend doesn't like dancing very much.
   B: Really? Neither do I, I must say.
e A: I was really ill last week!
   B: That's funny – so was I!
f A: Actually, I wasn't here last lesson.
   B: No, neither was I, unfortunately.
g A: We went to Istanbul for our holidays last year.
   B: What a coincidence, so did we!
h A: We didn't enjoy the film much.
   B: No, neither did we.

Recording 6

a I'm really thirsty today.
b I'm not feeling very well at the moment.
c I don't like this weather much.
d I watched that Julia Roberts film on TV last night.
e I was late for class today.
f I don't mind washing up, really.
g I hope we're not too late!
h I didn't sleep very well last night.

Consolidation Modules 7–11

Recording 1

ELIZA: Well, I live on my own now. I decided after my fourth husband died that I didn't want to marry again, and I like being independent. I still enjoy going to parties and meeting people – it's quite funny when I meet someone for the first time and they recognise me, but they can't remember the names of any of my films. They get embarrassed, but I don't mind. The last one was quite a few years ago, after all! I've lived here in Los Angeles for nearly forty years now, and I love the weather, and the people, but I feel I need a change, so maybe next year I'll do something exciting, like travel round the world. I've always wanted to go to Australia you know – so I should go, really, before it's too late!

PHILIP: I used to be the director of a large finance company. I had a really good salary, nice house, big car, all those things, but I was just working all the time, and I never saw my wife, or had time for my great passion – cooking. So, I decided, and one day – about three years ago – I just left my job, and we moved to a smaller house, got a smaller car, you know, and my wife and I opened a small restaurant. I did all the cooking at first, and it was very hard work – I thought 'I've made a mistake', but then we started to make some money, and we got a chef, and it was easier. Nowadays, I decide the menus, and I go to the market every day, to get fresh vegetables, fish, and I do some cooking. We're certainly not as rich as we were, and we work long hours, but I think we're much happier. Maybe next year we can have a holiday – our first one in three years!

Tapescripts

CARLA: I never go shopping myself – well not very often – I really hate it. All those crowds of people, and you can never find exactly what you want. That's what gave me the idea for the Internet company, you know, buy clothes, things for the house, presents, etcetera over the Internet, and the things are cheaper, too, of course. I was so surprised when the business grew so quickly – I suppose there are lots of people out there who hate shopping too! I still can't believe that the company is only a year old and it's already worth one and a half million! I don't really think of myself as a businesswoman – it was just luck, really. I think I'll probably sell the company in two or three years' time. Then I can stop work and have that great big family that I've always wanted, and go and live in a huge house in the countryside.

Module 12

Recording 1

VALERIE: When I was young we were very poor. My father died in the war, and we couldn't afford clothes. We never had any new ones, they were always other people's old ones and even when I got married myself, when my children were small, we didn't have much money, so I always had to make our clothes myself, mine and the children's. I didn't buy many things from the shops, so now I'm older, and we've got a bit of money, I do like to have nice things, I must say, good quality clothes, good labels. Of course, there are lots of designer things I would never buy. Some of the perfume and cosmetics and those things are a ridiculous price. I don't understand why people waste their money on them. But we do like to have nice clothes and a nice car, things like that. After all, you only live once, don't you? Why not enjoy it?

NICOLA: It really worries me the way young people today are so obsessed by these designer labels. I mean these trainers that cost over £100. I feel really sorry for parents who don't have any money with their children asking for these things. What do they do? The cheaper clothes are usually just as good, but the kids won't have them. I think the whole thing's crazy. It really makes me angry.

RORY: Some people I know, the only thing they're interested in is clothes, you know, designer T-shirts, and jeans and everything. and I think that's a bit stupid. But I don't agree with my mum either. She thinks you should just get the cheapest trainers and the cheapest jeans, but she doesn't understand that other people notice these things, and you feel really stupid if you're the person wearing the cheap ones. You just don't look good when everyone else has got the designer ones. You don't look cool.

Recording 4

a It's a hat which protects your head from the sun.
b It's a person who designs clothes.
c It's stuff that you use to wash your hands – not water!
d It's a person who sells flowers.
e It's a long leather thing that stops your trousers from falling down!
f It's a machine which answers the phone for you when you're busy.
g It's make-up that women (and sometimes men!) wear on their mouths.
h They're a special kind of shoe which you wear in summer.
i It's a person who sells meat.
j They're gold or silver things which people wear in their ears.

Recording 5

N = Neil   L = Lucy
N: Hello, Neil Lack.
L: Hi, it's me.
N: Hi!
L: Listen, just a quick call. I'm packing for the weekend, and I just want to check what we want to take with us.
N: Oh, I don't know, the usual things, toothbrushes, underwear, clothes, shoes …
L: Well yes, obviously, but any special clothes?
N: Shorts and T-shirts because it'll probably be quite hot walking round sightseeing and comfortable shoes. Actually, you can pack my brown shoes, because they're my best ones for walking around all day.
L: Yes. Do you think we'll need pullovers for the evening?
N: Probably, and put in those plastic raincoats just in case it rains.
L: And we'd better pack something smart if we're going to the theatre on Saturday night.
N: Yeah, put in my blue suit and that new shirt.
L: OK, and what about other things apart from clothes. Obviously passports, tickets, money, travellers' cheques. Do we need our driving licences?
N: We're not planning to hire a car, are we?
L: No but, well, anyway. What else?
N: A guidebook. That little yellow one's really good. A phrasebook … and don't forget the camera. You always forget the camera!
L: What about you? It's not my job to remember everything you know!
N: And what about sun cream? It might get really hot.
L: We can buy that there if we need it, can't we?
N: Yeah, I suppose so. Oh, before I forget, can you pack my razor and shaving cream?
L: Yeah, sure. Anything else?
N: Can't think of anything. Listen, I'll phone you back if I do, I've got a meeting now. I'll see you at the check-in desk at five, OK?
L: Yeah, see you then. Don't be late!
N: I won't!
L: I'm really excited, aren't you? I'm really looking forward to it!
N: Yeah, me too! See you later!
L: See you, bye. Take care.

Recording 6

a A: Lisa? Hi, I'm just going to the supermarket. What shall I get for dinner tonight?
  B: Oh, I don't know. Well, why don't we have pasta. You know, with some of that fish sauce. That's easy and quick …
  A: OK then, and is there anything else we need? What about pudding?
  B: Oh, let's have my favourite – double chocolate ice cream …
  A: All right. All right. I'll get some wine, too. See you later, then.
b A: Are you OK there, sir? Do you need any help?
  B: Well, yes, actually. I'm looking for a Christmas present for my mother and I'm not sure what …
  A: I see, well, how about this perfume? It's called 'Heaven Scent' It's very popular with the more mature woman.
  B: I don't think so, really. I'm never sure with perfume.
  A: Yes, it can be difficult, can't it? Now. let's see. You could buy her a really nice lipstick. Now this range has some lovely colours …
  B: Yes, maybe I'll do that. Which one do you think would be…
c A: … and I must get something to take back for Francesca. What do you think I should get?
  B: Er, how about one of those ashtrays we saw in that little souvenir shop by the bridge?
  A: Oh, come on, Ricky, be serious. They were horrible. And anyway she doesn't smoke!
  B: Well, I don't know. What about getting her a purse, a really good leather one.
  A: Good idea. Thanks!

165

Tapescripts

d A: Now, here are the children's sports shoes. Oh, these are nice, look. Why don't you try these on?
   B: Oh, Mum. Nobody wears trainers like that. Can't I have these?
   A: Oh, they're much more expensive. Don't you want that backpack we saw?
   B: Yes, 'course I do!
   A: Well, you can't have that and the expensive trainers. So shall we ask the assistant for your size in these?
   B: I suppose so.

Recording 8
Why don't we have pasta?
Let's have my favourite.
How about this perfume?
You could buy her a really nice lipstick.
What about getting her a purse?
Shall we ask the assistant for your size in these?

Module 13

Recording 2
a ten years   b your last birthday   c week
d nine o'clock this morning   e months and months   f last summer
g ages   h the weekend   i winter   j a long time   k he was born
l his life

Recording 4 (missing words / phrases only)
Zelda Markovitch
(1) three   (2) has been working   (3) two years ago
(4) no experience

Max Robertson
(1) fifty   (2) all his life   (3) forty
(4) seventy-six

Module 14

Recording 1
1 There are too many old people here for me, and not enough young people.
2 It's so dirty and smelly. There's too much traffic and noise.
3 The best thing is the nightlife. There are a lot of cafés and restaurants and places to go in the evening. You're never bored. I love it.
4 There are a few nice restaurants and little pubs, but there aren't many good shops. There aren't any clothes shops for example, that's a big problem about living here.
5 There isn't enough green space. There are too many buildings everywhere and streets and cars and people everywhere. I really miss the open space.
6 The people aren't really very friendly, I must say …
7 There are some lovely old houses and traditional shops. I like the old butcher's and there's a good baker's. They're really friendly and they sell lovely food.

Recording 3
J = Jeff   C = Cindy
J: Hello?
C: Hello, can I speak to Jeff, please?
J: Yes, speaking
C: Oh, hi. This is Cindy Kemble. Mark said you live quite near me and maybe you could give me a lift on Saturday.
J: Yes, of course, no problem. Did he tell you how to get to my house?
C: No, he said the nearest underground station is Manor House.
J: OK, well when you come out of Manor House station, take the Finsbury Park exit and turn left. Then go up Green Lanes with Finsbury Park on your left.
C: Uhuh.
J: So you go past the park and there's a bridge in front of you, so keep going towards the bridge, and take the road on the left just before you get to the bridge. That's Lothair Road.
C: OK, turn left before the bridge …
J: Yeah, actually it's opposite a big supermarket.
C: OK, right.
J: OK? Then my road's the second turning on the left, Venetia Road.
C: Sorry?
J: Venetia, V-E-N-E-T-I-A.
C: Uhuh. OK, got that.
J: Fine, well my house is at the beginning of the road. It's number four, the second house on your right.
C: Fine, I think I'll find it OK. It sounds quite a long way …
J: No, no not at all. It takes about ten minutes, honestly!
C: All right then, see you on Saturday. What time?
J: Oh, about 1.30, I suppose …
C: OK, bye.
J: Bye.

Recording 4
Sandra One of my favourite rooms when I was a child was my grandmother's living room, her 'back room' she called it. It was quite a small room, very, very full of old-fashioned wooden furniture that she'd got as wedding presents forty or so years earlier. She didn't have central heating, so in the winter there was always a real fire in the fireplace, and when it was cold we used to spend all our time sitting in big armchairs in front of the fire drinking cups of hot tea and talking and talking.
The room was full of little ornaments that my grandmother had collected, things that children love, lots of little china animals and people. There were also lots and lots of books in the room because my grandmother was a great reader, and cupboards full of interesting things, and old-fashioned toys that she had kept from when my mother was a little girl, china things with flowers and roses on them. My sister and I thought they were more beautiful than the modern things my mother had. I think I spent some of the happiest days of my childhood in that room talking to Nana and playing with those old toys.

Tom Well one of my favourite rooms is actually a café, which I often go to with friends for lunch at the weekend, or just for coffee. I sometimes stay for ages just reading the newspaper there. It's in a fairly quiet street, near some somes and the whole of the front is one big window, so you can sit and watch the people go by if you want. The kitchen and bar are at the back and there are only about twelve tables. The room's not very big and it's got bare wooden floors and a mixture of second-hand wooden furniture, so it doesn't look too neat and tidy. And the lighting's just right, not to bright. It's decorated in light blue and a nice bright yellow colour, and there are always lots of paintings on the walls by local artists. I love the atmosphere there. It's very friendly, and they play the kind of music I like, jazz or soul, but not to loud. I like it because I always feel really relaxed there when everyone's rushing past outside. I just sit back and enjoy my coffee and my newspaper, with the music and the noise of the coffee machine in the background …

Tapescripts

Module 15

Recording 1 (missing words/phrases only)
1 They lived   2 She'd asked him   3 I'll never help
4 He'd invested   5 We believed   6 I'll borrow

Recording 2
A young couple were having a romantic dinner at an expensive restaurant. They saw an old lady sitting alone, looking at them. They smiled politely, but were a little surprised when the old lady came over to their table. The old lady told the young woman that she looked just like her daughter who she said had died a year ago. She said it would make her very happy if they said, 'Goodbye, Mum' when she left the restaurant. How could they refuse? A few minutes later, the old lady stood up to leave. The two diners waved, as she had asked them, and said goodbye as the old lady walked out. When the couple received their bill, however, they saw that it included the cost of the old lady's meal. They called over the manager and asked him what had happened. 'The bill includes the charge for your mother's meal, he explained. She said you would pay.'

Recording 4
EC = Edward Carson   IN = Interviewer
EC: And so I think it's time I gave my side of the story. A number of the things that appeared in the newspapers are simply not true. I don't feel that I stole the money, more that I borrowed it. I didn't actually think I was stealing it, but the newspapers said it was £60,000 … which really is not true …
IN: What, it was less than that, or …
EC: Yes, it was much less, much, much less.
IN: How much did you in fact steal?
EC: Well, I borrowed probably about £20,000.
IN: Well that's quite a lot, isn't it?
EC: Twenty two maybe, certainly not more than that.
IN: And what happened then … after you'd taken the money
EC: I had this idea, perhaps it was a crazy idea, but I believed it at the time, that I could win back the money I owed, at the roulette tables, I just wanted to do it all quickly so I could pay everyone back and get on with my life. So I got in my car and spent three days driving to the south of France. I drove to Monte Carlo.
IN: And what did you do there?
EC: I tried to get into the casino, but they refused to let me in. They refused to accept my bet. So I had to go back to England and I still wanted to win the money back somehow, so I went to the races and put a bet on, I think it was about £5,000 in fact, on a horse called Lucky Six.
IN: What made you choose that horse?
EC: Well, it was just a name really. And six is my lucky number.
IN: And what happened?
EC: It finished sixth. There were seven horses in the race.
IN: Oh dear.
EC: So I decided after that, I'd been unlucky in Monte Carlo, I'd been unlucky at the races … I thought, third time lucky, I'll invest it. So I invested some money, the rest of my money in fact, in an airline. It was an independent airline. A few days later, it collapsed, so I lost almost all the money I'd invested. I had only about £1,000 left, I was really in despair …
IN: So what did you do?
EC: Well, I didn't know what to do. I borrowed a car, it was my brother's car, in fact, and went for a drive. I just wanted to drive down to the cliffs, near where I lived and think about things. Think about what to do next, and, well a policeman stopped me because I was driving too fast. I knew the police were looking for me, so when I stopped, I told the policeman what had happened. At first he didn't believe me …
IN: But in the end, you went to prison.
EC: Yes, I spent a year in prison. I think that taught me a lesson, really …

Recording 5
1 The newspaper article said that Carson stole the money. Carson said he'd only borrowed it.
2 In the newspaper article it was £60,000. Carson said it was only £20,000 or £22,000.
3 Carson didn't fly to Monte Carlo, he drove there.
4 According to Carson, he only bet £5,000 on a horse, not £10,000.
5 The horse's name was Lucky Six, not Lucky Seven.
6 It finished sixth, not last.
7 He invested his money in an airline, not a travel company.
8 He didn't buy a car, he borrowed one from his brother.
9 He didn't plan to kill himself.
10 He went to prison for a year, not a month.

Recording 6
a
A: Is there somewhere I can change some money?
B: Sure, we can change it for you. or there's a bank across the square.
A: What's the exchange rate for US dollars?
B: It's marked up there. It's exactly one peso to the dollar.
A: OK, I'd like to change this into pesos, please. It's 200 American dollars.
B: Certainly, madam. That's one hundred pesos.
A: Thank you.
b
A: Oh look it says 'Exact money only' I haven't got any change. Have you got change for £5?
B: Let's see. What do you need?
A: It's £1.50 so I need a pound coin, and a fifty pence coin, or three fifties.
B: That's one, two, three, four pounds …
A: OK.
B: And two fifties. There you go.
A: Great, thanks.
c
A: Excuse me. How much are these earrings?
B: Which ones?
A: These ones here.
B: They're £20.
A: Oh, that's a bit expensive. How about these smaller ones.
B: They're £12.
A: OK, I'll take this pair, the smaller ones, these. Can I pay by credit card?
B: Well, I prefer cash.
d
A: Hello, I come from Italy, and I'm staying in England for a year. I'd like to open a bank account here. What documents do I need, please?
B: Right, we need to see your passport, of course.
A: Yes.
B: A letter from your employer or your place of study, if you're a student.
A: And that's all?
B: That's all, yes.
A: OK. And one other thing. Can I …
e
A: Excuse me, can we have the bill, please?
B: Together?
C: Yes, please.
B: OK. That's one glass of white wine, one mineral water …
C: One club sandwich …
B: All right. There you are.
A: Thanks. Is service included?
B: No.
A: OK, thank you.

167

Tapescripts

A: Do you think we should leave a tip?
B: How much is it?
A: Nine pounds fifty!
B: Oh, leave him £10. He has been very nice.

Recording 7
a What's the exchange rate for US dollars?
b I'd like to change this money into pesos, please. It's 200 American dollars.
c Have you got change for £5?
d Excuse me. How much are these earrings?
e OK, I'll take this pair.
f Can I pay by credit card?
g What documents do I need?
h Can we have the bill, please?
i Is service included?
j Do you think we should leave a tip?

Module 16

Recording 1
peace   peaceful   violence   violent
power   powerful   freedom   free
religion   religious   tragedy   tragic
strength   strong

Recording 3 (*missing words/phrases only*)
1 'll 2 'll 3 'd 4 'll 5 'd 6 'd 7 'll 8 'd

Consolidation modules 12–16

Recording 1
a
A: Excuse me!
B: Yes, madam.
A: I want to know, er, was my bedroom cleaned this morning?
B: Yes, all the rooms are cleaned every morning, madam.
A: Well. I have a bit of a problem, then.
B: Oh dear, madam, is your room not satisfactory?
A: No, it's not that. It's just that I can't find some earrings which I left on the table by the bed …
b
A: Tina, what's that matter?
B: Oh nothing really. It's just Jake.
A: Oh no, what's he done now?
B: Well, he said he saw me with another boy outside the cinema.
A: Is that true? Did you go to the cinema with someone else?
B: Yes, but it was just my friend Tom.
A: So did you tell Jake that?
B: Yes, of course I did, but he said he didn't believe me and then he said he never wanted to see me again!
A: Oh dear, come on, let's go and have a coffee and talk about it.
c
A: Hi, Paul. How was your holiday?
B: Oh, don't talk about it. It was really terrible!
A: Oh no. Why? What happened?
B: Well, the hotel was nothing like the photo in the brochure. The rooms were really small, the food was horrible, all the staff were rude …
A: How awful! But the other people were nice?

B: Well, they were nice, yes, but I don't think any of them were under fifty.
A: Oh dear. So you won't go there next year, then?
B: You're right. I wouldn't go there again if you gave me £10,000! I'm going to stay here next year!
d
A: Right then, madam, could you tell me exactly what happened?
B: Well, I got home at about nine o'clock, and I went straight through to the kitchen, to make a cup of coffee …
A: And you didn't notice anything unusual?
B: No. I was quite tired you see, and I was thinking about work, but when I went to the cupboard I stepped on some broken glass and then I saw that someone had broken the kitchen window. I was so shocked.
A: Yes, a very unpleasant experience for you. So what exactly was taken, do you think?
B: Well, all my jewellery, I'm sure from the bedroom, and some antique silver from a cupboard.
A: Were all these things insured, madam?
B: Well, I think so …
e
A: Ah, Anita. Is the design for the conference centre ready?
B: Er, no. I was …
A: But you know I need it for tomorrow morning and I asked you to stop work on everything else until you finished it.
B: I know, and I've been working on it all day, but I haven't finished it yet. I'm sorry.
A: Well, you'll just have to stay here until you finish it, then.
B: Yes, of course. It'll be on your desk by nine o'clock.

168